Barcode in back

ID0805322

FEARMONGER

HUMBER LIBRARIES LAKESHORE CAMPUS
3199 Lakeshore Blvd West
TORONTO, ON.   M8V 1K8

HUMBER LIBRARIES LAKESHORE CAMPUS
3199 Lakeshore Blvd West
TORONTO, ON.   M8V 1K8

FEARMONGER

STEPHEN HARPER'S TOUGH-ON-CRIME AGENDA

PAULA MALLEA

JAMES LORIMER & COMPANY LTD., PUBLISHERS
TORONTO

HUMBER LIBRARIES LAKESHORE CAMPUS
3199 Lakeshore Blvd West
TORONTO, ON.   M8V 1K8

Copyright © 2011 by Paula Mallea

All rights reserved. No part of this book may be reproduced or transmitted in any form or by any means, electronic or mechanical, including photocopying, or by any information storage or retrieval system, without permission in writing from the publisher.

James Lorimer & Company Ltd., Publishers acknowledges the support of the Ontario Arts Council. We acknowledge the financial support of the Government of Canada through the Canada Book Fund for our publishing activities. We acknowledge the support of the Canada Council for the Arts which last year invested $20.1 million in writing and publishing throughout Canada. We acknowledge the Government of Ontario through the Ontario Media Development Corporation's Ontario Book Initiative.

Cover design: Meghan Collins

Library and Archives Canada Cataloguing in Publication

Mallea, Paula, 1949-
        Fearmonger : Stephen Harper's tough on crime agenda / Paula Mallea.

Includes bibliographical references and index.
Also issued in electronic format.
ISBN 978-1-55277-898-2

        1. Crime prevention--Canada.   2. Crime--Government policy--Canada.
3. Criminal justice, Administration of-- Canada. 4. Imprisonment--Canada. 5. Canada-
-Politics and government--2006-. I. Title.

HV7434.C3M34 2011   364.4'0971   C2011-904412-9

James Lorimer & Company Ltd., Publishers
317 Adelaide Street West, Suite 1002
Toronto, ON, Canada
M5V 1P9
www.lorimer.ca

Printed and bound in Canada

For my parents, with love

THERE IS ALWAYS AN EASY SOLUTION TO EVERY HUMAN PROBLEM: NEAT, PLAUSIBLE AND WRONG.

—H. L. MENCKEN

CONTENTS

ACKNOWLEDGEMENTS

I owe a debt of gratitude to a number of people. In no particular order, they are: Armine Yalnizyan, Allan Manson, Anthony Doob, Paul Ropp, Steve Sullivan, and anonymous reviewers for reading parts of the manuscript and for providing me with invaluable research materials, advice, and support. To MPs Joe Comartin, Don Davies, and Marlene Jennings for their valuable input. To MP Maria Mourani for offering me an interview that I was unable to pursue. To Ivan Egrmajer and Brian Dagg for technical assistance. To all of those dedicated journalists who do far more than report sensational crimes and who provide hard research and insightful analyses: your names appear throughout this book. Many thanks.

Thank you to Diane Young, the editorial director at James Lorimer & Company Ltd., and to copy editor Laurie Miller.

Thank you to the Canadian Centre for Policy Alternatives for supporting the early stages of this research.

Thank you to the Ontario Arts Council for its generous support.

Most of all, thanks to John, with all my heart, for your unwavering support of me and of this project.

Any errors or omissions are my own.

INTRODUCTION

In 2006, the Conservative government led by Stephen Harper came to power on a tough-on-crime platform. Since then, it has introduced a staggering amount of crime legislation. In 2010, fully 38 per cent of all the legislation before Parliament related to criminal justice matters.

Many of the crime bills prescribe severe sentences and remove judicial discretion. Many others promote a harsher philosophy of corrections. Experts on criminal justice, including victims' advocates, criminologists, and even the Correctional Service of Canada, have been critical of the government's approach. Still, it was only when the jaw-dropping costs of the new measures became apparent that real resistance to the crime agenda emerged.

The Conservative government's refusal to provide estimates for the costs of its policies, including its tough-on-crime agenda, resulted in its being found in contempt of Parliament and then defeated. Still, the May 2011 election produced a Conservative majority, enabling it to begin passing its crime laws unimpeded.

Prime Minister Stephen Harper's swift reappointment of his ministers of justice and of public safety confirmed a determination to pursue its crime agenda, despite the criticisms. Within the first hundred days of a new administration, the Conservatives promised to pass an omnibus bill containing a bundle of crime measures. Among these would be harsher sentences for young offenders, for those charged with firearms offences, and for those charged with drug crimes.

The many respected experts who oppose the Conservative approach say it is reactionary and repressive. They maintain that longer sentences and harsher conditions of imprisonment are counterproductive and actually contribute to criminal tendencies rather than reduce them. They say that proactive, preventive policies are needed if the declining crime rate is to be further reduced. The Conservative government disagrees, claiming that crime is on the rise and that severe punishment will get violent offenders off the streets and act as a deterrent.

What follows is an attempt to set out these opposing views, advancing the best evidence available in an effort to encourage a sensible and product-ive conversation on criminal justice. This conversation begins by setting out the facts on crime rates in Canada. It talks about the experience of com-parable countries and the alternative methods being adopted elsewhere. It highlights the changing approach of the United States as that country retreats from excessive incarceration and chooses preventive options, while its crime rates, like ours, continue to fall.

This book examines a selected group of Conservative crime bills, some of which have already become law, in an effort to assess the probability of their effectiveness. In this context, it provides a critique of mandatory minimum sentencing regimes and their effect upon the ability of judges to impose just sentences in individual cases. It questions the effectiveness of incarceration as a deterrent to criminal activity and sets out the many hard-won and carefully crafted principles of sentencing provided for in the *Criminal Code of Canada*, which emphasizes that incarceration is to be the last resort. It also argues for the continued independence of the judiciary and its ability to exercise discretion in sentencing.

Central to the concerns of parliamentarians and the public is the poten-tial financial cost of the Conservatives' approach. Thus, the book sets out current and future estimated costs in some detail and compares these costs to the considerably lower cost of the alternatives. It then compares the suc-cess rates of such alternatives—prevention, diversion, and rehabilitation—to the known results of incarceration in harsh conditions with limited programming.

At least as important as the financial costs are the costs in human terms of a regime that relies heavily upon incarceration. Most prison inmates are already disadvantaged in some way. They may be mentally ill, sexually abused, addicted, illiterate, or homeless. They may have been marginalized because they are Aboriginal. Or they may suffer from a combination of these disadvantages. This book considers the effects of incarceration on these inmates, compared to the effects of alternative programs.

Crime victims are among those who recommend a more progressive approach to criminal justice, and they are among the most eloquent of advocates. Their place in this book is to challenge the Conservative government as it tries to appropriate their voices and to present their own view of what works to reduce crime and assist victims.

Alternatives to a tough-on-crime agenda are already being provided by communities and governments at every stage of the criminal justice system. Preventive programs, restorative justice, alternatives to prison, and rehabilitative programs designed to reduce recidivism are all being offered across the country. This book describes many of these programs and assesses them for cost-effectiveness and success rates.

Leaving ideology and personal beliefs aside, the question we need to ask is: What works to reduce crime and contribute to the safety and well-being of the community? Clearly, it is easier to create long prison sentences and harsh prison conditions than to craft complex solutions for complex problems. The Conservative government, in an effort to be seen "doing something" about crime, prefers a solution based upon a simple network of prisons rather than a more complex network of social services. When all the evidence is in, it is hard not to conclude that the Conservative approach to crime is at best misguided, and at worst likely to produce the opposite result from the one intended.

Intelligent, evidence-based, affordable, pragmatic, results-oriented public policy should be the goal of any criminal justice system. In the face of Mr. Harper's tough-on-crime agenda, it is necessary and urgent to start an informed public debate on the subject. This is one contribution to that conversation.

1: THE CONSERVATIVE GOVERNMENT AND ITS CRIME AGENDA

THE 2006 ELECTION

In preparation for the 2006 federal election, Stephen Harper's Conservative Party issued its agenda for criminal justice. Titled *Stand up for Security*, the document was very detailed.[1] It asserted that the Liberal record on safety and security had been weak, and that Liberals had put Canada on the road to drug legalization. Mr. Harper pledged to "crack down on crime."

The Conservative Party claimed that the homicide rate and other crimes were up,[2] and promised to deliver "serious time" for "serious crime":

> *A Conservative government will protect our communities from crime by insisting on tougher sentences for serious and repeat crime and by tightening parole. We will ensure truth in sentencing and put an end to the Liberal revolving door justice system. The drug, gang, and gun-related crimes plaguing our communities must be met by clear mandatory minimum prison sentences and an end to sentences being served at home. Parole must be a privilege to be earned, not a right to be demanded.*

The plan promised specific measures that would introduce mandatory minimum sentences for drug and other offences, reduce the use of conditional (non-custodial) sentences, create "three-strikes-you're-out" legislation for dangerous offenders, mandate consecutive sentences for multiple murders, prevent courts from giving extra credit for time served in remand,[3] and create a reverse onus for bail hearings on some firearms offences.[4]

Another branch of the plan promised fundamental and sweeping changes to the correctional system. "Faint hope" applications (allowing offenders serving life sentences to apply for an earlier eligibility date for parole) would be abolished. Statutory release (allowing offenders to be released under supervision at two-thirds of their sentence) would be replaced by "earned parole." Parole provisions would be toughened up. A constitutional amendment would prevent federal prisoners from being able to vote in elections.

The campaign platform also promised to place more police on the streets, invest more money in victims services and youth crime prevention programs, repeal the long-gun registry, get tougher on sex offenders, enact a national drug strategy, and treat young offenders more like adults (by ensuring anyone fourteen years or older charged with serious violent or repeat offences is automatically sentenced as an adult, and by adding deterrence and denunciation to sentencing principles for youth), thus sending more of them to prison for longer sentences.

The Liberal Party's campaign platform, while generally strong in areas of human rights and social programs, appeared to vie in harshness with the Conservative plan when it came to criminal justice.[5] It too claimed that homicides were up in 2004, without acknowledging that crime rates had been trending down. Liberals were concerned about drug trafficking and gang violence. An earlier Liberal effort to decriminalize marijuana was not mentioned. Except for a promise to fund a *Gun Violence and Gang Prevention Plan* and a *Rural Community Safety Plan*, there was no real commitment to prevention or treatment in the context of criminal justice.

The Liberals' platform showed that they could be just as tough-on-crime as the Conservatives. Their platform promised fewer conditional sentences, more law enforcement, stronger laws on the investigation of drug-impaired driving, and harsh penalties for auto theft and street racing. Liberals also outdid the Conservatives by promising to *double* mandatory minimums for gun-related crimes (their emphasis).

The New Democrats also recognized the dangers of being seen as soft on crime.[6] They claimed that violent crime had increased over twenty years, and also noted the homicide statistics for 2004. They described gun violence as a crisis, and produced a lengthy criminal justice platform. The three pillars of the plan were: to mete out tougher sentences on gun crime, and generally provide "firm punishment and deterrence"; to fund more law enforcement; and to fund more preventive programs, especially with respect to communities and youth. This platform thus made prevention an explicit part of its plan.

Unlike the Liberals and Conservatives, the New Democrats promised extensive investments in housing, child care, education and training, employment, youth programs, and community-based efforts—all in the context of criminal justice as part of "Ending Violence." The New Democrats also proposed a "non-punitive rule" with respect to adult use of marijuana, while supporting drug addiction programs. Like their rivals, though, they pandered to the tough-on-crime vote by promising mandatory minimum sentences, tougher sentencing for youth who use guns, and new laws dealing with methamphetamine production.

The Bloc Québécois argued for prevention and rehabilitation programs as opposed to punishment-oriented measures. Its platform said it favoured decriminalizing small amounts of marijuana, and focusing on rehabilitation and drug prevention programs rather than imprisonment, especially for young offenders.[7]

The Green Party argued for tackling the root causes of crime, and for a stronger role for restorative justice.[8] They wanted to regulate marijuana like alcohol and tobacco, and argued for higher penalties for gun-related crimes.

There was a swift response to the Conservative approach from experts in the field. They argued that higher incarceration rates do not drive down crime rates, that deterrence as a principle of sentencing does not work, and that mandatory minimum sentences are counterproductive and expensive. They deplored the dearth of investment in prevention and rehabilitation, and predicted a huge increase in numbers of prisoners and an urgent need for more prisons as a result.

There were some unlikely opponents to the Conservatives' tough-on-crime agenda. The Correctional Service of Canada, which administers the federal penitentiary system, responded to the Conservative campaign platform in an analysis obtained by the *Toronto Star* and reported on just before the 2006 election.[9] It said that the tough-on-crime agenda would dramatically increase prison populations. It asserted that mandatory minimum sentences (a linchpin of the Conservative agenda) do not have a deterrent effect upon offenders. It said that "the expense of long incarceration drains funds away from needed social programs that do prevent crime." And it maintained that the Conservative approach would "hit Aboriginal people the hardest, violate Charter rights of inmates, and likely not make for safer streets." The advice of the Correctional Service appears to have been ignored.

Another interested observer watching the Harper government's five-year effort to overhaul criminal justice offered a passionate response. Calling the agenda "dumb on crime," Conrad Black, a high-profile supporter of Prime Minister Harper and an ex-inmate, expressed strong feelings about the tough-on-crime agenda:[10]

> Canada's vocation is as the world's great liberal pioneer, to be tough on crime by treating its causes, reducing the unnecessary and hideously expensive demonization and segregation of the non-violent, and not... to be "dumb on crime" by stigmatizing and tormenting trivial offenders, and assuring that greater numbers of young and of native people are ground to powder in the criminal system. The government is in hot pursuit, without a warrant, of higher costs, more crime, more misery, and deeper roots among the most reactionary and uninformed voters. It is bad policy and shabby politics, and the government has those votes anyway so it is not clear why it is alienating the rest of us, who want a justice system based on decency, efficiency, and results, not oafish posturing.

The platform was given an unfortunate boost just before the 2006 election. The tragic death of Jane Creba, gunned down on Boxing Day in downtown Toronto by a young gang member, was seized upon by the Conservative Party as proof that guns, gangs, and drugs are becoming a more serious threat to Canadians. Conservative adviser Tom Flanagan, regrettably, saw it as a way of improving the party's chances at the polls.

He said, "Our internal polling had already established criminal justice as the issue area where we had the strongest lead over the Liberals, and Jane Creba's tragic death helped to make our position more salient to voters."[11]

The Conservatives won the 2006, election and formed a minority government. The thirty-ninth Parliament ran from April 3, 2006, to September 7, 2008. In the first session, fully 24 per cent of all Senate and House of Commons bills were related to crime (sixteen of sixty-eight bills). Nine of the sixteen bills received royal assent by the end of the session, among them a bill repealing conditional sentencing for certain offences and one creating the new offence of street racing.

During this first session, Justice Minister Vic Toews justified his efforts to impose more mandatory minimum sentences by saying that they had caused a "significant drop in crime" where they had been used in the United States.[12] Yet as early as 1970, Texas congressman George H. W. Bush supported a vote to repeal virtually all mandatory minimum sentences for drug offences. This legislation was supported by both Democrats and Republicans. Mr Bush said, "Contrary to what one might imagine, this bill will result in better justice and more appropriate sentences...We will undoubtedly have more equitable action by the courts, with actually more convictions where they are called for, and fewer disproportionate sentences."[13] He did so for reasons that have been followed in many other states over the ensuing forty years. Experienced practitioners, policy analysts, and researchers agree that mandatory minimum sentences are "a bad idea."[14] As the Correctional Service of Canada and many others have said, they provide no deterrent and they are very expensive.

Questions were raised almost immediately about the cost of Mr. Harper's crime agenda. It was apparent that more offenders would be incarcerated, but the government offered no estimates of the numbers of new inmates or of the expected added expense. Minister of Public Safety Stockwell Day claimed that the prison population would increase by about three or four hundred inmates.[15] His communications director said he plucked this number out of the air. Over time, the Conservatives offered various estimates from $90 million to $2 billion—all without providing a basis for their figures.

In the second session of Mr. Harper's first government (from October 16, 2007, to the election call on September 7, 2008), ten of sixty-five bills—15 per cent—related to crime. Of these, 40 per cent received royal assent, including Bill C-2, the *Tackling Violent Crime Act*, which included a number of separate pieces of legislation that had all died on the order paper when the first session ended.

Bill C-2 came into law in a circuitous way. The Conservatives first allowed their crime initiatives from the first session to die on the order paper. Then a month later they put forward the omnibus bill (C-2) containing five of the same measures. Some of these laws had previously been studied at length and carefully amended by all political parties in committee. Nevertheless, they were reintroduced in Bill C-2 in their original, unamended form.

These measures included laws relating to mandatory minimum sentences for certain firearms offences, an increase in the age of consent relating to sexual exploitation of children, new drug-impaired driving measures, and a reverse-onus provision for bail hearings on certain offences. Also included was a measure known to be highly unpalatable to the opposition—the new "three-strikes-you're-out" dangerous offender provision. Many parliamentarians did not want to see this law pass because of its apparently arbitrary nature, and because of its similarity to discredited three-strikes legislation in the United States. Many also believed that the law was too broad and would result in some offenders receiving the "dangerous offender" designation who did not deserve an indeterminate sentence of incarceration.

To encourage the opposition to vote for the legislation, Prime Minister Harper made Bill C-2 the subject of a confidence motion. The opposition parties thus had to vote for the bill unless they were prepared to bring on an election they did not want. They also knew they could not vote against publicly popular crime measures without risking the wrath of the voting public at some later date. Bill C-2 became law on February 28, 2008.

During this second session, the Conservatives introduced a number of other bills, including one that would overhaul the *Youth Criminal Justice Act* and another that would impose mandatory minimum sentences for drug offences. As in 2007, most of these bills died on the order paper when Mr. Harper called an early election in September 2008.

Early on, the Harper government had commissioned a sweeping review of the Correctional Service of Canada. The review panel, struck in April 2007, was given a mere fifty working days (later extended to six months) to produce its report.[16] The thirteen-item agenda would have represented a monumental task even if the panel had had adequate time and a research staff. It had neither.

The panel relied on a series of visits to federal prisons and interviews with corrections officials, representatives of the guards union, and some community-based justice partners. Virtually no experts in penology, criminology, criminal law, or other related fields were consulted.

The review panel was chaired by Rob Sampson. Mr. Sampson had been minister of correctional services in the Conservative government of Michael Harris in Ontario. As such, he was responsible for an effort to privatize Ontario prisons. This experiment failed when the Penetanguishene "super-jail" was returned to public sector management by a subsequent Liberal government after five years of being run by a Utah-based company.[17]

Other review panel members included a victims' rights advocate, a retired deputy police chief, the chief of a British Columbia First Nation, and a former chair of the National Parole Board. Only the latter could be said to have any familiarity with the operation of the correctional system. None of the five panelists had expertise in the area, nor did they have any training in assessing evidence about what works in corrections.

The resulting report, *A Roadmap to Strengthening Public Safety: Report of the Correctional Service of Canada Review Panel 2007*,[18] produced 109 recommendations. It did so without making reference to the considerable history of correctional policy and practice, and without a single reference to human rights. The report also ignored the many high-level commissions of inquiry which have looked into correctional policy and practice, including the Ouimet Report (1969), MacGuigan Report (1977), and Arbour Report (1996).

It was thus not surprising that the *Roadmap* recommended harsher treatment of inmates and less attention to the human rights of prisoners. As Craig Jones, former executive director of the John Howard Society of Canada said, "the die was cast for a specific outcome and specific recommendations as a consequence of the choice of members, their terms of reference, and their submission deadline."[19]

In a hard-hitting critique of the *Roadmap*, Michael Jackson and Graham Stewart said that its conclusions illustrate the "dangers of creating major 'transformative' policy virtually overnight by a largely unqualified group under a heavy cloud of political expediency."[20] They pointed out the many ways in which the *Roadmap* recommendations infringe upon the human rights of offenders.

The *Roadmap* was immediately adopted as government policy by Minister of Public Safety Stockwell Day. There were no further consultations. The *Roadmap* became the foundation for the Correctional Service's *Transformation Agenda*, reinforcing the Conservative government's determination to incarcerate more offenders for longer terms, and to make their time in custody more difficult.

Conrad Black was incensed at the recommendations of the *Roadmap*, calling them repressive:[21]

> The Roadmap is the self-serving work of reactionary, authoritarian palookas, what we might have expected 40 years ago from a committee of southern U.S. police chiefs. It is counter-intuitive and contra-historical. The crime rate has been declining for years, and there is no evidence cited to support any of the repression that is requested. It appears to defy a number of Supreme Court decisions, and is an affront, at least to the spirit of the Charter of Rights.

Despite many well-documented criticisms, the recommendations of the *Roadmap* have been enshrined in Conservative crime legislation. Accelerated parole review is no longer available to first-time, non-violent penitentiary inmates, producing the anomalous result that these inmates are unlikely to be granted parole at all. There is no longer a possibility of day parole at one-sixth of a federal sentence. The "faint hope" application has been repealed, meaning offenders serving life sentences have no possibility of applying for an earlier release at the fifteen-year mark.

Many other changes are being made at the Correctional Service of Canada that do not require legislation. The new *Transformation Agenda* reported in 2009 upon efforts, based on *Roadmap* recommendations, to "fundamentally transform federal corrections."[22] For example, in the first two years of the program steps taken to improve drug interdiction in the prisons included the hiring of thirty-two new security intelligence staff and twelve new detector-dog teams, and the purchase of x-ray machines and other drug detectors. Plans for the next two years (2008–2010) included the hiring of fifteen more dog teams and sixty-five more intelligence staff—for a total of ninety-seven new staff. These measures have a negative impact upon offenders' visits with family and friends, visits that are an important part of rehabilitation and reintegration.

This considerable effort and expenditure of resources dwarfs the meagre response to the need for mental health care in federal institutions. The Correctional Investigator (prison ombudsman) Howard Sapers says access to mental health care must be a top priority, since the number of inmates with mental illness is rising at an alarming rate. About 25 per cent of new admissions to the federal system have a mental illness. The Correctional Service has responded by hiring fifty-seven new staff (less than 60 per cent of those hired to collect intelligence about drugs), with no plan to hire more.

A number of other knowledgeable voices objected to the plan to incarcerate more people for longer. Toronto Police Chief Bill Blair said that prison should be reserved for "truly dangerous" criminals. "We're not talking hundreds or thousands here, we're talking a relatively small number of people," he said.[23] Those who commit crimes are "all human beings, they're all different. Some of them are going to respond positively if you give them better opportunities, better choices...We have to have hopeful redemption for those individuals to get them on the right path."

Rick Hansen, Calgary's chief of police, also said that we are sending too many of the wrong kind of people to jail.[24] He cited people who are on drugs, are mentally ill, or are not taking their medications. He wanted substance abusers to go to secure detoxification facilities, not to prison. He wanted others to be diverted as well.

No notice appears to have been taken of these experienced voices.

THE 2008 ELECTION

In the run-up to the 2008 election, Conservative campaign promises included an extensive and detailed list of longer prison sentences, fewer conditional sentences, and fundamental changes to the *Youth Criminal Justice Act* which would result in harsher sentences including more custody.[25] The Conservatives placed very little emphasis upon preventive or rehabilitative programs.

The Liberal Party in 2008 took a more measured approach, emphasizing preventive programs.[26] It promised to attack the "root causes" of crime, alleviating poverty and putting resources into housing and education. It again pledged more support for the RCMP. It supported some changes to the *Youth Criminal Justice Act*, but not the complete overhaul represented by Conservative proposals. Significantly, it promised to restore the Law Commission of Canada (abolished by the Harper government), and to assign it the immediate task of reviewing the sentencing provisions of the *Criminal Code*. Such a review has long been recommended by experts on sentencing.

The New Democratic Party in 2008 dropped its controversial suggestion of a "non-punitive rule" for adult marijuana use.[27] It recommended longer sentences for a number of offences, while offering to create new positions for police officers. In addition, it promised preventive measures such as a permanent youth gang diversion strategy and programs within the prison system to offer training, rehabilitation, and drug addiction treatment.

The Bloc Québécois again argued against the young offender amendments, but wanted to step up enforcement against gangs, abolish day parole at one-sixth of a sentence, and eliminate statutory release altogether.[28] They wanted to abolish 2-for-1 credit for remand time, as well. In this way, they positioned themselves as tough on crime, except for young offenders.

The Greens dropped their advocacy for marijuana regulation and referred only in general terms to women's rights, pay equity, the Kelowna Accord, and other matters that did not directly affect criminal justice.[29]

Opposition parties appeared again to be positioning themselves so that no one could accuse them of being "soft on crime." At the same time, they were making an effort to support progressive measures for prevention and rehabilitation.

Shortly after Mr. Harper won the 2008 election with another minority, he prorogued Parliament. Little legislative activity had occurred. The second session began on January 26, 2009, and ran until Mr. Harper again prorogued on December 30, 2009. During the 2009 session, his government introduced a number of crime measures, both new and old. Twenty of the seventy bills (29 per cent) in this session related to crime. Only three (15 per cent) received royal assent before prorogation.

The most notable of the three crime bills that did become law during this session of Parliament was Bill C-25, known as the "Truth in Sentencing" law. This law removes the convention of providing two days of credit for each day an offender spends in remand ("2-for-1") when calculating a sentence.[30] The 2-for-1 credit was typically provided for two reasons: conditions in remand are especially harsh, allowing for no programming or treatment, and the time spent there is "dead time": it does not count toward parole after sentencing.

The new law reduces the credit to 1-for-1, which looks equitable to the untrained eye, but which actually produces a mathematical inequity between similar offenders, depending on whether or not they are granted bail. The offender who is granted bail will end up serving less time overall than the identically positioned offender who fails to obtain a release on bail pending trial (see Chapter 4).

Although this inequity was canvassed thoroughly in committee, opposition parties did not block the legislation. The new law results in offenders spending more time in prison, causing additional expense to the correctional system. The bill was voted on and passed without any financial estimates being provided. Parliamentarians had no idea what Bill C-25 was likely to cost, and nothing more was heard about costs in 2009. The Liberals made a formal request to the Parliamentary Budget Office to provide estimates, but no report was received until mid-2010.

Shortly before Prime Minister Harper prorogued Parliament on December 30, 2009, Justice Minister Rob Nicholson accused the Liberal-dominated Senate of holding up his crime legislation. He said, "I have a busy criminal law agenda but, [after] getting it stuck in the Senate and having it bogged down there for month after month, I know the game that they are playing."[31] He said that Liberal senators were "trying to stall these things and they are doing the dirty work for the Liberals in the House of Commons."

Prime Minister Harper also claimed that the Senate had been obstructionist:[32]

> *Our government is serious about getting tough on crime. Since*
> *we were first elected, we have made it one of our highest*

> *priorities. The Liberals have abused their Senate majority by obstructing and eviscerating law and order measures that are urgently needed and strongly supported by Canadians.*

Incensed by this characterization of the actions of the Senate, Senator James S. Cowan penned a letter to the Justice Minister setting out in detail how the crime laws had not been obstructed by the Senate, but had been delayed by the government's own actions. Legislation had not been brought forward in a timely fashion. As well, delays had been caused by the Prime Minister's decisions to call an early election and to prorogue Parliament twice. It was not the fault of the Senate. He then made a serious accusation:[33]

> *It is difficult to take a law-and-order agenda seriously when it is argued with so little respect for facts. Justice above all depends upon truth. As our country's Minister of Justice and the Attorney General of Canada, your first allegiance must always be to the truth, far beyond any political or partisan gamesmanship. Our system of justice depends upon it. How can Canadians have any confidence in their justice system, if the person responsible for that system...is prepared to play fast and loose with the truth?*

As Senator Cowan pointed out, seventeen crime bills had been introduced by the government during 2009. Some of these were back for the second time after dying on the order paper when Prime Minister Harper took the country into the 2008 election. Two of those were passed by the Senate and were now law.

The fifteen other bills that were "urgently needed" died on the order paper when Prime Minister Harper chose, for reasons that remain unclear, to prorogue Parliament again in December 2009. By that date, only three of the bills had made it to the Senate.[34] None of the other twelve bills in the session had been passed by the House of Commons before prorogation, and most of them had never been brought before the House at all.

In the third and final session of the fortieth Parliament, which began on March 3, 2010, fully 38 per cent of the total legislative agenda (twenty-eight of seventy-three bills) was devoted to cracking down on crime. Of those twenty-eight bills, ten had received royal assent (36 per cent) and become law by the time the government fell on March 25, 2011—eight of them on March 23. Among these were bills abolishing the "faint hope" provision and accelerated parole reviews.

During 2010, the government made further changes to the criminal justice system without passing legislation. Justice Minister Nicholson chose the summer recess to pass regulations increasing sentences and providing for additional surveillance opportunities, saying these changes targeted organized crime.[35] He was able to make the changes by executive decision of the federal cabinet, without debate and without the need to pass legislation.

The new regulations established longer sentences; a broader use of wiretaps; permission to seize proceeds of crime; and tougher bail, parole, and sentencing conditions. It was a simple matter of adding a number of existing *Criminal Code* offences to the "serious crimes" category. These included: keeping a common gaming or betting house; betting, pool-selling, and book-making; committing offences in relation to lotteries and games of chance; cheating while playing a game, or in holding the stakes for a game, or in betting; keeping a common bawdy-house; and a number of offences related to illegal drugs.

Long-time observer Lawrence Martin said that the measures were less about tackling organized crime than about going after the "small-time players."[36] As he noted, under the new regulations, "Canadians can be headed off to the slammer for five years or more for selling a few ounces of marijuana, bookmaking on a game of checkers or operating a prostitution ring with two hookers." At the same time, the new surveillance opportunities were substantial.

Other ways of influencing the crime agenda without passing legislation have also been employed. For example, Conservative supporters or sympathizers have been appointed to important posts affecting the administration of criminal justice. Dozens of recent appointees to the National Parole Board are people who have close links to, or have donated money to, the Conservative Party.[37] While it is not unusual for any party in power to use such posts as patronage appointments, in this case it appears that the appointments have had a tangible effect upon parole board decisions.

National Parole Board data show steady drops in the percentage of successful day parole or full parole applicants since the Conservatives came to power in 2006. For day parole, the number fell from 74 per cent to 66 per cent between 2005–06 and 2009–10. For full parole, the difference was from 45 per cent (2005–06) to 41 per cent (2009–10).

The panels that determine who should be recommended for judicial appointments have also been redesigned. Partisan political appointments to these panels can be said to compromise the independence of the judicial system, and putting law enforcement officers on them sends another clear signal. Public Safety Minister Vic Toews has nonetheless appointed police officers to these panels, despite the strong opposition of Chief Justice of the Supreme Court Beverley McLachlin, the Canadian Judicial Council, the Federation of Law Societies of Canada, and Ontario's Chief Justice and Attorney General.[38] The Chief Justice and the Canadian Judicial Council warned that the independence of the judiciary was "in peril" and that it must be free to make rulings "irrespective of political or ideological considerations."[39]

The opposition, meanwhile, has seemed unable to stop the barrage of crime legislation. It was not until 2011 that Liberal leader Michael Ignatieff announced his party's opposition to a centrepiece of the Conservative crime agenda. He said the Liberals would vote against the new mandatory minimum sentences for drug offences.[40] Saying, "This bill isn't tough on crime, it's dumb on crime," he went on:

> We're all in favour of cracking down on serious criminals, but this bill doesn't distinguish between massive grow-ops and a first-time offender with a small amount. What's more, the Conservatives won't tell us what the fiscal implications of this bill are. How many billions will it cost? How many mega-prisons will have to be built? For these reasons we just can't support it.

With this, the Liberals joined the New Democratic Party and the Bloc Québécois in opposing the bill. It was the first potentially effective resistance to the tough-on-crime agenda. Now that the Conservatives enjoy a majority in Parliament, however, any such resistance will be moot.

It was only in 2010 that Parliament and the Canadian public received their first inkling about the colossal costs of the new crime laws, thanks to the Parliamentary Budget Officer, Kevin Page. He published calculations for just one piece of crime legislation (Bill C-25) and found that it would result in 4,189 additional headcounts in the federal prison system (close to ten times Mr. Day's estimate for his entire crime agenda).[41] Mr. Page's estimate of the cost for this one law was $5.1 billion over five years, which would more than double the Correctional Services budget.

This new information commanded the attention of the opposition and of the public, and in late 2010 the Liberals requested full financial estimates for three files: the crime legislation, corporate tax cuts, and the fighter jet purchase. The Conservative government refused to provide this information, saying it was the subject of cabinet confidence. Speaker Peter Milliken was asked for a ruling, and he found that in refusing to provide the information, the Conservative government was in prima facie contempt of Parliament. The matter was sent to committee for deliberation. It confirmed the Speaker's prima facie finding. A motion of non-confidence was passed by the House of Commons on March 25, 2011, bringing the government down and propelling Canada into an election.

THE 2011 ELECTION

In their 2011 campaign document entitled "Here for Canada," Mr. Harper's Conservatives accused the opposition of promoting a soft-on-crime ideology that apologizes for criminals.[42] They said Conservatives share the "common-sense beliefs of law-abiding Canadians," and that is why tackling crime is one of their highest priorities. Crime was one of five main areas that the platform addressed.[43]

The platform again placed heavy emphasis upon increased sentencing and the creation of new criminal offences. Elder abuse would be tackled by adding "vulnerability due to age" to the list of aggravating factors in sentencing. There would be a new mandatory minimum sentence to tackle the industry in contraband tobacco. Victims would be assisted by a mandatory surcharge on offenders (which goes to the provinces to provide victim services), and by an increased Employment Insurance benefit for parents of murdered children. There would be new laws to combat human trafficking.

The centrepiece of the platform was a promise to resurrect eleven pieces of crime legislation, bundling them into an omnibus bill, and passing them within the first 100 days of their new mandate.

With respect to its approach to corrections, the Conservative platform talked only about eliminating illicit drugs from prisons. It did not talk about treating addictions or mental illness, or funding further programming aimed at rehabilitation. It did not refer to harm reduction as a potential approach to the health issues surrounding intravenous drug use in prison.

Missing from the Harper crime strategy was any reference to the risk factors for crime. There was no promise to fund preventive programs or to support communities in their efforts to reduce crime. Instead, the platform justified its heavy emphasis on punishment by claiming that "in recent years the scales of justice have tipped too far in favour of the rights of criminals at the expense of law-abiding citizens."

The Liberal platform did not propose specific crime measures, instead talking in more general terms about "stronger, safer communities."[44] It said criminals must be punished but "more prisons alone will not make our communities safer and stronger." It claimed that "the Harper government's narrow preoccupation concerning our communities has been punishing crime, and exploiting fear." In this way, the Liberals began to distinguish their approach to criminal justice from that of the Conservatives.

In a section entitled "Stronger, Safer Communities," the Liberals talked at length about poverty and homelessness and what can be done about them. The platform referred to mental illness and disability as hampering citizens' ability to participate fully and safely in Canadian life. It recognized the importance of community activity in creating a safer context, and said that the federal government needed to be a stronger supporter of volunteers, non-governmental organizations, and community action, even when they express opinions contrary to the government's. Respect for others' views was an overriding theme.

The platform explained how a Liberal government would change the long-gun registry to make it more palatable to gun owners and more useful to law enforcement agencies. (The Conservatives promised again to scrap the registry.) The Liberal platform promised to do a better job of managing the

RCMP. It also promised to set up a national task force to try to find out what happened to the 580 Aboriginal women who have been reported missing or murdered, and what can be done to prevent further tragedies of this kind.

On the whole, the Liberal platform recognized the complexity of the issues and did not offer simplistic solutions.

The New Democratic Party set out the five first steps that an NDP government would take, if elected. None of them had to do with crime. In discussing the crime agenda, it emphasized "prevention, policing, and prosecution." It promised more support for crime prevention within communities, especially for programs directed at youth. This included increased support for the National Crime Prevention Centre and for the Youth Gang Prevention Fund.[45] It said it would fund a Correctional Anti-Gang Strategy, aimed at stopping gang recruitment within prisons. Adopting a recommendation of the Prison Ombudsman, it promised to provide treatment for mentally ill prisoners.

The platform also promised 2,500 new policing positions, said it would create new offences for home invasions and carjackings, and would make gang recruiting illegal. It would also support a stronger citizen's arrest law.

Although the New Democratic Party officially supports the legalization of marijuana, party leader Jack Layton was less than clear about this fact during the campaign. He said it was an important issue to debate, and claimed there was nothing positive about the Conservative approach, "which is to put a criminal cast on absolutely everything...they don't like."[46]

Mr. Layton was particularly adamant that safe injection sites like InSite, in Vancouver, should be established across the country.[47] He said that InSite's approach had been shown in study after study to be effective at reducing crime related to the drug trade:

> It really fits in with that notion of prevention. To try to drive people further and further into an underground world simply accelerates and magnifies the amount of crime that you are going to have associated with it.

On the whole, New Democrats attempted to show that they were not "soft on crime," while placing the emphasis more on prevention and rehabilitation. Mr. Layton said it was ridiculous that "Mr. Harper seems to think preventing crime is being soft on crime."[48]

Both the Liberal and New Democratic leaders broadened their progressive stances during the campaign, and particularly during the debates.[49] They both promised to provide more assistance to victims and to work harder on prevention. Michael Ignatieff, the Liberal leader, said that the prime minister was promoting the politics of fear. Mr. Layton talked about tackling the underlying issues related to crime: housing, violence against women, the plight of Aboriginal people, and so on. Both opposition leaders appealed to evidence rather than to ideology as the driver of their public policy development.

The Bloc Québécois platform talked about justice rather than retribution only, and used strong words to condemn the Conservative approach.[50] They said it was "demagogic, alarmist, and dogmatic." The priority of the Bloc was to provide rehabilitation and reintegration for young offenders. They wanted to get tough on organized crime, street gangs, and white collar criminals. They did not wish to see judges turned into "prison sentence dispensing machines." In this way, the Bloc tried to appeal to its full range of voters as well.

The Greens were not preoccupied with the criminal justice file in 2011.[51] They wanted to legalize and tax marijuana, while initiating a national campaign to discourage its use (as with tobacco). They wanted to prosecute white collar crime. Otherwise, their platform on criminal justice was thin.

As the campaign progressed, criminal justice issues dropped off the radar screen. The prime minister convinced voters that they should fear a possible opposition coalition and argued that, to avoid such a result, Canadians should give him a majority government. When election day arrived on May 2, 2011, voters accepted his argument that Conservatives were better managers of the economy. They gave him his majority, thus allowing him unfettered power to advance his agenda.

Eleven outstanding crime bills will be bundled in the new omnibus bill. They include heavy mandatory minimum sentences for drug crimes and sexual assaults against children, and an increase in sentences for young offenders. For a long list of offences, there will be no more conditional sentencing (house arrest). Pardons will be harder to obtain and will not be available to some offenders. Offenders serving time outside Canada will find it harder to obtain a transfer back home. More tools will be provided to law enforcement to fight high-technology crime and terrorism. And mega-trials will be streamlined.

The Harper government can now pass all this without fear of effective opposition. The new opposition NDP will be impotent to do more than recommend changes in committee and exert moral suasion on the Conservatives. Unless Mr. Harper's own members of Parliament or Senators vote against the tough-on-crime agenda, it will become law.

2: CRIME RATES VERSUS INCARCERATION RATES: THE FACTS

Prime Minister Stephen Harper has rejected the idea of evidence-based justice policies, saying researchers are trying to[1]

> pacify Canadians with statistics...Your personal experiences and impressions are wrong, they say; crime is really not a problem. These apologists remind me of the scene from the Wizard of Oz when the Wizard says, "Pay no attention to the man behind the curtain."

Thus, the prime minister consigns statistics to the dustbin as though they were part of a fairy tale. He prefers to rely upon his own personal beliefs about what the public wants.

CRIME RATES ACCORDING TO STATISTICS CANADA

Mr. Harper claims that crime is on the rise in Canada. Statistics Canada, however, says that crime has been declining for more than twenty years. Only one of these propositions can be correct. It is critical that the public understand the facts if there is to be any hope of influencing the government.

The crime rate statistics in Canada are clear. In 2008, the crime rate was the lowest in the last twenty-five years.[2] Since peaking in 1991, the rate has declined steadily, dropping 3 per cent in one year (from 2008) and 17 per cent over the past decade (from 1999).

The property crime rate has declined by 50 per cent since 1991, and in 2008 was also at its lowest in the last twenty-five years. Violent crime peaked in 1992, and decreased by 14 per cent to 2008. The 2008 violent crime rate was the lowest recorded since 1989.

Figure 1. Police-reported crime rate has been decreasing since 1991

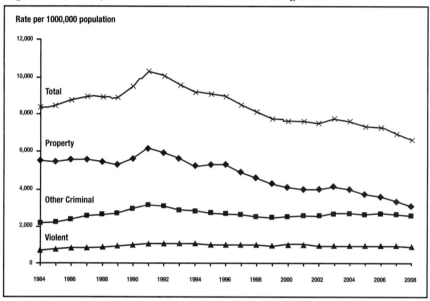

Source: Uniform Crime Reporting Survey. Canadian Centre for Justice Statistics. Statistics Canada.

Some critics who are prepared to accept that crime rates are declining in general will nevertheless insist that violent crime is on the rise. This is not true. The Crime Severity Indexes show sharp declines since 2006, and significant declines over the past decade. The Crime Severity Indexes are a measure of the seriousness of police-reported crime and were created by Statistics Canada in consultation with police chiefs, provincial justice departments, and academics. The Crime Severity Index decreased 4 per cent in one year (from 2008) and 22 per cent over the past decade (from 1999).

Statistics Canada reports decreases in rates of crime for many of those offences which the public fears most.[3] For example:

> *The term "serious assault" refers to two forms of assault: assault*
> *with a weapon or causing bodily harm...and aggravated assault,*
> *whereby the victim is wounded, maimed, disfigured or whose*

*life is endangered...Together, there were just over 57,000 such
incidents reported to police in 2009...Following nearly 25 years
of gradual increase, the rate of serious assault fell for the second
year in a row in 2009, down 3 per cent.*

Figure 2. Police-reported Crime Severity Indexes, 1999–2009

index

Note: *Indexes have been standardized, with 2006 as the base year equal to 100.*

Source: *Statistics Canada, Canadian Centre for Justice Statistics, Uniform
Crime Reporting Survey.*

The rate of reported sexual assault has also been declining since its peak
in 1993. It has decreased by 4 per cent since 2008.

The rate of robberies has been declining since its peak in the early 1990s.
There has also been a decrease in the use of weapons in robberies over the
past decade. The use of firearms in robberies dropped from 20 per cent to
15 per cent between 1999 and 2009, while the use of knives dropped from
36 per cent to 30 per cent during the same decade.

Rates of break-ins have dropped 42 per cent since 1999. Rates of auto
thefts have dropped 40 per cent from 1999 (including a drop of 15 per cent
in the one year from 2008).

Rates of drug offences are also down 6 per cent from 2008, including a

21 per cent drop in cocaine offences.

The traditional youth crime rate (the volume of youth accused) is about the same as it was in 1999, but youth crime *severity* is 7 per cent lower than in 1999. The youth *violent* Crime Severity Index remained stable from 2008 to 2009 after dropping in 2007. This stability continues despite far fewer youths being incarcerated under the new *Youth Criminal Justice Act*.[4] In fact, between 2003–2004 (the year the new *Act* came into effect) and 2008–2009, the average number of youth in detention (following conviction) fell a full 42 per cent.

Figure 3. Police-reported Youth Crime Severity Indexes, Canada, 1999–2009

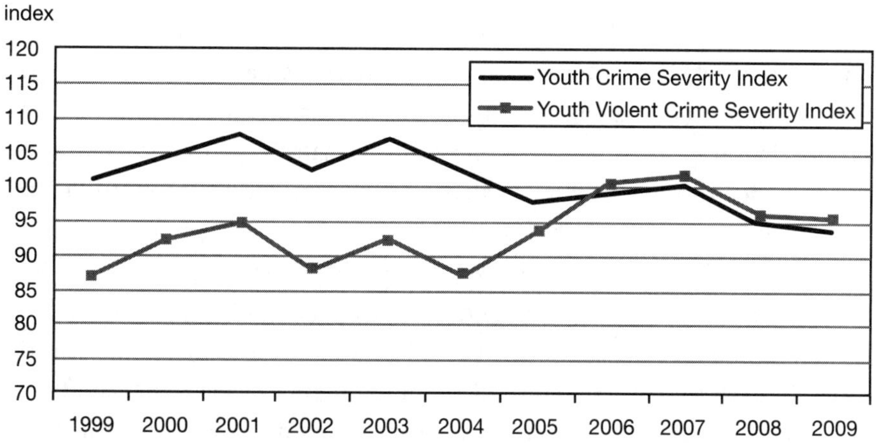

Note: Indexes have been standardized, with 2006 as the base year equal to 100.

Source: Statistics Canada, Canadian Centre for Justice Statistics, Uniform Crime Reporting Survey.

Put another way, under the old legislation Canada was unnecessarily incarcerating hundreds of young people.

There has been much publicity about the "guns, gangs, and drugs" that the Prime Minister says are an "epidemic."[5] The media reported endlessly on the "summer of the gun" in Toronto. The tragic death of Jane Creba was callously used as an illustration of how much gun crime existed in the city. In fact, Jane Creba's death was a highly publicized aberration, and the rate of such offences has dropped ever since that tragedy occurred. In 2009, the rate of firearms offences was down 10 per cent from 1999 figures.[6] As well, it will surprise many that Toronto has the third-lowest Crime Severity Index among thirty-three Canadian metropolitan areas.[7]

"Administrative" charges inflate crime rate numbers considerably. These amounted to 25 per cent of charges in adult court in 2008.[8] They include failure to appear in court, failure to comply with a court order, breach of probation, or being unlawfully at large. These are all victimless crimes. While they may be associated with more substantive charges (but not always), those substantive offences are most often property offences and not crimes against persons. Many, if not most, administrative charges relate to such breaches as failing to report to police when required, failing to inform authorities of a change of address, drinking alcohol when prohibited, and so on.

The inclusion of administrative charges in crime rates inflates the final numbers if what we are most concerned about is harm to victims or to property. In 2003–2004, 31 per cent of all cases before adult criminal courts involved at least one administrative charge, up from 22 per cent about a decade earlier.[9] Public Safety Canada says that the proportion has settled at 25 per cent in 2008, as noted.

More specifically, according to the Statistics Canada figures for 2006-2007, administrative charges accounted for 24 per cent of all charges in adult court.[10] The next offences on the list fall far short of this proportion. These were impaired driving (9 per cent), common assault (8 per cent), and theft (7.5 per cent). Other violent crimes appear even farther down the list, including major assault (4 per cent), weapons charges (3 per cent), robbery (1 per cent), sexual assault (1 per cent), and attempted murder and homicide (less than 1 per cent). Drugs charges come in at 3 per cent (possession) and 2.5 per cent (trafficking). Break-and-enter charges account for only about 3 per cent. Looking at the range of offences, then, it is clear that Canada's incidence of crime is vastly reduced if we discount the administrative charges and consider only those charges which cause actual harm to property or persons.

The Harper government also spreads fear about released prisoners who reoffend, implying that recidivism is rampant and that the Canadian justice system is a "revolving door." On the contrary, statistics show that the rate of reoffending (including violent and non-violent offences) has been dropping steadily for years from an already low rate.[11]

For example, day parolees (who used to be eligible for release after serving one-sixth of their sentences) have been highly successful when released to their communities.[12] Over the past decade, successful completion of day parole was over 80 per cent. More than 10 per cent of those parolees who were returned to prison were guilty only of a breach of conditions. And in 2008–2009, 2.8 per cent were revoked for a non-violent offence, while only 0.5 per cent were revoked for a violent offence. The total number of successful completions in that year was 3,073. This record speaks well for the system of day parole. Ironically, one of the laws passed two days before the Harper government fell in 2011 prohibits offenders from obtaining day parole after serving one-sixth of their sentences.

Full parolees have also been mainly successful upon release. These offenders become eligible for parole after serving one-third of their sentences, after satisfying the National Parole Board that they are no longer a risk to the public. The percentage of full paroles that were successfully completed increased in 2008–2009, and the rate of completion has been over 70 per cent since 1999–2000. Once again, breaches of conditions accounted for most of the revocations, at a rate of just under 20 per cent. In 2008–2009, 6.7 per cent of full paroles were revoked for a non-violent offence, and 0.8 per cent for a violent offence.

Finally, looking at the numbers for those released on statutory release (by which inmates are automatically released under supervision at two-thirds of their sentence), only a very few inmates were returned for reoffending. About 60 per cent of statutory releases have been successfully completed since 1999–2000. Around 30 per cent were revoked due to a breach of conditions. Significantly, 8.4 per cent were revoked due to a non-violent offence, while only 1.3 per cent were revoked due to a violent offence in 2008–2009. Again, the rate of reoffending is small; yet the *Roadmap* recommends the elimination of statutory release.

So it can be concluded with confidence that Canada's crime rate has been declining for over twenty years, and that fears about violent crime and recidivism are largely unfounded. The Harper government nonetheless continues to assert that crime is on the rise, and a recent report by the Macdonald-Laurier Institute has been produced to provide support for this position.[13] Although the author of the report does not claim to be a statistician, and although he offers no supporting evidence or sources for his arguments, his report attacks Statistics Canada's methodology and conclusions.

Scott Newark, in his report, says that Statistics Canada would get better results if it worked more closely with law-enforcement agencies.[14] Julie McAuley, director of StatsCan's Canadian Centre for Justice Statistics, replies that StatsCan is continually consulting with the Canadian Association of Chiefs of Police, as well as with criminologists, academics, and other experts. She points particularly to their involvement in developing the Crime Severity Index, which is severely criticized in Newark's report. Ron Melchers, a criminologist at the University of Ottawa, says that Mr. Newark "doesn't know what the Crime Severity Index is. It's not intended to be quantitative or numerical. He criticizes it for being something it's not intended to be, which is kind of bizarre."

A convincing refutation of the Newark report has been provided by two respected experts: Edward Greenspan, a renowned criminal lawyer, and Anthony Doob,[15] a criminologist who has been dealing with these statistics for more than thirty years.[16] They contend that Mr. Newark compares figures that cannot be compared, presents figures that are not accurate, and ignores evidence supporting the conclusion that crime is decreasing.

For example, Mr. Newark expresses concern that Statistics Canada does not include crime rates for all criminal offences. Mr. Greenspan and Dr. Doob point out that this information is freely available on the Statistics Canada website. Mr. Newark provides numbers that he says show violent crime going up from 1999 to 2009. He does not correct for population growth, however, and thus is reporting absolute numbers and not crime *rates* at all. The crime *rates* are clearly declining. He also says that youth violent crime has increased 100 per cent in three years, but his numbers are unaccountably wrong: instead of reporting 1,957 such crimes in 2001 (the correct Statistics Canada number), he reports 956. In 2008, the number of such crimes was 1,887, a clear decrease from 2001.

Mr. Newark even disputes the accuracy of Statistics Canada's homicide rate, saying it does not convey the reality. He says homicides are "arguably decreasing because of the increased quality of medical care," and not because there are fewer actual attempts to kill. If his thesis were correct, then the number of attempted murders should be on the rise, but it is not. In addition, an offender can be convicted of attempted murder even where there are no life-threatening injuries or any injuries at all. Thus, attempted murder numbers, even if they were on the rise, would not account for any decrease in the homicide rate.

When asked for a comment about the confrontation between Statistics Canada and Mr. Newark, Justice Minister Nicholson's office replied, "Unlike the opposition, we do not use statistics as an excuse not to get tough on criminals...One victim of crime is still too many."[17]

One victim of crime is certainly too many. But as Greenspan and Doob say, "Crime rates have nothing to do with tougher laws or harsher sentencing. The fact is that crime rates go up and down. In recent years, they've gone down." The government's punitive approach is not going to affect this.

THE GOVERNMENT VERSUS STATISTICS CANADA

The Conservative government says that Statistics Canada's entire system of gathering statistics is biased. Minister Toews believes that Statistics Canada's methods are systematically and massively understating crime rates. He claims that there is a high volume of unreported crime and that these numbers ought to be included in the analyses. Following his lead, Stockwell Day made headlines in August 2010 when he claimed that thousands of new prison cells were needed because of the "alarming" rates of unreported crime.[18] He cited a Statistics Canada victimization survey that showed rates of reporting were marginally down.

Every few years, Statistics Canada does do a victimization survey that deals with a select group of crimes. According to criminologist Anthony Doob, the last two surveys concluded that people are indeed reporting less by a few percentage points.[19] Dr. Doob then talked about what those numbers might represent.

For example, anyone who uses the Internet will likely have received spam emails offering a small fortune in exchange for helping with a bank transaction. This fits the definition of attempted fraud. Virtually no one reports it. People whose bicycles are stolen often do not report the crime unless they plan to make an insurance claim. They know that the police are at work on more serious crime and so do not bring forward these kinds of complaints.

The same is true for occasional shoplifting and any number of other offences.

Mr. Newark also claimed that people do not report crime because of fear of reprisals. This is not supported by the evidence. The most recent report on victimization from Statistics Canada provides us with the full range of reasons people do not report crime.[20] Fear of revenge by the offender is second-last as a reason for failing to report, and is provided as a reason by only 6 per cent to 7 per cent of respondents.

The Conservative government says its tough-on-crime agenda is designed to "restore faith in the justice system." However, the same victimization report shows that "no confidence in criminal justice system" is a factor in failing to report crimes for only about 14 per cent of respondents. Thus, a failure of confidence in the system is not a major problem among victims.

The reasons people give for not reporting crime seem eminently sensible, and mainly save law enforcement a lot of work that would produce dubious results. For example, they cite that the offence was not important enough to report (70 per cent) or that they felt the police would not be able to do anything about it anyway (60 per cent). Many respondents (40 per cent) dealt with the matter in another way, and many (35 per cent) decided that it was a personal matter, and so did not report. About the same proportion (35 per cent) stated that they did not want the police to be involved, while some felt that the police would not help them (20 per cent). There were some who felt the police would be biased (10 per cent) and others who feared publicity or news coverage (5 per cent). Finally, about 10 per cent of respondents did not report offences because no items had been taken or the items had been recovered, or because their insurance would not cover the loss. It is hard to see how including thousands of such unreported offences would give the government useful information for designing policy options.

Despite efforts by the government to frighten Canadians, Statistics Canada's *Juristat* also found that 93 per cent of Canadians were "satisfied with their personal safety" (48 per cent were *very* satisfied). Victimization rates in 2009 were stable as compared to 2004. The alarmist tone of Mr. Newark's report is thus puzzling, and his analysis does not support the conclusion that "many of us appear to have accepted more crime as inevitable."

INCARCERATION RATES VERSUS CRIME RATES

Since the Conservative government is appealing to victimization statistics to justify its punishment-oriented policies, it is important to look at the relationship between victimization and imprisonment rates. Tapio Lappi-Seppälä of Finland has compared the rates and has found that there is no relationship between the two.[21] For example, he found that in Scandinavia and the United States, victimization rates are "practically identical," but that imprisonment rates in the United States were staggeringly high compared to those in Scandinavia. Thus, more incarceration does not lead to less victimization.[22]

Research also does not show a relationship between crime rates and incarceration rates. Dr. Doob has done an impressive amount of research into this issue. He finds that the only thing that seems to account for high or low incarceration rates is the choice of public policy.[23]

The following two charts created by Dr. Doob show that Canada's crime rate and that of the United States follow approximately the same trajectory, rising upwards to the early 1990s and then trending downwards.[24]

Figures 4 and 5. United States and Canadian Crime Rates

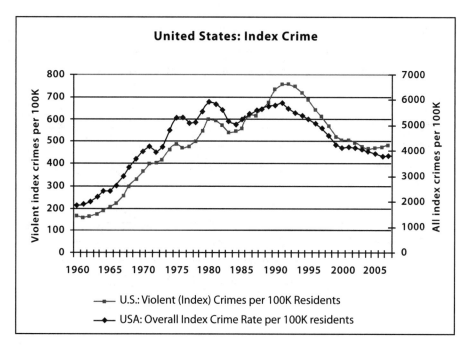

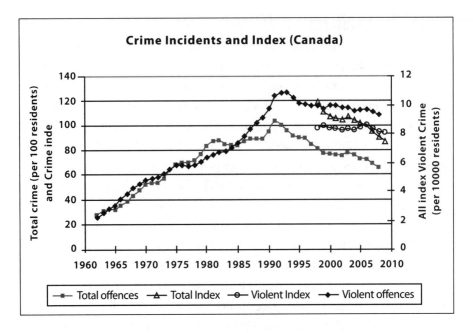

However, looking at the comparison between Canada's incarceration rate over those years and that of the United States, we see a dramatic difference.

Figures 6 and 7. United States and Canadian Imprisonment Rates

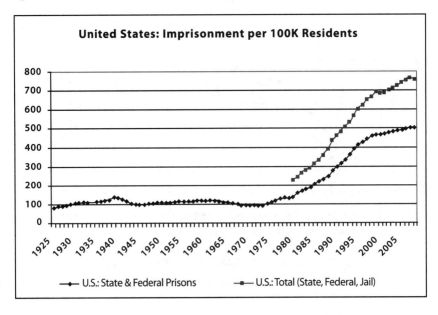

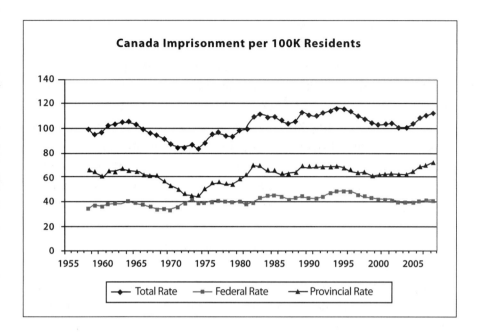

Canada Imprisonment per 100K Residents

Whereas the United States' rate of incarceration went up from 166 per 100,000 of population (in 1970) to 756 (in 2007-2008), Canada's has risen only slightly since the 1950s, and in 2008 Canada incarcerated only 112 people per 100,000 of population. The incarceration rate in the United States remained relatively flat until the 1980s. Interestingly, it was just when crime rates began to tail off that the United States went on an orgy of incarceration. Since no other Western country followed this trend to high incarceration rates and since other Western countries present similar decreasing crime rates over those years, it is fair to conclude that the high level of incarceration in the United States did not account for its decreasing crime rate. There are many factors which create a climate likely to result in criminal offences. The incarceration rate is not one of them.

It is a fact that imprisonment rates may be reduced significantly without an adverse effect upon crime rates. Readers may be surprised to learn which governments have presided over such a reduction. Ronald Reagan first became governor of California when the incarceration rate was 146 per 100,000. Four years later, in 1972, it was 96 per 100,000, a reduction of 34 per cent. Mr. Reagan was happy to take credit for this reduction in the prison population, remarking that only a conservative governor could get away with it. Any liberal, he knew, would be excoriated for doing the same.[25]

Margaret Thatcher, too, while a strictly law-and-order prime minister of Great Britain, was unwilling to pass laws that would add to incarceration numbers. This was largely because she knew how expensive imprisonment is. Consequently, during her tenure, from 1979 to 1990, the incarceration rate barely budged (from eight-five per 100,000 to eighty-eight).

There is a lesson here for advocates of incarceration. Savings in the billions can be produced by reducing the numbers in prison, with no discernible negative effect upon crime rates. Many states in the United States have taken a hard look at their deficits and have begun to slash imprisonment rates.[26] California has just been ordered by the courts to reduce its prison population by 40,000 over two years.[27]

Professor Neil Boyd, Associate Director of Criminology at Simon Fraser University, cites recent research that compares about thirty nation-states and shows that there is "no systematic relationship between rates of imprisonment and rates of crime. The extent to which a given country imprisons its citizens has no meaningful connection to the extent of crime that it experiences."[28]

Finland is an example.[29] It has made a concerted effort to reduce imprisonment over the past fifty years. At the beginning of the 1950s, Finland had 200 prisoners per 100,000; but by the 1990s it had reached the Nordic level of around sixty. Lappi-Seppälä notes that Finland substantially reduced its incarceration rate without disturbing "the symmetry of the Nordic crime rates." He concludes that "crime and incarceration rates are fairly independent of one another; each rises and falls according to its own laws and dynamics."

Lappi-Seppälä, Boyd, and Doob are not outliers when it comes to this assessment. The work of D. Greenberg, H. von Hofer, J. Sutton, and R. Ruddell support the same conclusions.[30] All of them agree that differences in the use of imprisonment cannot be explained by the level and trends in criminality.

If crime rates do not fluctuate according to the number of offenders who are incarcerated, then what does cause crime rates to rise or fall? Statistics Canada confirms that one influential factor is demography.[31] For example, people aged fifteen to twenty-four are responsible for much of the crime. Any time there is a bulge in that age group, the crime rate is likely to rise. Similarly, when the population begins to age (as the baby boomers are doing now), crime rates decline. Other influential factors noted by Statistics Canada are unemployment rates, alcohol consumption trends, and shifts in inflation. We will see that drug addiction, untreated mental illness, poverty, homelessness, the effects of colonization, previous abuse, and many other risk factors contribute to crime statistics.

If incarceration rates run on their own trajectory, independent of what the trend is in crime rates, then it is important to ask why the Harper government is introducing dozens of laws designed to consign ever-larger numbers of citizens to prison. The government is not basing its legislation upon statistics, research, experience, or common sense. If there is anything to be afraid of, this is it—a government determined to punish thousands of Canadians at immense cost to the Treasury and to our human dignity.

3: MANDATORY MINIMUM SENTENCES AND THE MYTH OF DETERRENCE

APPROACHES TO SENTENCING

The Conservative government's tough-on-crime agenda is specifically designed to produce a higher incarceration rate with longer sentences. Mr. Harper and his ministers are pursuing this goal with fixed determination. Canada appears to be striving for a gold medal in the incarceration Olympics.[1]

From the outset, ministers of the Crown have made it clear that they do not trust judges to carry out their sentencing mandate responsibly. This is why the government is creating a multitude of mandatory minimum sentences that remove judges' discretion to apply an appropriate sentence in each individual case for each individual offender. Those who are close observers of our judicial system say that Canada's judiciary applies the law responsibly. Judges hand down harsh sentences when necessary and craft appropriate, workable alternatives where justified. Appeal courts rectify any errors.

Nonetheless, the Conservatives are highly critical of the judiciary and of its relationship to the executive branch of government. Prime Minister Harper has been heard to say that he wants judges appointed who are tough on crime. He was sharply criticized for this by a former chief justice of the Supreme Court, Antonio Lamer, who pointed out how inappropriate Mr. Harper's comments were. "I must say I was taken aback. The prime minister is going the wrong route as regards the independence of the judiciary. He's trying to interfere with the sentencing process."[2]

Public Safety Minister Toews has also been pointed in his complaints about judges. As Justice Minister of Manitoba, he said judges, unlike parliamentarians, "are not well-placed to understand and represent the social, economic, and political values of the public."[3] He also described one of Canada's most respected jurists, Louise Arbour, United Nations High Commissioner for Human Rights and former Supreme Court justice, as a "disgrace." This comment came in the context of a Liberal request that the House of Commons acknowledge Justice Arbour's work at the United Nations upon her retirement from that position. Mr. Toews objected, saying, "The comments that Louise Arbour has made in respect of the state of Israel and the people of Israel are, in fact, a disgrace and I stand by those words." He was referring to her call for the protection of civilians during the 2006 Israel-Lebanon war, when she said that "the scale of killings...could engage the personal criminal responsibility of those involved." Her comments were interpreted by some as anti-Israel.[4]

More recently, Immigration Minister Jason Kenney launched an attack upon federal court judges with whose decisions he disagreed.[5] In a public speech to the University of Western Ontario's law faculty, he said that judges were deciding cases "seemingly on a whim." He suggested that they were preventing him from properly administering the immigration program. It is not clear why judicial decisions that differ from Mr. Kenney's own preferred outcome would prevent him from administering his department, since he has the power to change any laws which he feels are being interpreted improperly. Nevertheless, he maintained that "most Canadians share my despair at such decisions" and went on to present accounts of a few cases which observers described as "highly selective, incomplete...misleading [and]...just plain wrong."[6]

The Conservative government also has difficulty in accepting judicial interpretation of constitutional issues. A tension between the executive and the judiciary has existed throughout Canada's history, because the parliamentary system was set up to ensure that there are adequate checks and balances. Thus, for a court to rule in opposition to a sitting government's agenda is neither unusual nor inappropriate.

Mr. Toews views the matter differently. In criticizing Supreme Court of Canada decisions, he has accused a former chief justice of overseeing a "frenzy of constitutional experimentation."[7] He titled one speech, "Abuse of the Charter by the Supreme Court."[8] He has continually criticized the judiciary in its implementation of the *Charter*,[9] failing, it seems, to realize that the *Canadian Charter of Rights and Freedoms* was enacted precisely for the purpose of protecting the rights of Canadians against government abuse.

The tension between the Supreme Court of Canada and the Conservative government came to a head with the court's judgement in the Omar Khadr case.[10] It found that Mr. Khadr's rights under the *Charter* have been and continue to be violated by his treatment in Guatanamo Bay. The court did not order the government to request Khadr's repatriation, but it did say that "courts are empowered to make orders ensuring that the government's foreign affairs prerogative is exercised in accordance with the constitution."[11]

No past government has ever ignored such a strong declaration from the Supreme Court of Canada. To date, however, no action has been taken by the Harper government and nothing further has been heard from the Court. Omar Khadr is still at Guantanamo Bay. He is the only Western detainee whose home country has refused to request his repatriation.

The relationship between the executive and judiciary has thus been uneasy since the accession of Mr. Harper's government. Conservative efforts to erode the sentencing function and to influence the selection of judges appear directed to upsetting the usual balance by diminishing the independence of the judiciary in favour of the powers of Parliament.

Usually a fierce supporter of the Harper government, Conrad Black has been thunderstruck at the approach of the government to the sentencing power. Any attempt at summary would lose the flavour of his forceful argument. He says:[12]

> The government should run, not walk, to the dustbin to deposit there its proposals...for larger prisons, longer criminal sentences, and harsher treatment of inmates...
>
> The government is inching at a pace appropriate to the ponderous mind of the average correctional officer down the path laid out by its Roadmap to Greater Public Security. The most recent leaps backwards have been on mandatory minimum sentences, harsher marijuana laws, and extension of almost all

sentences, all bad, unjust, and expensive mistakes. Mandatory Minimum Sentences [are] a political catchy method of avoiding the perceived problem of soft-hearted ninnies as judges, letting people off lightly. It has been a catastrophic failure in the United States, from which the designers of the Roadmap have cribbed it, and emulating it in Canada would be an outrage... There is no rationale or excuse for confining those who are not physically dangerous, nor for reducing their access to treatment, which is cheaper, more effective, and more humane than prison, though less likely to appeal to knuckle-dragging deadbeats of the jail'em, flog'em, hang'em school.

Put another way, "Prisons are not a sign of a successful society. Building them when they're not even needed is a wasteful folly."[13]

Canadians take a more nuanced approach to crime and punishment than they are generally given credit for. A January 2007 survey of public attitudes concluded that "the strongest public support lay with the restorative justice objectives of promoting a sense of responsibility in the offender and securing reparation for the crime victim."[14] The authors found that there was less support for principles of deterrence and incapacitation than for restorative justice. People generally agreed with the idea of mandatory minimum sentences, but added the important caveat that judges be allowed to exercise discretion outside the minimum—something the Conservative agenda does not contemplate.

In order to understand fully the challenge that Canadian judges face in sentencing, it is important to understand what their mandate is. Several amendments to the *Criminal Code of Canada* have been made since 1995, setting down in detail what factors judges are expected to consider when imposing sentence. The list is long and comprehensive, and it is used by judges each and every time they sentence an offender.

The basic principles are set out in s. 718 of the *Code*. It lists denunciation and deterrence as two principles of sentencing, and these are the two upon which the Conservative government has relied virtually exclusively. Next on the list is the separation of the offender from society—but only "where necessary." This is a signal to judges that incarceration is a last resort and not the first or even a second resort. The last three principles promote the rehabilitation of the offender, reparation of harm to victims, and the encouragement of a sense of responsibility in offenders as well as acknowledgement of the harm they have done.

These last three objectives make it clear that there is much more to be considered than punishment, prison sentences, and some vague notion of deterrence when dealing with an offender. The *Criminal Code* brings victims into the picture in a very prominent way, and also requires that rehabilitation be a part of a judge's consideration, as well the restoration of balance in the community.

According to the Supreme Court of Canada, these principles were enacted because Parliament wished to mandate the expanded use of restorative principles in sentencing. Significantly, this was done because of the proven general failure of incarceration to rehabilitate offenders and reintegrate them into society.[15]

Judges are expected to consider a list of additional sentencing principles that are set out in s. 718.2 of the *Code*. These enumerate the aggravating or mitigating factors that warrant the judge's consideration, and which will affect his or her decision on sentence. The circumstances of an offence will be considered aggravating if the offence was a hate crime, spouse or child abuse, abuse by someone like a teacher or a priest who is in a position of trust, an organized crime or gang offence, or terrorism. Many of these factors attempt to respond to the special needs and position of victims.

If that were not enough, there is a list of four further considerations attached to s. 718.2. The first factor is simply designed to ensure a degree of parity in sentencing. It says that a sentence should be similar to that imposed on similar offenders in similar cases. Once mandatory minimum sentencing laws come into effect, all semblance of parity will be lost, since the identical minimum will be applied to offenders who are differently situated and whose offences are different in their details. Judges will be thwarted in their task, and the *Criminal Code* parity provision will no longer be meaningful.

The other three factors are specifically intended to restrain the use of incarceration. Consecutive sentences should not result in "unduly long or harsh" sentences. No offender should be deprived of liberty "if less restrictive" sanctions are appropriate in the circumstances. And "all available sanctions other than imprisonment that are reasonable in the circumstances" should be considered, especially for Aboriginal offenders. It could not be clearer, that judges are to restrain their use of incarceration.

THE MYTH OF DETERRENCE

Those are the general principles of sentencing. Among them is deterrence, which is also a stated aim of the Conservative government. It says its legislation is intended to take violent, repeat offenders off the streets and to stop "revolving door" justice or recidivism. The only way longer sentences might achieve these objectives would be by way of specific deterrence (removing the offender himself from society for a longer period of time), or by general deterrence. For general deterrence to work, a potential offender is supposed to be deterred from committing crimes because he or she expects to be caught, knows what the consequences will be, and wishes to avoid them. The public policy decision to increase incarceration thus relies largely upon a belief in the effectiveness of deterrence.

If there were a deterrent effect to long sentences, heavy use of incarceration, and mandatory minimum sentences, then the United States should have one of the lowest crime rates anywhere. Its incarceration rate eclipses the rate in Canada by close to 700 per cent. There has, however, been no concomitant decline in crime rates in the United States. Crime rate trends in Canada and the United States, as we have seen, are comparable.[16] The United States is incarcerating nearly seven times as much of its population as Canada, but with no perceptible positive effect upon its crime rate.

The more people you lock up, the less dangerous each extra prisoner is likely to be.[17] The state of Florida provides a case in point. Over the past thirteen years, the proportion of new prisoners in the system who had committed violent crimes fell by 28 per cent, but those doing time for "other" crimes increased by 189 per cent.[18] The "other" crimes were non-violent offences that involved neither drugs nor theft, such as driving with a suspended licence.

Some parts of the United States are beginning to buck the trend. New York State cut its incarceration rate by 15 per cent between 1997 and 2007, while violent crime dropped by an astonishing 40 per cent.[19] Mississippi has reduced the proportion of sentences that non-violent offenders must serve from 85 per cent to 25 per cent. Texas is using more non-custodial sentences, substituting a stronger probation system and community-based programs for the mentally ill and for low-level drug addicts.[20] The crime rate there has dropped by 10 per cent over five years, to its lowest level since 1973.

Most recently, über-conservative Newt Gingrich, former Republican speaker of the House of Representatives, has written that the United States is spending 300 per cent more on corrections than it did twenty-five years ago ($68 billion). He argues that it is not worth it.[21]

> *Our prisons might be worth the current cost if the recidivism rate were not so high but, according to the Bureau of Justice Statistics, half of the prisoners released this year are expected to be back in prison within three years. If your prison policies are failing half the time, and we know there are more humane, effective alternatives, it is time to fundamentally rethink how we treat and rehabilitate our prisoners.*

In fact, a number of high-profile American conservatives have declared themselves against an over-reliance upon incarceration.[22] Newt Gingrich has been joined by Edwin Meese (attorney-general under Ronald Reagan) and William J. Bennett (former "drug czar" under George H. W. Bush). They have issued a "Right on Crime" statement. In it they call for more cost-effective approaches that enhance public safety. They insist that prisons are "not the solution for every type of offender." Their approach is supported by recent research, which shows that incarceration does not produce lower victimization rates, and that other countries impose much shorter sentences without any increase in crime rates.[23] Mr. Gingrich's new liberal position has surprised observers in the United States, and is far more progressive than anything being proposed by the Harper government.

A similar movement is afoot in Britain. Justice Secretary Ken Clarke, a Conservative, bemoans the consequences of the previous Labour government's expensive crime initiatives.[24] These increased the cost of prisons by two-thirds and sent the prison population soaring. Clarke's stated intention is to find effective ways of punishing criminals while reducing public spending—the opposite of what the Harper government is doing. Clarke says, "Prison is not the answer for every offender. It can harden some non-violent, low-risk individuals, who come out as greater threats to society."

Other Western countries are also lowering their levels of incarceration. The Netherlands has begun to use more non-custodial sentences, and both the prison population and the crime rate have fallen.[25] In 2001, the Dutch allowed judges to order community service for crimes that had previously earned six months in jail. By 2008, 40 per cent of criminal trials were ending with community service orders.[26] In 2009, the country was able to close eight jails.

Where does Canada stand among comparable Western countries in its incarceration rate? Statistics show that we are already very tough on crime. While the United States outstrips every country in the world with its rate of 743 prisoners per 100,000 of population, most Western industrialized countries fall between 200 and 60.[27] The most recent figures show Canada at 117, somewhat below England, Scotland, Wales, New Zealand, and Australia but well above every other Western European country. As the example of Finland shows (see Chapter 8), cutting our rate in half, to around sixty per 100,000, should be entirely possible without triggering a rise in the crime rate.

As we have noted, the effectiveness of general deterrence (imposing a sentence designed to discourage other potential offenders) depends upon the potential offender's expectation of two things: getting caught, and being sentenced harshly.

The likelihood of getting caught usually depends upon the amount of funding placed in law enforcement and the community, and the amount of publicity accorded to these efforts. The theory is that if the offender has heard about these and calculates that he might get caught, he might think twice.[28] The fact is, though, that many offenders act on impulse, and they all plan not to get caught. The notion that they might go to prison never comes up. Deterrence in these circumstances will not work.

Sanjeev Anand, a University of Alberta law professor and former prosecutor, says people are "buying Ottawa's message. They are not thinking the way criminals think. Most criminal acts are impulsive; they are not well thought out."[29] Craig Jones, former executive director of the John Howard

Society, says that not even repeat offenders are thinking about the sentences they might face.[30] "They will tell you very specifically: 'I wasn't thinking about the sentence. I was thinking about how best not to get caught.'" The Canadian Safety Council weighs in: "There is little demonstrable correlation between the severity of sentences imposed and the volume of offences recorded. [The] greatest impact on patterns of offending is publicizing apprehension rates, or increasing the prospect of being caught."[31] More recent research has also concluded that shifting funds from imprisonment to targeted policing, thus increasing the likelihood of apprehension and punishment, may be effective in reducing both crime and imprisonment.[32]

Judge John Reilly of Alberta writes about his own education with respect to deterrence.[33] Our criminal justice system is "based on the assumption that the best way to modify behaviour is to instill fear through punishment or the threat of punishment," he says. Starting out as a hard-line, punishment-oriented young crown attorney and judge, he later came to believe that alternative methods of behaviour modification based on "relationship, understanding, reconciliation, restitution, and even forgiveness" produced lower rates of recidivism. He thinks that reliance on denunciation and deterrence is "archaic and wrong...futile, wasteful, and counterproductive."[34]

The Correctional Service of Canada, too, has stated its opinion on the subject. In an analysis obtained by the *Toronto Star*, the Correctional Service says that research shows mandatory minimums do not have a deterrent or educative effect.[35] In fact, the Correctional Service says the "tough on crime" proposals will probably not make for safer streets. This is a startling conclusion, by people who should know, that the government's claims about improved public safety are baseless.

Consider the following example. Fred and Jim are two ordinary young men with good jobs who are long-time friends and who think they are clever. They joke about the stupidity of bank robbers, who do not seem to know how to carry off a crime without getting caught. Fred and Jim muse that they could easily design the perfect crime. At first they discuss it only in theoretical terms, but gradually they become caught up in the idea, and soon they are out buying a gun and a camera and renting a van.

They know that the crimes (kidnapping and extortion) they are about to commit are very serious. They know that the punishment if they get caught will be severe. But they are sure their plan is sophisticated. Instead of going to the bank and demanding money from the teller, they decide to go to the home of the bank manager and kidnap his wife. They tie her up, place her in the van, and take a photo of her to show to her husband.

They then proceed to the bank, where Fred waits in the getaway van and Jim goes to the bank manager's office with the photo and gun to demand money. The bank manager tells Jim that he does not keep money in his office, but if he can be allowed to step out for a moment, he will be right back with some cash. He returns with a security guard, and that is the end of the perfect crime.

If this seems like an incredible story, be assured that it has all the hallmarks of most of the crime that keeps the courts busy. The deterrent effect of prison sentences is not considered—not even by otherwise intelligent, methodical, knowledgeable people. How is deterrence then supposed to work for the more typical offenders who may be mentally ill, high on drugs, or otherwise incapable of sound judgement in the moment?

It is clear that the people most intimately connected to the delivery of criminal justice do not think prison sentences deter crime, which is additional justification for asking a new Law Reform Commission of Canada to examine and address this in the *Criminal Code*. It also provides ample justification for seeking alternative methods of sentencing, and for funding programs designed to prevent crime before it happens.

The Conservative government raises the spectre of recidivism as a reason for longer sentencing regimes. Specific deterrence, in the form of prison sentences, is designed to encourage the individual offender not to reoffend. Leaving aside the potential for an offender's committing offences within the prison, it is important to note that long sentences are likely to make an offender *more* inclined to offend upon release, not less. Research concludes that recidivism rates are the same whether an offender is given probation, a suspended sentence, or a prison sentence,[36] and that longer prison sentences are no more effective at preventing reoffending than shorter ones.[37] Finally, and significantly, young people sent to prison are *more* likely to reoffend than those who receive community sanctions.[38] Thus, it is difficult to justify the use of incarceration as a specific deterrent. Other sanctions are far more effective.

A 1999 meta-analysis from the University of New Brunswick, for example, reviewed research on recidivism, covering more than fifty studies and 336,052 offenders, and concluded that neither prison sentences in general nor longer prison sentences will reduce recidivism.[39] They found, instead, that prison produced a slight *increase* in recidivism (3 per cent), with lower-risk offenders more negatively affected by the prison experience. Rather than "scaring people straight," in other words, imprisonment for lower-risk offenders increases the likelihood of recidivism.[40] According to Public Safety Canada,[41] the New Brunswick study shows that, regardless of the type of analysis employed, "no evidence for a crime deterrent function was found" from the use of imprisonment.

The authors of this study set out the implications for public policy. They conclude that prisons should not be used "with the expectation of reducing criminal behaviour." They note that excessive use of imprisonment has enormous cost implications. They also recommend "repeated, comprehensive assessments of offenders' attitudes, values, and behaviours" during incarceration to determine who is being adversely affected by imprisonment.

In a plea for less rather than more incarceration, Serge Ménard, Justice Critic for the Bloc Québécois, was eloquent. M. Ménard's impeccable credentials make him eminently suited to comment. He practised criminal law for many years in serious and high-profile cases, worked closely with the police to defeat organized crime, and is highly respected in the profession. He says:[42]

> Although intervention is necessary, sentence length and severity have relatively little effect...Fear of getting caught is what deters people from committing crimes...Most people think getting caught and ending up with a criminal record is bad enough.

MANDATORY MINIMUM SENTENCES

Another central plank in the Conservative approach to criminal justice is the mandatory minimum sentence. This is offered by the Conservative government as a means to their stated ends of denunciation and deterrence. But, "If the only tool you have is a hammer, you tend to see every problem as a nail,"[43] as psychologist Abraham Maslow famously said. The Conservative government has seized upon incarceration—and mandatory minimum sentences in particular—to hammer down large numbers of offences and offenders. This approach to criminal justice is simplistic, but the issues are complex. They require complex and thoughtful solutions.

When the Conservatives won the 2006 election, Canada already had a number of mandatory minimum sentences on the books, almost all of them created since 1995. Eight were imposed in the wake of the École Polytechnique massacre in Montreal. Twelve came into being in 2005, when the Liberal government was fighting "soft on crime" accusations. More than twenty have been created or increased since the Conservatives came to power. Many, many more are being proposed in new legislation.

For politicians, the beauty of mandatory minimum sentences is that they are quick and easy to impose. They give the impression that the government is doing something about crime. This relieves the government of having to attack underlying problems in any serious way.

The government maintains that mandatory minimum sentences will ensure that the severity of the sentence will match the severity of the crime. In fact, mandatory minimums provide a one-size-fits-all solution, catching large numbers of less serious offenders in a very wide net. The guarantee of uniformity results in gross injustices.

This emphasis on mandatory minimums is interesting in that Justice Minister Rob Nicholson was vice-chair of a parliamentary committee in 1988 that recommended mandatory minimum sentences *not* be used except in the case of repeat violent sexual offenders.[44] Trying to explain the minister's new and contradictory position on mandatory minimum sentences, his director of communications writes that the justice system and the drug world are different now from what they were twenty-two years ago, and so the government's response has also changed. "Parliament," she writes, "is expected to draft and enact laws that clearly articulate the legislators' intent, which is reflective of the values of the citizens who elected them." She does not explain what has changed in twenty years. Two additional studies prepared for the Justice Department (in 2002 and 2005) also said that mandatory minimums do not reduce crime.

To take one example, under the mandatory minimum regime, in a case where an offender has been convicted of several firearms offences or drug offences, the sentence will have to reflect the new mandatory minimum sentences for each offence. That means that each individual offence will attract a minimum sentence (five years, for some offences). If the sentences are imposed as consecutive, it will be impossible for a judge to produce a sentence that is not excessively long, thus contravening one of the sentencing principles set down by the *Criminal Code*.

Similarly, how is a judge to consider "less restrictive" sanctions, as he or she is required to do by the *Criminal Code*, when faced with mandatory minimum sentences? He or she will be unable to fulfil the obligations of a judge under that sentencing principle. The same holds true for the principle that requires imprisonment to be the last resort, especially in cases involving Aboriginal offenders.

Much of the Harper government's proposed legislation is thus diametrically opposed to the approach adopted by Canada's *Criminal Code*. Years of close consideration led to the enshrinement of these sentencing principles, but the current government intends to brush them aside, and to do so in a way that can only present a dilemma for those charged with dispensing justice.

A short example will illustrate why judges require the flexibility offered by the *Code*'s current provisions. Imagine a headline that says, "Attempt by Father to Kill Three Children Nets a Conditional Sentence." This is an instance to which, without full information, people are likely to respond, "How outrageous. What a slap on the wrist. He should go to jail for life."

Then the circumstances are explained. A father of three small children, a dedicated family man, suddenly loses his wife to cancer. He is left alone in his grief to care for the children and shoulder all of the responsibilities of the home and work. He falls into a deep depression and, when it seems impossible to go on, places his children and himself into the family vehicle in the garage and turns on the engine. His clear intent is to end the lives of all of them. In only a few moments he comes to his senses, turns the car off, brings the children back into the home unharmed and unaware of the crisis, and they resume their normal lives.

Some time later, one of the children happens to mention the event to her teacher. The teacher, as she is obliged to do by law, reports it to the authorities. The father is charged with three counts of attempted murder.

The judge, after much deliberation and with the concurrence of all sides, decides it is appropriate to impose a conditional sentence, allowing the father to continue looking after his children in the home, and with a requirement that he seek therapy.

Would any right-thinking person have done otherwise?

Mandatory minimum sentencing regimes are changing fast in the United States. In New York, the state government has repealed most mandatory minimums for drug offences.[45] As noted earlier, in 1970, George H. W. Bush voted as a congressman to repeal mandatory minimums for drug offences.[46] Michigan reduced its incarceration rate by 19 per cent in the three years ending in 2009. The abolition of mandatory minimums, notably supported by Michigan's prosecutors, was largely responsible for the change.[47]

University of Minnesota law professor Michael Tonry conducted a 2009 study based on at least sixteen studies of justice systems, including that of the United States.[48] He concluded:

> *The greatest gap between knowledge and policy in American sentencing concerns mandatory penalties. Experienced practitioners, policy analysts, and researchers have long agreed that mandatory penalties in all their forms—from one-year add-ons for gun use in violent crimes in the 1950s and 1960s, through 10-, 20-, and 30-year federal minimums for drug offences in the 1980s, to three-strikes laws in the 1990s—are a bad idea.*

The preference for mandatory minimum sentences by the Harper government is thus all the more puzzling. In its effort to imitate all things Republican, it seems to have missed the mark by about thirty years—during which time the United States has started rethinking its position. While the US is pulling back from policies that lead to over-incarceration, Canada is doggedly pursuing prison as the solution for virtually every wrong.

Graham Stewart points out that, until 2006, Canada had been doing criminal justice differently for about thirty years, encouraging rehabilitation rather than long sentences. As a result, he says, Canada had better results than the United States at a fraction of the cost. "Why," he says, "would we decide to go the American route? The only reason I could identify in our discussion is that, whereas it's bad corrections, it's good politics."[49]

Craig Jones suggests that the Harper approach is based upon a "bedrock economic model" of the sort now recognized as neoliberal.[50] Briefly put, this says that if you increase the price of something, demand for it goes down. In the context of crime, then, it is presumed that if you increase the cost of crime (prison), people will decide not to commit criminal offences. This rather strained analogy adapts Chicago School of Economics theory to criminal justice theory in a way that accords nicely with the economic models most admired by the Harper government. It is another way of justifying deterrence as a prime objective, and mandatory minimum sentences as a tool to this end.

Many Canadians, though, object strenuously to this simplistic and heartless approach. One judge says, "What judges are always concerned with is that, when the occasional exception comes along, we cannot do the right thing. There are cases where a mandatory minimum is simply too harsh."[51] An observer says that these sentiments seem to be shared by "an overwhelming number of lawyers, judges, and legal academics. They call mandatory minimum sentences ineffective, contradictory of bedrock sentencing principles, and downright cruel in specific cases."[52]

One twenty-year Crown Attorney in Victoria calls the proposed drug mandatory minimums "simplistic, harmful, and dysfunctional."[53] Robert Mulligan also reminds us of a fail-safe which never seems to figure in the thinking of the Conservative government. If a trial judge produces a sentence which is clearly inappropriate for the circumstances and the offender, this can and will be remedied on appeal. That is how the system is supposed to work, and it works well. Only about 1 per cent of indictable sentences are ever appealed—a testament to how often trial judges do get it right.

One justification offered for imposing mandatory minimums is to ensure predictability and consistency in sentencing. This is at first sight an admirable goal, but it ignores the fact that criminal justice deals with individuals. The simplistic formula of mandatory minimums is more likely to deliver injustice than anything a judge might do under the current system.

The Harper government is plainly not influenced by decisions of the

Supreme Court of Canada on the subject of mandatory minimums. Speaking for a unanimous court in 2000, Mme. Justice Louise Arbour spoke of the potential harm that mandatory minimum sentences can generate:[54]

> ...[S]entences that are unjustly severe are more likely to inspire contempt and resentment than to foster compliance with the law. It is a well-established principle of the criminal justice system that judges must strive to impose a sentence tailored to the individual case.

Consider the following example. Joe, high on drugs, runs into a bank, waves a gun around and threatens the tellers. His brother Jake waits at the door of the bank and acts as a lookout. Joe gets away with a small amount of cash, and he and Jake are driven by another brother, Ken, away from the scene. In a panic, they drive home to Mom and she throws the mask and gloves into the dumpster. Then the police arrive, and they are all arrested.

Joe will receive a minimum of four years for use of a firearm in the commission of a robbery. Jake will receive a minimum of four years for standing lookout, which makes him a party to the offence. Ken will receive the same four-year minimum sentence because, as the driver of the getaway car, he is a party to the offence. Mom will receive the same four-year minimum sentence because she aided and abetted the offence. Does this result appear to be fair and just?

Alan Borovoy, former counsel for the Canadian Civil Liberties Association, provides another, real-life example.[55] Ontario Provincial Police Officer Stanley Levant shot a fleeing suspect in 1994 during a split-second, high-stress confrontation. Because of his spotless record and the desperate situation, he received six months in jail. Sentenced under the current mandatory minimum regime, he would have received an automatic four years with no right of appeal.

Mr. Borovoy went on to comment on the Harper government's newly proposed firearms mandatory minimums. Officer Levant, under the new law, would have received a minimum of five years rather than four years. Mr. Borovoy laughed: "As though anybody contemplating a gun-related crime would not be deterred by a four-year possibility—but would be deterred by a five-year possibility."

Former Supreme Court of Canada Justice John Major says that mandatory minimum sentences are not a good idea because no two crimes are the same.[56] He concurs with former judges Herb Allard and Wally Opal that proposed mandatory minimums will end up in *Charter* challenges at the Supreme Court. He cites as an example the former seven-year minimum for importing drugs like marijuana. The Prison for Women was full of these cases in the 1970s. Prosecutors began routinely to drop smuggling charges down to "possession for the purpose" in order to avoid the seven-year minimum. The mandatory minimum sentence was finally ruled by the Supreme Court to be cruel and unusual punishment, and was declared unconstitutional.

As an example of the anomalous effect of the seven-year minimum, MP Serge Ménard cited the real-life example of a woman who accepted some packages for a friend who was away. The packages contained illicit drugs. Both the woman and her friend were convicted of importation and both received the minimum of seven years.

M. Ménard put forward an example to illustrate the effect of the proposed new drug law. If someone offers his friend a joint and the friend says no, the person offering the drug is still a trafficker within the meaning of the law. Under new mandatory minimums, if that person had ever previously been convicted of a drug offence, the offence would attract a minimum sentence of one year. If the person had proffered the drug near a school, or an area normally frequented by youth (a mall, a park) or if a young person was in the room at the time, or if the person who refused the drug was a youth, the minimum sentence would be two years.

Judge Allard talks about the one-year minimum that used to attach to auto theft. He notes that this was the mandated sentence, even in cases where a young person took a car for a joy-ride and returned it to its owner without damage. The judge had no discretion to lower the sentence.

If the concern is that "sentencing is in chaos," as expert Allan Manson suggests, then what is required is a thoughtful, analytical approach to the issue.[57] Because the many principles of sentencing in the *Criminal Code* are not stated in order of priority, judges give different weight to different aspects. It is like a buffet, Professor Manson says, and you don't know whether a judge is going to choose the beef or the tofu. Depending upon the choice, the sentence might be very different from jurisdiction to jurisdiction and from judge to judge. Professor Manson recommends the establishment of a sentencing commission to introduce "a measure of coherence to sentencing practices." Other jurisdictions in Britain and the United States have done so, and it would seem to be a sensible way to establish reliable, consistent sentencing.

UNINTENDED CONSEQUENCES

A number of unintended consequences come with a regime of mandated longer sentences. If judges no longer enjoy the trust of the government and lose their discretion to impose sentence, that responsibility will eventually be shouldered by others in the system. These will be people who have no training and no obligation with respect to an appropriate disposition for an offender. For example, as already noted, prosecutors may simply decide not to prosecute the offence as charged. They will instead adjust the facts, leaving some out if necessary, and proceed on a lesser included offence that has no mandatory minimum.

Respected jurist David Cole agrees that this will be one result of mandatory minimums. He gives as an example the situation in American jurisdictions where use of a firearm in the commission of an offence (as here) dictates a minimum sentence:[58]

> The Americans have this phenomenon in which the prosecution
> "swallows the gun." In other words, the prosecutor makes the
> gun go away so that the judge doesn't hear about it. We are
> concerned about taking those kinds of important decisions away
> from the public arena and into the private arena.

There are many ways that prosecutors can adjust cases in order to avoid what they regard to be too harsh a sentence. They can do so by not mentioning that a drug deal occurred in a school yard, or by not proving the amount of a fraud was over $1 million, or in a hundred other ways. This should not be left to the discretion of the prosecution. Crown Attorneys do not want the responsibility, which properly belongs to the judge. What purpose is served by removing discretion from judges and handing it to prosecutors?

Further distorting the system, some victims will decide not to report offences if they know that a harsh jail sentence is likely to result. Police officers, too, will decide to lay lesser charges or not to lay charges at all. People will refuse to sit on juries or will refuse to convict. In the United States, this is known as "jury nullification," and it has a storied history through the eras of Prohibition and in the Jim-Crow-era South. Juries just follow their conscience, defy the law, and refuse to convict.

Other consequences to the criminal justice system will ensue as a result of mandatory minimums and other lengthy sentences. Offenders who are facing long minimum sentences will fight their charges fiercely. There will be fewer guilty pleas, resulting in a multitude of court hearings. More personnel and more infrastructure will be required. Courts will become more clogged than they already are.

Since very few accused will plead guilty, very few will benefit from the shorter sentence that often comes with a guilty plea. Thus, offenders will occupy more time and space in the prison system, causing even more serious overcrowding, violence, and misery, to say nothing of the money required to house them.

A gross injustice will be visited upon some accused persons who are actually innocent of their charges. Some of them will plead guilty to lesser charges rather than face the awful certainty of the mandatory minimum sentence attached to the full offence. Thus the justice system will be distorted in the most fundamental way, and wrongful convictions will increase, which are likely to generate appeals in the future.

There can be no doubt that much of the new legislation will be subjected to scrutiny under the *Charter* at great expense. This head-on collision between the laws and the *Charter* has been anticipated by public servants from the moment the laws were drafted. In normal times, a Justice Minister signs an "executive certification" which says that any new piece of legislation complies with the *Charter*. Under the Harper government, though, according to one insider, legislation has been pushed through "despite stern internal warnings that it would likely violate *Charter* provisions.[59] This source said:

MANDATORY MINIMUM SENTENCES AND THE MYTH OF DETERRENCE

[The Conservatives] made a lot of campaign promises that were either ill-advised or not workable. Then, when they came into power, they were hell-bent on making them happen...Very often, there have been instances where very fine Department of Justice legal minds would say: "You can't do that because the Charter says X or Y." The answer from the minister would be: "I can't take that to caucus. We'll just have to barrel ahead."...The prevailing attitude was: "We'll sign the certification saying that this is Charter-proof and let the judiciary fix it later." There is a real fix-it-later attitude.

In summary, the government is drafting draconian sentencing laws designed to fill prisons, while doing little or nothing likely to apprehend and incarcerate the dangerous, violent offenders they keep telling us about, and certainly nothing to prevent crimes from happening in the first place. Nothing in the proposed laws would have helped in stopping a Clifford Olson or a Willie Pickton before they started to commit their appalling crimes. Nothing in the new legislation would have helped law enforcement agencies prevent the repetition of those crimes. Instead, the Conservative government is taking a superficial approach to a complex system, an approach guaranteed to cause more problems than it solves.

4: A CLOSER LOOK AT THE CONSERVATIVES' CRIME LAWS

Of the seventy-three bills before the Senate and House of Commons when the government fell in March 2011, twenty-eight bills, or 38 per cent, dealt in some way with the criminal justice file. Several bills were passed, including the *Tackling Violent Crime Act* and the *Truth in Sentencing Act*. Many others were winding their way through the system.

The Conservative government claims that its crime legislation is to remove dangerous, repeat offenders from the streets and to tackle the problem of "guns, gangs, and drugs." The Prime Minister has everyone in his caucus repeating this mantra. Marjorie LeBreton, government leader in the Senate, while defending Mr. Harper's appointment of another socially conservative Senator, said: "It'll strengthen our hand in dealing with justice bills, especially ones having to do with the youth criminal justice system. Guns and gangs and drugs. That's where Don Meredith will be really helpful."[1] MP Julian Fantino, a former Toronto police chief, took a hard line long before being elected: "Violent crime is up, it's been up, it's been going up for years, and now we're seeing an explosion of guns and violence."[2]

The Prime Minister himself is a master at fearmongering. In a speech to the Canadian Professional Police Association, he said:[3]

> *If we are to protect our Canadian way of life, we need to crack down on gun, gang and drug crime.*

Canadians are tired of talk. They want action, and they want it now.

...They've told us they want to be able to go about their daily lives without having to worry about getting hit by a stray bullet fired by a gang member,

Or being killed by a street racer losing control of his stolen vehicle.

They've told us they want to get real on crime.

And they want to put an end to gang, gun and drug violence.

Yet most of the legislation being offered as a solution will not prevent crime. It will merely weigh in after the event and create harsh penalties. Attorney General of New Brunswick Kelly Lamrock says, "Being tough on crime doesn't mean what you do after the crime's already been committed; it's what you do to make sure the crime doesn't happen in the first place. For us that means being tough on crime [in New Brunswick], and we are."[4]

2-FOR-1 CREDIT FOR PRE-TRIAL CUSTODY

Bill C-25, or *The Truth in Sentencing Act*, came into force on February 22, 2010. It eliminates the judicial convention of allowing two days for every one served in pre-trial custody when determining a sentence ("2-for-1"). This approach provided credit to offenders because of the appalling conditions in remand centres where they are held pre-trial, because of the lack of programming in these centres, and because the time spent in remand is "dead time"—meaning that it is not included when calculating the ever-important release date after sentencing.

Inmates in remand have not yet been convicted of any crime. Some have not yet even had a bail hearing. Some have had a bail hearing, but failed to convince the court that they are a good risk for release, and so have been denied bail. Others have been ordered released on conditions, but have been unable to fulfil one or more of those conditions. People often fail to meet bail conditions when they are unable to provide a fixed address or find someone who can sign as surety. (A surety is like a guarantor who agrees to ensure the accused's compliance with bail conditions, failing which the surety will have to forfeit an amount of money stipulated by the judge.) The remand population in Canada overall has almost doubled in the last ten years, due mainly to large numbers of accused being unable to satisfy their bail conditions.[5] This means that a judge has been satisfied that an accused could safely be released into the community, but that accused was unable to meet the necessary conditions.

The pool of remand inmates includes people charged with extremely violent crimes like murder, people charged with less serious offences like shoplifting, and everything in between. People of all ages are held together. Some will have long criminal records, and others will have none at all. Some will be sick with addiction withdrawal or will have other health issues. Many will suffer from a mental illness. There is extreme overcrowding in remand facilities, with all the attendant health risks. There is in most facilities absolutely nothing to do all day—no programs, no routine. Inmates are left to sit in their cells virtually all day, with relief only coming when they are shuffled into armoured vehicles and taken to court.

Statistics show that 65 per cent of those on remand are eventually convicted.[6] Fully 30 per cent have their charges withdrawn or stayed. The remainder are acquitted. Yet they are all treated exactly the same way in the remand centre.

A shocking description of the Don Jail in Toronto emerges from the story of Jeff Munro.[7] A schizophrenic, he had been picked up for exposing himself on the street. He had been sent to the Centre for Addiction and Mental Health many times before by police. This time, however, he was sent to the infamous Don. There he was punched and kicked to death by inmates who accused him of stealing a bag of chips. This is a description of the Don Jail in 2010:

> The prison is a cement box, the floor, walls and steel bars all painted a neutral white caked with grime. It's noisy, each of the units filled with the sounds of men shouting, banging the bars and arguing; wall-mounted TVs blare different channels. With hundreds of men living in cramped quarters, many of them taken directly off the streets, the smell is intense. The sound of the toilets is so loud, prisoners follow a self-imposed no-flushing policy throughout the night, and in the morning, the stench

of human waste is unbearable. Drugs move freely through the
Don, though correctional officers say that the odd whiff of pot
is a welcome respite from the stink of urine, vomit and sweat.
The jail is also overrun with mice, cockroaches and a generous
variety of infectious diseases.

Clearly, no one should have to endure these kinds of conditions for months and years—and yet many do.

It has been suggested that remand prisoners abuse the 2-for-1 convention by intentionally accumulating remand time in order to get a shorter sentence later. The attorneys general of both Alberta and Manitoba, who encouraged the passage of C-25, were among those claiming that accused persons were "banking" remand time in "many cases."[8] This was also the opinion of the federal government.[9] Defence lawyers, on the other hand, maintain that banking time rarely happens. In view of the conditions that exist in remand, it is hard to imagine that many offenders would prefer shorter prison time to shorter remand time.

Aside from ignoring the shocking conditions in remand, Bill C-25 also creates sentences that are inequitable. Cheryl Webster, a criminologist at the University of Ottawa, points out that 2-for-1 was adopted as a convention for the very purpose of producing parity at the sentencing end.[10] Once sentenced, every day after conviction provides an offender with 1.5 days' credit toward his release date (because prisoners are currently released at two-thirds of their sentence if they do not achieve parole). This is not true for pre-conviction time (remand or "dead" time). So without at least a 1.5-for-1 offset, there is no parity in the actual sentences. Yet Parliament settled for 1-for-1, which is clearly inequitable.

Imagine two equally-situated offenders, Bob and Doug, who commit the same offence. Bob makes bail but Doug does not. When convicted, each receives the equivalent of ninety days as a sentence. Doug has already spent thirty days in remand.

Bob (who was out of custody) serves sixty days and then is released because the provincial system allows offenders one-third of their sentence off as remission.

Doug is sentenced to sixty days because, under Bill C-25, he is allowed one day for each day in custody. Thus thirty days are subtracted from what would have been his ninety-day sentence. Doug then has to serve two-thirds of sixty days, or forty days. Adding up his time in remand (thirty days) and his sentenced time (forty days) produces a total of seventy days. This is ten days or 17 per cent more time than Bob, even though both committed the same crime in the same circumstances, and have the same background. Bill C-25, which purports to provide equity, actually does the opposite. 1.5-for-1 should be the legal minimum if parity is the goal.

The question arises: why did our legislators set 1-for-1 as the basic formula (with a special application to ask for an increase), when it should mathematically be 1.5-for-1 (providing parity, with an option to apply for more)? This error was pointed out by a number of experts at the parliamentary committees. David Daubney, General Counsel for the Criminal Law Policy Section at the Department of Justice, agreed that, under the 1-for-1 formula, offenders who serve remand time will finally serve more time than those fortunate enough to make bail.[11] Time in remand actually *adds* to the final tally of time served. Faced with the patent unfairness of the new regime, Justice Minister Nicholson pronounced, irrelevantly, "Bad behaviour should not be rewarded."[12]

Justice Minister Nicholson also tried to justify C-25 by claiming that, in the past, there were "many cases" in which offenders were provided with an enhanced credit above 2-for-1, and that he felt this to be inappropriate.[13] Allan Manson, who is an expert in the area of sentencing, says that enhanced credits have been rare, and that he was only able to find twenty-five such cases in the past seven years.

Parliamentarians were not the only ones failing to grasp the implications of C-25. Expert witnesses appearing before the Senate Committee admitted they did not understand the sentence calculation issue. The attorneys-general of both Alberta and Manitoba said they would need "time to consider" the sentence calculation, signalling that it had played no part in their thinking as they promoted and supported the legislation.[14] They also admitted that the Western attorneys-general who had pushed so hard for a law were recommending the equitable formula of 1.5-for-1, and not the inequitable 1-for-1 at all.

The Harper government argued that C-25 was necessary because the courts are clogged and the law would make the system more efficient. Matthew MacGarvey of the Law Union of Ontario, for example, testified that in Ontario the time required to get to trial has nearly doubled since 1992.[15] Yet with Bill C-25 the government has added a new administrative burden to the remand courts, which will actually add to the backlogs.

This is because Bill C-25 allows offenders to apply for additional credit above the 1-for-1 formula if they can show "circumstances justify" an increase. This additional step will add significantly to the time and cost of processing bail court prisoners. Allan Manson pointed out to the Senate Standing Committee that 85,000 people were sentenced to custody in 2008.[16] Under C-25, virtually all of them would have applied for an increase to the remand credit. If this adds even five or ten minutes to each hearing, it is easy to imagine how the backlog will grow.

What is entailed in applying for enhanced credit? For one thing, offenders will call evidence as to the conditions of remand when asking for the increase. This is already happening. One person working at a detention centre in Toronto said he was being subpoenaed about three times a week to give such evidence.[17] Crown counsel agree that there will be more bail hearings and they will be longer. Jamie Chaffe, President of the Canadian Association of Crown Counsel, says there will be a "substantial impact" because bail courts will now be engaged in what is essentially a sentencing exercise.[18] Also, the legacy of the *Askov* case is looming. This means that if delays become too lengthy, *Charter* provisions will be invoked to argue for the release of unconvicted remand prisoners.[19] It happened before; it can happen again.

Martin Friedland, QC, a highly respected expert in criminal law, concluded from his research that being held in remand affected virtually all aspects of an accused's criminal case. Astoundingly, he found:[20]

> ...a clear relationship between custody pending trial and the trial itself. Not only was custody likely a factor in inducing guilty pleas, but those not in custody during trial were more likely to be acquitted than those in custody, and, if convicted, were more likely to receive lighter sentences.

Thus, an accused person who is held in remand prior to trial is more likely to get convicted and then to receive a longer sentence. This could be invoked as another argument for providing enhanced credit for remand time.

Justice Canada in 2009 found that there were great disparities across the country as to time spent in remand.[21] In 2008, the average stay in remand in Winnipeg was 120 days, compared with 17 days in Toronto and 54 in Whitehorse. Interestingly, although the information in the Justice Canada study was cited in a secret memorandum to cabinet, it was never made known to parliamentarians as they debated Bill C-25.[22] In other words, the Conservative government knew about problems with what they were proposing, but they did not make the information available to the House of Commons or the Senate. The broad disparities across jurisdictions provide another argument for permitting judges to exercise discretion with respect to credit for remand time.

There are other disparities as well. The abolition of 2-for-1 credit will unfairly target the disadvantaged, and in particular, Aboriginal people. Winnipeg is a good example, as a large proportion of those in remand are Aboriginal. Aboriginal people tend to be poorer, both economically and socially. They often cannot afford to pay their bail. And for various reasons they are rarely able to advocate for themselves.

There is a much simpler and fairer solution to the wrangling over how to deal with remand time. Instead of calculating an offender's sentence from the day he is sentenced, courts should calculate it from the first day of custody. This would not take account of the harsh conditions in remand, but it would at least avoid the more obvious inequity of the current system. The Canadian Sentencing Commission recommended this solution twenty years ago.[23]

It is hard to avoid the conclusion that the government had other reasons than efficiency and fairness for introducing this law. The Supreme Court of Canada has determined that living in pre-trial custody is a punishment in and of itself, and thus has endorsed 2-for-1. Judges wrestle every day with decisions about release, giving careful thought to the facts and the circumstances of each individual accused. Bill C-25 is an example of the Conservative government's effort to remove discretion from judges and tie their hands when it comes to the sentencing function.

The Harper government cynically used the news of the day to manipulate people into accepting this unfair regime, and parliamentarians into voting for it. The recent high-profile case of the "Toronto 18" had produced a scenario in which Amin Mohamed Durrani spent three years, seven months and eighteen days in pre-trial custody.[24] When he was finally convicted, his sentence was one day. Under the 2-for-1 formula, the judge gave the offender credit for seven and a half years. Since this was virtually identical to the sentence that the judge had in mind for the offences, the judge determined that the offender had already served his time. This was a fair disposition, but headlines blared "ONE DAY" without adequately explaining the rationale. Thus, the public and members of Parliament were given the impression that the system was broken and needed to be fixed.

When faced with the unpalatable facts about the colossal costs Bill C-25 would engender ($5.1 billion over five years),[25] Public Safety Minister Vic Toews retorted, "We understand there is a cost to keeping dangerous criminals behind bars. And, we're willing to pay it because it's a far cry from the costs to victims and society of having violent criminals on our streets."[26] However, passing legislation that keeps offenders in prison longer does not help fight violent crime. Such legislation takes effect only after the crime has been committed.

In a discussion at the Standing Senate Committee, criminologist Anthony Doob pointed out that the burgeoning numbers of accused persons in remand were not the result of dangerous "guns, gangs, and drugs" anyway. He said there was a simpler explanation: "It is part of our culture that we simply hold people in pre-trial detention."[27] Perhaps this partly explains why the Conservative government persists in retributive, counterproductive legislation. Mr. Harper believes that Canadians want to punish certain people. We don't care what it costs. We don't care if it works.

Whoever we are as a people, and whether or not we are prepared to accept this characterization of our national identity, the justice system is already preparing to adjust to the new reality. Justice David Cole predicted that the elimination of 2-for-1 would prompt judges to start thinking about how to compensate.[28] He said they would force trials to be held more quickly and might also "start compensating by intentionally lowering sentences"—an area in which they still have discretion as long as there is no mandatory minimum. Judges understand what remand conditions are like and why offenders should be provided with special credit for dead time. Contrary to the implication in the name given to the bill, there was never any lie in sentencing.

A recent court decision in Ontario provincial court has proven Justice Cole's predictions to be accurate. Judge Melvyn Green decided that Bill C-25 was constitutional. He also, however, recognized that it would produce injustice between identical offenders, depending on whether they were held in remand or released on bail.[29] He said that if this were widely known it "could only contribute to a sense of public outrage or abhorrence; a palpable sense of unfairness." Accordingly, since he could no longer apply the 2-for-1 convention, he instead adjusted the sentence for one Marvin Johnson. Mr. Johnson had been in remand for twelve months. The sentence imposed by Judge Green meant that he would be released within three days.

A summary of Mr. Johnson's circumstances illustrates the way in which the Conservative government is misdirecting its efforts to fight crime. Mr. Johnson was abandoned by his alcoholic father at age four, and by the age of forty was a homeless crack addict.[30] He had fifteen convictions since 1998, nine of them for trafficking drugs in small amounts to support his habit. He was caught selling $20 worth of cocaine to an undercover officer. He had never been in a drug treatment program.

As the *Globe and Mail* editorial writer said:

> *Should Canada be spending so much time and energy debating how long to keep Marvin Johnson in jail? Wouldn't it be more productive to figure out how to improve services for children who grow up in Marvin Johnson's straitened circumstances? Wouldn't it be better to work on treatment or supportive housing options for Marvin Johnson?*

It is expected that some judges will follow the lead of Judge Green while others will not. This will once again result in disparities between jurisdictions. Those who disagree with Judge Green's approach will impose their usual sentences, while incidentally pushing the number and length of court hearings inexorably up, as offenders object to the unfair treatment. While such a result could easily have been anticipated, and might have been prevented, Bill C-25 is now law and many more offenders are spending more time in prison, and chafing under the injustice.

YOUNG OFFENDERS

New proposals to amend the *Youth Criminal Justice Act* are among the most troublesome of those the government has put forward. Bill C-4: "Sébastien's Law (Protecting the Public from Violent Young Offenders)" is named after a young victim whose life was tragically and violently ended by a group of youths.[31] It had not become law at the end of the fortieth Parliament, but was destined to be passed as part of the omnibus bill the Conservatives promised during the 2011 election campaign.

The Conservative government claims that it has based its new, much harsher young offender legislation upon two things: the recommendations of Commissioner Nunn of Nova Scotia, and the results of country-wide consultations held in 2008. Yet Nunn's report found that the current *Youth Criminal Justice Act* was an "intelligent, modern, and advanced approach to dealing with youths involved in criminal activities."[32] It said that Canada was "far ahead of other countries in its treatment of youth in conflict with the law." It went on to make recommendations that were intended to "tweak" some parts of the *Act*, inadvertently opening the door for the Conservative government to justify levying more custodial sentences.

The report on the 2008 country-wide consultations, once it was finally made public, did not support the punitive approach presented in Sébastien's Law either. At the Standing Committee on Justice and Human Rights, committee members pointed out that there was "little support [in the report] for changes to the [*Youth Criminal Justice Act*] at this time."[33] MP Joe Comartin, a member of the committee, noted that the report did not agree that general deterrence works (that is, that tough sentences deter other potential offenders) and that it made no comment at all about specific deterrence (the idea of deterring the offender himself from reoffending). Nevertheless, the Conservative government put the principle of deterrence front and centre in the new bill. (Mr. Comartin also pointed out that the government ignored the comments of prosecutors where they disagreed with its intentions.)

Liberal justice critic Marlene Jennings demanded to know how the government had arrived at its position on youth crime in the face of the consultation report, which said:

> *Legislation cannot prevent crime, reduce crime or protect the public. Changing legislation will not change behaviour. The YCJA should not be changed just for the sake of change. There was an overwhelming consensus that the perceived flaws are not in the legislation; the flaws are in the system.*

The provisions of Sébastien's Law will roll back the considerable advances achieved by the *Youth Criminal Justice Act* since 2003. Before that time, Canada's *Young Offenders Act* had resulted in one of the highest incarceration rates of young offenders in the Western world. The new *Youth Criminal Justice Act* was adopted at that time with the express purpose of diverting young people away from the criminal justice system and dealing with their offences in alternative ways.

The success of the *Youth Criminal Justice Act* has been borne out by the statistics. Although the number of youth committing offences has remained relatively stable since 1999, the total number of crimes committed by youth is down.[34] Between 2002–2003 (the last year of the old *Young Offenders Act*) and 2006–2007, 26 per cent fewer cases were heard in youth court. And between 2003–2004 and 2008–2009, the average number of youth in detention following conviction fell a full 42 per cent.

To be clear, the drop in incarceration rates was *not* followed by an increase in the youth crime rate. On the contrary, the crime rate has been generally dropping since the *Youth Criminal Justice Act* came into force. Put another way, under the old *Young Offenders Act* Canada was incarcerating at least 42 per cent more youth than was necessary to control crime. It is one of the starkest examples of how incarceration rates bear virtually no relationship to crime rates.

Public Safety Canada says that the rate of youth charged has been decreasing since 1991, and that in 2003, "There was a notable decrease in all major crime categories, in part attributable to the implementation of the *Youth Criminal Justice Act* (YCJA) in April 2003, which places greater emphasis on diversion."[35]

Figure 8. Rate of Youths Charged per 100,000 Youth, 1989–2008

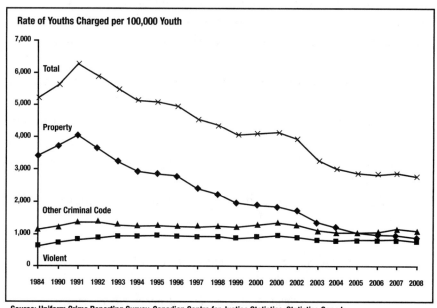

Source: Uniform Crime Reporting Survey. Canadian Centre for Justice Statistics. Statistics Canada.

Notes: For criminal justice purposes, youth are defined under Canadian law as persons aged twelve to seventeen years. Violent crimes include homicide, attempted murder, assault, sexual offences, abduction and robbery. Property crimes include break and enter, motor vehicle thefts, other thefts, possession of stolen goods and fraud. In 2008, 43.3 per cent of all youths charged with violent crimes were charged with assault level 1 (minor assault).

Despite the Statistics Canada evidence, Justice Minister Nicholson insists that youth violent crime has risen 30 per cent since 1991, and 12 per cent from 1997–2006.[36] These two views cannot both be right. Mr. Comartin pointed out to Mr. Nicholson that he was being selective in his use of the available data, relying upon a spike in youth crime in 2006, rather than more appropriately looking at the trend over time. As the graph shows, youth crime fell again after 2006, and has fallen a long way since its highest level in 1991.

The Violent Crime Severity Index for youth has been stable between 2001 and 2009 (see Figure 3). It should be emphasized that, in 2008, 43.3 per cent of all youths charged with violent crimes were charged with assault level 1, which is minor assault (see note to Figure 8, above). Thus, close to half of the violent crimes committed by youth are categorized as minor.

Opinions about the effectiveness of the *Youth Criminal Justice Act* cover the full range. The Canadian Bar Association has pronounced it an "unmitigated success."[37] Prime Minister Harper has pronounced it an "unmitigated failure."[38]

A British study, published by the Prison Reform Trust, describes Canada's *Youth Criminal Justice Act* as a "very progressive piece of legislation, one of the most progressive in relation to youth crime passed by a jurisdiction in the English-speaking Western world in a number of years."[39] The authors point out that custody is "one of the surest ways to grow the adult prison population of the future."

Canadian experts also praise the *Youth Criminal Justice Act* for its excellent results:[40]

> *Without increasing recorded youth crime, the YCJA has resulted in a very significant reduction in the use of courts and custody for adolescent offenders in Canada and hence has allowed a significant reduction in spending on youth courts and custody facilities, a reduction generally accompanied by shifting resources to community-based programs.*

These experts also note that Sébastien's Law will send more young people to jail and that "sending more young people into custody would increase the cost of youth justice services without increasing public safety."[41] Nicholas Bala, a respected youth justice expert at Queen's University's law faculty, calls the legislation "an example of pandering to public misperceptions about youth crime."[42]

Frank Addario, past president of the Criminal Lawyers' Association, made an impassioned appeal to the legislators.[43] He pointed out that causes of youth violence are closely linked to fetal alcohol syndrome, violence in the home, and poverty. He views Sébastien's Law as "another attempt to simplify what's really a complex social issue in order to condense it into a digestible election issue."

Statistics, research, and international plaudits aside, though, the government continues its unwavering course to more custody with less diversion and rehabilitation for young offenders.

One important change in the proposed legislation will add denunciation and deterrence to the principles of sentencing for youth. We have already noted that deterrence does not, generally speaking, work. Research shows deterrence especially does not work for young people because they "frequently act impulsively and often do not have the necessary intellectual capability to fully assess the consequences of their actions."[44] Sébastien's Law turns the whole philosophy of the *Youth Criminal Justice Act* on its head, by inserting principles of sentencing that apply to adults, and that had been purposely omitted from the sentencing of youths. This begins a march toward treating youths like adults, an approach the Supreme Court of Canada has explicitly rejected.

The Supreme Court of Canada has noted that the *Youth Criminal Justice Act* introduced an entirely different sentencing regime.[45] The Court approved of the new approach by saying that there must be a presumption of diminished culpability of youth.[46] The Court has held that "there is a rebuttable presumption of diminished blameworthiness or culpability in young persons by reason of the fact that they are more vulnerable, less mature and less able to exercise moral judgment."[47]

Attorney General of New Brunswick Kelly Lamrock says that "by adding deterrence and denunciation and making the youth system more like an adult system, we've destroyed the whole point of having a system that works to prevent young people from reoffending."[48] He deplores the legislation in the strongest terms.

The Canadian Bar Association says that the *Youth Criminal Justice Act* "attempted to strike an appropriate balance between 'toughening up' measures to deal with serious violent offenders and pursuing a more restorative approach through increased emphasis on alternative measures for non-violent offenders."[49]

> *The purpose of sentencing under the YCJA is to hold a young*
> *person accountable for an offence through the imposition of just*
> *sanctions that have meaningful consequences promoting his or*
> *her rehabilitation and reintegration into society, thereby con-*
> *tributing to the long-term protection of the public...[The YCJA]*
> *provides that the sentence imposed must be proportionate to the*
> *seriousness of the offence and to the degree of responsibility of*
> *the young person for that offence and afford the best chances for*
> *rehabilitation and reintegration into society. It must also be the*
> *least restrictive sentence that is capable of achieving the senten-*
> *cing purpose and must in no case be greater than punishment*
> *appropriate for an adult.*

The Supreme Court of Canada has been very clear that a "violent offence" does not include an offence solely against property.[50] Sébastien's Law, however, defines a "serious offence" to include offences against property.

The Court also excludes from its definition of "violent offence" any offence in which bodily harm is only reasonably foreseeable. The Court's definition requires that the young person actually cause, attempt to cause, or threaten to cause bodily harm.[51] Sébastien's Law would change that. "[A]n offence that endangers the life or safety of another person by creating a substantial likelihood of causing bodily harm" is now classified as a "violent offence." This is exactly the type of offence which the *Youth Criminal Justice Act* wished to remove from the young offenders legislation, because youngsters do not have the same capability as adults to foresee the likely consequences of their behaviour.

For example, a youngster goes for a joyride in a stolen car and is seen speeding in an area where there are pedestrians. He returns the car undamaged, and no one is harmed. Under the new definition, this young person could be facing jail time.

Sébastien's Law would require courts to consider adult sentences for serious crimes, thus encouraging courts to impose longer sentences than they do now. The plan would also allow courts to lift publication bans in certain cases, something which has been shown to militate against the rehabilitation of young offenders. While Justice Minister Nicholson says his proposals are aimed at "out-of-control, repeat offenders,"[52] nothing in the new bill targets such offenders. All kinds of young people will be caught up in the net.

Remarkably, Sébastien's Law would also permit sentencing judges to take into account evidence of previous brushes with the law ("extrajudicial sanctions") whether or not there was ever a charge or conviction. New Brunswick Attorney General Lamrock speaks passionately about how this will hamstring efforts to help youngsters in trouble with the law:[53]

> *This is one of the first times the Parliament of Canada has proposed a bill that criminalizes intervention...This bill allows judges, when sentencing, to look at past participation in programs for substance abuse or mental health, or even at things as simple as police warnings.*

As Mr. Lamrock points out, the bill says that these interventions can now count against the youngster when he does come before a judge. The results will be perverse:

> *By saying that participating—whether in sentencing circles, whether in community service, whether in counselling—now counts against kids later on in sentencing, we're going to have more kids lawyering up, we're going to go to more trials, and we're going to have kids getting help far less quickly. From our perspective, it would be a mistake to criminalize participation in the very programs that the evidence suggests are working in New Brunswick to keep people safer and to make sure that they don't do it again.*

Mr. Lamrock says that his government works to meet the unique needs of each young offender, whether these be poverty, abuse, mental illness, or other difficulties.[54] New Brunswick strives to avoid incarceration. Mr. Lamrock calls the Conservative government's proposed changes "one-size-fits-all," and says they will result in more serious problems than if we allow judges, lawyers, and professionals working directly with young persons to do their jobs.

Under Sébastien's Law, there are far more opportunities to incarcerate youth. Yet we know that prisons are "schools for crime," especially for young people. A 2009 study in Montreal concluded that:[55]

> Teenagers who come into contact with the justice system are nearly seven times more likely to be arrested for offences as adults, compared to youths of the same age with a similar history of criminal behaviour but who have not been taken into the justice system. The situation is apparently even more alarming for young persons who are incarcerated.

Some of the strongest evidence in support of choosing alternatives to incarceration comes from Quebec. Serge Ménard, justice critic for the Bloc Québécois, pointed out that since 1985, the youth crime rate in Quebec has been from 50 per cent to 66 per cent lower than in the rest of Canada.[56] In 2008, there were 50 per cent fewer victims in his province compared to other provinces and territories. One would expect a federal government to take notice of this remarkable record and to try to emulate the process that led to such an excellent outcome.

M. Ménard said that Quebec produced these excellent results by taking a different approach—one which concentrated on staffing and long-term investment, rather than on building prisons. In the 1980s, the federal government provided money to provinces for capital infrastructure (building prisons) which Quebec had to turn down because it was trying to reduce incarceration, not increase it. M. Ménard said that for the amount of money required to imprison a young person for a year (about $100,000), he could hire two to three professionals to work with that youngster, and produce much better results.

MP Carol Lavallée of the Bloc said the Quebec approach delivers good legal aid, a rehabilitation incentive program, an offender education program, and probation services. Quebec did a complete overhaul of preliminary intervention programs under its 1977 Youth Protection Act.[57] All of this effort has produced enviable results.

If there were any doubt that incarceration has an exceptionally negative effect on young people, the example of the new Roy McMurtry Youth

Centre in Ontario provides ample evidence.[58] Opened in July 2009, the jail was supposed to turn troubled youth into future responsible citizens. It was supposed to provide the best programming in safe conditions.

Ontario child advocate Irwin Elman, however, has reported that the facility is not safe, and that there have been serious allegations of abuse, lack of programming, and even of food. "It doesn't feel safe and it isn't safe," Mr. Elman said.[59] Staff and detainees alike report escalating violence, lack of programming, and questionable body-cavity searches for missing items such as, unaccountably, a DVD. This is not how Canada should be treating its young offenders, yet the new legislation would consign more of them to such conditions for longer sentences.

Canada's recent history with two diametrically-opposed approaches to youth criminal justice (the *Young Offenders Act* and the *Youth Criminal Justice Act*) amply demonstrates that the hard-line, punishment-oriented, pro-incarceration approach is the one that produces more young repeat offenders. Sébastien's Law will do nothing to achieve the government's stated purpose, which is to take violent, repeat offenders off the streets.

HOUSE ARREST

Bill C-16, the *Ending House Arrest for Property and Other Serious Crimes by Serious and Violent Offenders Act*, implies that serious and violent offenders are being allowed to serve their sentences at home under house arrest. This is misleading. Conditional sentences are not available for offenders who pose a danger to the community, and they are not available to an offender whose sentence would otherwise be more than two years. Under a conditional sentence, the offender is required to serve his sentence, though not in prison, under conditions set down by the judge.

One of these conditions may be that the offender serve his sentence under house arrest. House arrest comes with its own stringent conditions. For example, an offender may be ordered not to leave the place where he is serving his sentence except for medical or other pressing reasons. When he does leave, he may have to be accompanied by his surety at all times. He may be told to refrain from drugs and alcoholic beverages. There may be a curfew or community service. There may be electronic monitoring. Any breach of the specified conditions results in the offender serving his full sentence in custody.

Contrary to popular belief, conditional sentences are not a slap on the wrist. They are often longer than a jail term would have been, and the conditions are often more strict than those applied to parolees or probationers.

The Supreme Court of Canada has said that, while probation is appropriate for the rehabilitation of offenders, conditional sentencing provides both rehabilitation and punishment.[60] For this reason, conditions are more restrictive than for probation. The Court went on to say that house arrest should be a common requirement of conditional sentences, and that conditional sentences are in fact custodial sentences that are not served in an institution.

Conditional sentences were first established when Parliament realized that the collateral consequences of incarceration were too high.[61] These consequences include increased financial costs, increased exposure of first offenders to career criminals, low rehabilitative success of prisons. Research shows that "putting people in jail rather than 'non-custodial sanctions' actually increases the likelihood they will reoffend."[62]

As an alternative to incarceration, conditional sentences offer considerable advantages. Depending on the conditions imposed, they can sometimes allow an offender to keep a job, support his or her family, continue education or training, and make restitution to the victim. In doing so, conditional sentences relieve the public purse of the burden of paying for incarceration, as well as for the social assistance needed to keep a family for whom a source of income has been lost. It permits victims to seek restitution that would not be possible with the offender in custody. And it allows for young offenders and others to get the much-needed education or training that will steer them away from further offending. As well, conditional sentencing allows judges to impose a condition requiring the offender to get treatment for addictions or other problems, which is not allowed in a probation order.[63]

When Prime Minister Harper announced Bill C-16, he said that 30 per cent of offenders on conditional sentences are sent back to jail for breaching their conditions. Statistics Canada again disagrees. It says that adults under supervision serving conditional sentences are far less likely to become reinvolved with the correctional system within twelve months of sentence completion than are those who do time in custody. Statistics Canada says there has been only 15 per cent reinvolvement of those with conditional sentences, compared to 30 per cent reinvolvement of those who have been incarcerated.

It is important to note that the vast majority of those sent back to jail to serve their sentences had not even broken another law. They were reincarcerated simply because they violated their curfew or were unable to provide an address or otherwise failed to comply with their conditions.

The Harper government says conditional sentences are too light a punishment, and are in any case inappropriate for "serious violent offences." But, as noted, conditional sentences have never been available for violent offences. As well, Bill C-16 goes far beyond dealing with violent offences and removes the potential for conditional sentencing for many non-violent offences as well.

As we have noted, the Supreme Court of Canada has expressly ruled that offences solely against property are not considered to be violent crimes.[64] Bill C-16, however, adds another thirty-eight offences to the list of those for which conditional sentencing is not available, among them many that are solely property offences. Some of the new offences are forging passports, bribery of judicial officers, bribery of officers, perjury, giving contradictory evidence with an intent to mislead, fabricating evidence, public servant refusing to deliver property, stopping mail with intent, drawing documents without authority, obtaining based on forged document, making counterfeit money, and possession of counterfeit money.

It would be interesting to hear the rationale behind removing the availability of house arrest for a person convicted of drawing a document without authority. Is this the violent offender for whom the Conservative government believes incarceration is needed? Is a prison sentence likely to deter others who may be contemplating drawing a document without authority? And why would anyone recommend eliminating house arrest for such an offence when we know that just fifteen conditional sentences save the system $1 million per year?[65] That is about $66,700 per year per offender.

The Correctional Service of Canada says that conditional sentences have "generally worked well and garnered praise from sentencing experts around the world."[66] Conditional sentences are imposed in fewer than 5 per cent of all cases, but have reduced admissions to provincial jails by 13 per cent with no negative impact on crime rates.

In 2008, 8.6 per cent of adults in the correctional system (federal and provincial/territorial) were serving conditional sentences, according to Statistics Canada. The cost of conditional sentences at that time (2006–2007) was $2,398.05/year, compared to an average (in 2010) of $84,225 for a provincial inmate and $147,467 for a federal inmate.[67]

Even the listed offences that are deemed to be violent cast the net very wide. Causing "bodily harm" can be something as small as causing a cut finger, or a bruise in a bar fight. "Abduction" may include the act of a parent removing a child for a day without the permission of the other parent. These are not the serious violent offences that most people might expect will be caught by this legislation—but they can be and they will.

In 2006, Emile Therien was the president of the Canada Safety Council. He argued in support of conditional sentencing, saying that there is evidence that long prison sentences without remedial programs may actually increase the chances of reoffending after release.[68] He also pointed out that conditional sentencing makes sense from a safety standpoint, because there is the potential to establish an environment for positive behaviour change.

More recently, Mr. Therien has written that conditional sentences hold far more potential for rehabilitation and restorative justice than do terms of imprisonment.[69] While incarceration may protect the public from the offender during the time served, a conditional sentence is far more likely to prevent the offender from continuing to endanger the public once the sentence is over.

Once again, statistics, research, and support from both Canadian experts and those abroad have all been ignored in the Conservative government's push to incarcerate more offenders. If Bill C-16 becomes law (and it will form part of the new majority government's omnibus bill), there will be increased costs both in financial terms and in terms of human misery. Recidivism numbers will also start to increase—something no victim or ordinary citizen wants to see.

FAINT HOPE

Bill S-6, the *Serious Time for the Most Serious Crime Act*, implies that serious crimes do not attract serious sentences in Canada.[70] In fact, Canada already sentences serious offences much more harshly than other Western democracies. For example, with respect to first-degree murder (S-6 applies only to murder and high treason), Canadians spend far more time in custody than in similar countries.[71]

Figure 9. Average Time in Custody for First-Degree Murder in Western Democracies.

Table 1 – Average Time Spent in Custody

Country	Time Served (years)
New Zealand	11.0
Scotland	11.2
Sweden	12.0
Belgium	12.7
Australia	14.8
United States: Life sentence with parole	18.5
United States: Life sentence without parole	29.0
CANADA	28.4

Source: Department of Justice Canada, "Fair and Effective Sentencing: A Canadian Approach to Sentencing Policy" October 2005.

In Canada, the average time spent in prison for first-degree murder is 28.4 years. This is a far longer sentence than has been imposed for murder even in our own history. Before 1961 (when Parliament first distinguished between "capital" and "non-capital" murder), the average time spent in custody, according to the Correctional Service of Canada, was 19.6 years. This dropped to an average of 15.8 years (for capital crimes) and 14.6 (for non-capital crimes) between 1961 and 1976. In 1976, Parliament abolished capital punishment, and the average time in prison shot up to 22.4 years. It has been increasing ever since.[72]

Canadians serving time for first-degree murder spend on average 17.4 years more in prison than they would in New Zealand, and about ten years more than they would even in the United States, which is well known for its long sentences. The only sentence longer in the US is "life without parole" (which is not a sentence available in Canada) in which an American offender will still spend only about six months longer in custody than a Canadian.

The average time spent in custody for murder in the comparison countries is fifteen years. This is exactly the number of years chosen by Canadian legislators for eligibility for the "faint hope" application. This is a process by which offenders serving life for murder may apply to be considered for parole fifteen years into their sentence rather than waiting the longer period set by the legislation or the court (up to twenty-five years).

This is called a "faint" hope application because it is so difficult for offenders to satisfy the many requirements of the law. Few inmates attempt to navigate the process, and very few are ever released under it. Between 1987 and 2009, according to Public Safety Canada, a total of 991 offenders were eligible to apply for this early release. There were court decisions in 173 of those, and 143 offenders were deemed eligible for release. The average number released per year has thus been six.[73]

According to Correctional Service of Canada statistics, of the 130 offenders who were actually released under "faint hope" up to April 21, 2009, 101 were living in their communities, fourteen were back in custody, eleven had died, one was out on bail, and three had been deported. The return rate to prison for these offenders is thus about 10 per cent. Many or most of these would have been returned for technical violations, and not for new offences. Compare this with the return rate for those released on statutory release in 2006-2007. Some 41.9 per cent were returned to prison in that year, the vast majority of which were for technical violations of their conditions (30.7 per cent of all those released under the program).[74]

The process involved in "faint hope" applications was rigorous, and ensured that only offenders who did not pose a threat to public safety and were likely to succeed in their communities were ever released early. The applicant had first to convince a judge to be allowed to apply for "faint hope" release. If successful at this level, then the application had to be approved unanimously by a jury of twelve citizens. This ensured that the community itself was involved in deciding whether or not the offender was a good risk. Upon passing this hurdle, the inmate still had to make a presentation to the National Parole Board. Very few offenders even attempted the "faint hope" process, as the chances of succeeding at every level were slim. Any applicant that did achieve release under "faint hope" would remain under supervision by the Correctional Service of Canada for the rest of his or her life.

The "faint hope" clause was designed to encourage offenders to work hard at their rehabilitation and reintegration plans while in prison. It did offer a slight hope of earlier release, and this distant prospect lessened prisoners' despair. It provided a reason for inmates to refrain from violence and confrontation, and eased the safety concerns of staff and offenders alike.

Bill S-6 became law just before the Harper government fell in 2011. The law abolished the "faint hope" application altogether for those convicted from then on. It also made the application even more stringent for inmates who were already in the system. Although they will still be able to apply for "faint hope" release, now they may apply only two times (not five, as before). They also have a very limited period in which to make the application (ninety days from the day they reach the fifteen-year mark in their sentences).

Even more importantly, the fundamental test for a successful application has been changed. Whereas the offender used to be required to satisfy the judge that he had a "reasonable prospect" of success, the test is now the much more difficult one of showing a "substantial likelihood" of success. This is designed to ensure that the hurdle is too high for virtually all applicants.

What "faint hope" applications used to represent was an opportunity for the system to show some flexibility in the case of offenders who were at low risk for reoffending, and who had already paid a very heavy debt to society. Such flexibility and exercise of discretion—whether by the judge or by the community members of the jury, or by the National Parole Board— attracted the disapproval of Harper government parliamentarians, and have been eliminated.

The bill's sponsor said that its "sole purpose" was to restore faith in the justice system.[75] But there was no evidence that people had lost faith in the justice system, or that the "faint hope" clause affected their opinions one way or the other. We are left to speculate as to what might have motivated the abolition of "faint hope."

Lacking full information as to what "faint hope" was, and how hard it was to achieve, the public knew only what the government told them—that it meant killers got out of jail early. People do not want killers getting out of jail early. If they had been told, however, that twenty-five years is actually getting out very late, by Western standards, and that successful applicants are unlikely ever to reoffend (1.3 per cent), then it is likely that Canadians would have been more supportive of the idea of "faint hope."

Victims, in whose name the government repeatedly dedicated this legislation, understand that offenders will be released, whether earlier or later.[76] They know that the best outcome for public safety lies in the rehabilitation of the offender, not in continued punishment. They prefer the government to do more to help victims manage the criminal justice process, whether at the trial stage, the appeal stage, or the release stage. This legislation does not do that.

Statistics, research, and long experience show that "faint hope" was a humane and successful program which showed the better side of a very harsh system. Abolishing it will increase human misery, endanger offenders and staff alike, and cost the system millions of dollars in lengthier incarceration, more litigation, and more recidivism upon later release.

PAROLE PROVISIONS

In 1992, the *Corrections and Conditional Release Act* made changes to the system of release from prison. It eliminated the notion of earned remission and replaced it with today's "statutory release," in which offenders who do not obtain parole are released at two-thirds of their sentence under supervision in the community. It also instituted a new system of accelerated parole reviews.

The government has so far resisted the advice of the *Roadmap* in one respect: it has chosen not to eliminate statutory release. However, it has passed Bill C-59, which abolishes the accelerated parole reviews for first-time, non-violent offenders. This means that offenders who used to be eligible for accelerated parole review can no longer apply for day parole at one-sixth of their sentence. The new law has been made retroactive to the extent that offenders who have not served one-sixth of their sentences at the time of the passing of the bill will not be eligible for accelerated parole reviews.

Correctional Services of Canada says that accelerated parole reviews were intended to "provide for formal recognition in law that non-violent and violent offenders should not be subject to the same conditional release process."[77] The *Roadmap*, on the other hand, said that accelerated reviews should be abolished because of the high recidivism rates of these offenders. Yet in 2007-2008, only six out of 831 (0.7 per cent) of such offenders were revoked for a violent offence, while six out of 527 (1 per cent) who were released under the regular parole procedure were revoked for a violent offence.[78] With respect to non-violent offences, there were somewhat higher reoffending rates for prisoners released as a result of accelerated reviews compared to regular releases (8.6 per cent and 4 per cent). In neither case do the statistics on recidivism justify the abolition of accelerated parole reviews. As Jackson and Stewart said in their critique of the *Roadmap*, "Misusing statistics to create exaggerated fears while ignoring the mass of contrary evidence mocks serious public policy development."[79]

The possibly unintended result of abolishing accelerated parole reviews is that virtually all short-term, non-violent offenders will be disqualified altogether from obtaining parole. This is because there will simply not be enough time for them to complete the regular parole process, which involves being assessed and placed in an appropriate institution, having a correctional plan designed, and then completing the required programs and applying for parole. Thus, paradoxically, it will be first-time, non-violent offenders who will most likely have to serve out their entire sentences.

The federal Correctional Investigator says that only about 25 per cent of federal prisoners are receiving the "core program" required to successfully apply for parole. This is the set of programs that specifically deals with the underlying factors that must be addressed to reduce the likelihood of further offending.[80] It is not designed to compel offenders to "earn" release, but to make them less of a risk to society upon release.

Costs to the correctional system will increase as a result of C-59. All of those cases which were dealt with by accelerated reviews will now have to go through the entire parole application process, including a full parole board hearing. And inmates will spend much longer in prison, driving up costs and provoking more overcrowding and violence.

REDUNDANT AND OPPORTUNISTIC LAWS

A number of crime laws being introduced by the Conservative government are of questionable utility because they are redundant. One example is a bill which created a new offence of "auto theft." This offence was always adequately prosecuted under the theft provisions of the *Criminal Code*. Among other things, the new law increases the maximum sentence for auto theft from ten years to fourteen years, and applies a mandatory minimum sentence of six months if the offender is convicted of three or more auto thefts.[81] This is another "three-strikes-you're-out" law, which leaves judges no discretion to adjust for individual circumstances, and which will ultimately distort the delivery of justice.

The new "street racing" offence also used to be adequately prosecuted under "dangerous driving" and "criminal negligence" laws. The new law mainly adds to the page count of the *Criminal Code* (which is beginning to take on the aspect of the *Income Tax Act*) without making substantive changes. But it gives the appearance of "doing something" about crime. Again, the main change is with respect to sentencing: there is now a higher maximum sentence available to judges. People who work in criminal law argue that the maximums are unlikely to be used in any event.[82] This is because the allowable maximums were already very high, and most judges have been reluctant to impose them in the past.

Undeterred, the minister of justice insists that, even if the law is not applied, the new maximum prison sentences will send a clear message that street racing will not be tolerated.[83] He says that the creation of a new "street racing" law will educate Canadian society about the unacceptable risks associated with the activity. This is an interesting position for the minister of justice to take. He has just created a new crime with long maximum sentences that he admits may not be applied, and then explains his actions by saying that the law will at least provide education to Canadians. A better approach might be to provide education in the normal way and do so before the offence occurs.

At least one law-enforcement officer has suggested that the higher the risk associated with an activity (that is, the higher the potential sentence for something like street racing), the *more* likely that some people will be attracted to the activity.[84] This turns the tables on the deterrence argument in a very interesting way. Support for this proposition can be seen in European countries, where the countries with the most drug use tend to be those which have the heaviest sanctions.[85]

Laws like these do, however, create an illusion that the Harper government is doing something about crime. Auto theft and street racing have been in the news, and so a swift if redundant response capitalizes on an opportunity for favourable press coverage. The laws may not add anything to our ability to curb crime, but they are smart politically.

The government has been quick to respond to incidents of notoriety as they hit the press. Each time the government reacts, it does so with new legislation, hastily drafted, and with little thought as to the full ramifications of the laws it is proposing. Incarceration is always a central feature.

White-collar crime was one area where the Conservative government moved quickly to capitalize on a recent scandal involving a Ponzi scheme. The Earl Jones story broke in the summer of 2009, and by October 21, 2009, Bill C-52 (now Bill C-21) was introduced in the House of Commons. First entitled the *Retribution on Behalf of Victims of White Collar Crime Act*, the bill is now called the Standing *Up for Victims of White Collar Crime Act*.

The bill does make some gestures toward victims—imposing new obligations on judges to consider ordering restitution, adding certain aggravating factors for consideration on sentencing, and allowing for community impact statements and a new type of prohibition order. But the real meat of the bill is the mandatory minimum sentence of two years for fraud over $1 million.

The government imposed this minimum sentence even though it could present no statistics on the current trend of sentencing for fraud of this magnitude.[86] Many think that the bill is redundant because judges would normally sentence in this range anyway. Some experts say that, "While Bill C-21 may help to change the perception that Canada is soft on financial crime, on its own it will do little to change the reality."[87]

The reason that Messrs. Caylor and Groia give for this failure to change the reality is that the government has not allocated the resources necessary to investigate and prosecute white-collar crime effectively. Instead, the new legislation imposes more obligations upon the system, which does not have the resources to carry them out effectively. The Crown will be required to quantify the proceeds of a fraud if it wishes to request the mandatory minimum sentence, which would not be easy even if funding were ample. More accused persons will refuse to plead guilty because of the mandatory minimum, further clogging up the system. Finally, the system has no ability to distribute the assets of a fraud among a large number of victims.

For all these reasons, it is expected that the new fraud law will cause further delays and more expense to the system without delivering the relief to victims that it promises.

In another case, the Prime Minister and two senior cabinet ministers recently travelled to Toronto to announce a new law on citizen's arrests where they participated in a media scrum. The new law they were extolling was described by one observer as "truly laughable."[88]

The case prompting the new legislation involved a citizen's arrest by shopkeeper David Chen. Mr. Chen was charged with assault and forcible confinement by over-enthusiastic police and then prosecuted by over-zealous Crown Attorneys. The judge in the case promptly acquitted Mr. Chen. After that court decision, it is highly unlikely that such charges would ever be brought again in similar circumstances. The perceived problem was already solved.

Why, then, the huge amount of attention, time, and money spent drafting a new law? One observer of the high-powered photo-op in Toronto was skeptical:[89]

> Yesterday's appearance may have been more about "optics"…
> Is this the most compelling issue Canada faces today? That
> a Prime Minister and two cabinet ministers should come to
> Toronto, should leave Parliament, to unveil a new sentence to be
> added to the Criminal Code that is really redundant given court
> rulings? So I think this is very much about optics.

Another probable motivation would be to distract the public from the compelling issues that really do matter. As has been noted, there are many files with serious national and international implications, but the government does not want the media raising these or the public demanding answers to difficult questions.

This government has also chosen to make life more difficult for those ex-offenders who are succeeding in their lives upon release. The notoriety of the cases involved made it well-nigh impossible for the opposition to resist Bill C23-B, for example, which made it more difficult or impossible to obtain a pardon. Yet the negative effects of the law on most ex-offenders will far outweigh the value of abolishing pardons for a few high-profile cases.

In the summer of 2010, notorious offender Graham James (a hockey coach convicted of sexually assaulting his players) was discovered to be working in Guadalajara, having obtained a pardon with respect to his crimes. The public outcry was predictable. Bill C23-B (the *Eliminating Pardons for Serious Crimes Act*) was immediately introduced, and received royal assent with unseemly haste.

The new law replaces the word "pardon" with the phrase "record suspension," which is generally agreed to be more descriptive of the process. It increases the amount of time an offender must wait to apply for a pardon from three to five years for a summary conviction offence and from five to ten years for an indictable offence. Many feel that this is a very long period of ineligibility for people whose job prospects depend upon their obtaining a "record suspension." Only 4 per cent of all those obtaining pardons since 1970 (some 400,000 souls) have reoffended. Thus, it is odd that the government should make the process more difficult for all potential applicants.

There is also a "three-strikes-you're-out" aspect of the bill, which makes anyone who has been convicted of three indictable offences ineligible for a pardon. Since many indictable offences have no violent component, and many more are not "serious" crimes in the scale of *Criminal Code* offences, this again seems like a draconian, one-size-fits-all response to a mainly non-existent problem.

Current plans to increase the fee for the pardon application from $50 to $150 and then to $631 militate against its objective of getting people back to work.[90] How is a person on social assistance expected to pay the fee to get the job that will enable him to get off social assistance? Catch-22 does not begin to describe this situation.

The government's timing was no accident for another reason—the prospect of Karla Homolka, a notorious offender, soon becoming eligible for a pardon. According to the National Parole Board, fully 25 per cent of all applicants are turned down,[91] and one might expect that Karla Homolka would be among these. Nonetheless, Bill C-23B passed easily. It was politically astute if not a policy triumph.

These are just some of the crime laws introduced by the Conservative government over five years. Its approach to criminal justice appears to be mainly punishment oriented and politically opportunistic. It relies upon the public's lack of knowledge about criminal justice issues, and upon the fear it can engender from select headlines. The 2-for-1, young offenders, and parole laws are substantive efforts to roll back a more humane and effective criminal justice system. Some other laws are mere efforts to capitalize on the moment.

Most Canadians, provided with full information, would think twice about supporting the ideology behind much of the Harper Conservatives' flawed crime legislation. It is probable that we are not unlike our American counterparts, 90 per cent of whom favour reducing prison time and creating a stronger probation and parole system.[92] The Harper crime laws enhance neither public safety nor our reputation as a nation of compassion and good sense.

5: DRUG LEGISLATION

The Conservatives' drug legislation (Bill S-10) deserves special attention because of its ramifications for large numbers of ordinary Canadians. The Conservative government takes a particularly moralistic and rigid approach to matters concerning illicit drugs, despite widely divergent views expressed by the public. Its drug legislation will be in the omnibus crime bill promised by the Conservative majority government in 2011.

The way Western democracies have categorized various psychotropic, hallucinogenic, and mood-enhancing drugs as legal or illegal is not based on rational argument. If public health concerns were the basis for these decisions, tobacco would be illegal. If concerns about violence and family breakdown were the explanation, alcohol would be illegal. If potential harm through misuse/abuse were the reason, it would be harder to obtain oxycodone (an opioid in the same family as morphine and heroin but easily obtained by prescription) than marijuana (which is illegal).

Our methods of dealing with the drugs we have declared to be illegal have been similarly irrational. The early-twentieth-century experiment with the prohibition of alcohol was a disastrous failure and was reversed only after much violence and social disruption. Nearly a century later, we appear not to have learned from this history. Prohibition as a means of controlling the use of drugs has proven conclusively and emphatically to be ineffective and counterproductive. We continue to imprison thousands of users of drugs less harmful than tobacco and alcohol, and Bill S-10 contemplates an even harsher regime.

THE NEW DRUG LAW

Bill S-10 would establish dozens of new mandatory minimum sentences for a whole range of drug offences. The legislation is broadly and vaguely drafted and will ensnare many ordinary Canadians, who will serve long sentences. The "aggravating factors" and "health and safety factors" that serve to increase prison sentences are broad, vague, and complex, and will be variously interpreted to the point that the appeal courts will find themselves busy. There will also be *Charter* challenges based upon the harshness of the regime.

Meanwhile, support for abolishing drug prohibition comes from some surprising quarters. Tom Flanagan, a former adviser to Prime Minister Harper and one of the masterminds behind the Conservative election win in 2006, has been outspoken on the subject: "Moralistic legislation produces widespread law-breaking, indeed an entire illegal industry, while the pariah product becomes more available than ever."[1]

His disapproval of "moralistic" legislation is interesting in that the Prime Minister himself takes a moralistic view. Mr. Harper has declared that, "Drugs are not bad because they are illegal; they are illegal because they are bad."[2] He and his colleagues do not appear to make the distinction between the drug and the abuse of the drug. If they did, they would see the efficacy of treating drugs as public health issues, not as problems for the criminal justice system.

Mr. Flanagan lists the damage caused by prohibition:[3] corruption, criminality, civil war in drug-producing and drug-transporting countries like Colombia and Afghanistan, an increase in property crime as the addicted seek to feed their habit, and the involvement of organized crime and gangs that run production, transportation, smuggling, and money-laundering. In addition, there are the consequences for law enforcement. He describes what he calls the "hypertrophic growth of the state's security and surveillance apparatus, arbitrary searches and seizure of property, pointless criminalization of innocent activities, and growth of genuine criminality as a spinoff from the trade in forbidden drugs."

That is quite a list. Some serious thought is needed as to how to avoid these consequences, and to provide a complex response to what is a complex issue. However, the sum total of the government's efforts with respect to drug laws consists in imposing a multitude of mandatory minimum sentences. Expert Neil Boyd, who specializes in drug laws, says the Harper agenda is not based on fact, or data relevant to public health, or empirical evidence.[4] "That's not what they care about. Stephen Harper is an ideologue, publicly committed to increasing imprisonment for a greater range of criminal offences and personally in favour of the death penalty."

The Conservative government claims the new penalties are directed toward "organized crime" and that they will get violent criminals off the street, yet the government does not indicate how this will work. The new sentences will mainly catch small players while largely benefiting the top echelons of the drug trade. As one seasoned observer points out, it will not be the Sopranos who will be caught by the new laws. It will be the three stoners growing pot in the basement.[5]

Justice Minister Nicholson, though, insists that his legislation was only meant to punish small amounts of marijuana if they were intended for "sale" (which pushes the gravity of the offence up a category to "trafficking" from "simple possession"). However, "trafficking" does not mean only "selling." It includes "giving" and "sharing." Hence, every casual user of marijuana who shares his marijuana or gives some away will be caught by the legislation.

Dr. Thomas Kerr (Research Scientist at the British Columbia Centre for Excellence in HIV/AIDS) says that mandatory minimum sentences will not be more effective against drug dealers and kingpins than against ordinary users.[6] The big players who traffic in large quantities of illegal drugs keep themselves at a distance from more visible street dealing, and so are rarely captured:

> Instead, it is people who are addicted and involved in small-scale, street-level drug distribution to support their addictions who commonly end up being charged with drug trafficking and who would bear the brunt of minimum mandatory sentences for drug dealing.

Deterrence is known not to work. Neil Boyd refers to sentencing patterns in Canada over past decades.[7] Up to the 1970s, the courts used to be extremely harsh on drug use. Fully 70 per cent of those in possession of marijuana went to jail, and 80 to 90 per cent of those in possession of heroin and cocaine went to jail. The result? Illegal drug use escalated. It is another illustration of the disconnect between incarceration rates and crime rates. As Boyd says, "It is a very powerful piece of evidence to suggest that what is driving the extent of use that we experience are not the penalties the judiciary imposes."

In full agreement, criminologist Anthony Doob says, "Very few criminals have any idea what sentencing ranges pertain to particular offences, let alone being deterred by the prospect of drawing a certain sentence."[8] Looking at the complicated sentencing regime set up by Bill S-10, it is easy to see what Dr. Doob means. The list of offences, aggravating factors (List A and List B), and health and safety factors is so involved that charts had to be created by the Department of Justice to enable people to understand the legislation. This is the chart dealing with cannabis and marijuana:[9]

Figure 9. The Chart Setting Out New Marijuana Sentences

Annex B:
Proposed New Mandatory Sentences for Serious Drug Offences
Schedule II drugs (cannabis and marijuana)

	OFFENCE	MANDATORY PENALTY			NOTES
		w/Aggravating Factors – List A[1]	w/Aggravating Factors – List B[2]	w/Health and Safety Factors[3]	
[1]	Trafficking		1 YEAR	2 YEARS	n/a	Offence would have to involve more than 3 kg of cannabis marijuana or cannabis resin
[2]	Possession for the Purpose of Trafficking		1 YEAR	2 YEARS	n/a	Offence would have to involve more than 3kg of cannabis marijuana or cannabis resin
[3]	Importing/ Exporting	1 YEAR	n/a	n/a	n/a	Offence is committed for the purpose of trafficking

	OFFENCE		MANDATORY PENALTY			NOTES
			w/Aggravating Factors – List A[1]	w/Aggravating Factors – List B[2]	w/Health and Safety Factors[3]	
[4]	Possession for the Purpose of Exporting	1 YEAR	n/a	n/a	n/a	Offence is committed for the purpose of trafficking
[5]	Production, 6–200 plants	6 MOS	n/a	n/a	9 MOS	Offence is committed for the purpose of trafficking. Maximum penalty will be increased to 14 years imprisonment.
[6]	Production, 201–500 plants	1 YEAR	n/a	n/a	18 MOS	Maximum penalty will be increased to 14 years imprisonment
[7]	Production, more than 500 plants	2 YEARS	n/a	n/a	3 YEARS	Maximum penalty will be increased to 14 years imprisonment
[8]	Production of oil or resin	1 YEAR	n/a	n/a	18 MOS	Offence is committed for the purpose of trafficking

*Source: Backgrounder: Penalties for organized drug crime act
(Ottawa: Department of Justice, May 2010).*

[1]Aggravating Factors List A

The aggravating factors include offences committed:

- for the benefit of organized crime
- involving use or threat of violence
- involving use or threat of use of weapons
- by someone who was previously convicted of a designated drug offence or had served a term of imprisonment for a designated substance offence in the previous 10 years
- through the abuse of authority or position or by abusing access to restricted area to
- commit the offence of importation/exportation and possession to export

[2]Aggravating Factors List B

The aggravating factors include offences committed:

- in a prison
- in or near a school, in or near an area normally frequented by youth or in the presence of youth

- in concert with a youth
- in relation to a youth (e.g. selling to a youth)

[3]Health and Safety Factors

- the accused used real property that belongs to a third party to commit the offence
- the production constituted a potential security, health or safety hazard to children who were in the location where the offence was committed or in the immediate area
- the production constituted a potential public safety hazard in a residential area
- the accused placed or set a trap

It is hard to imagine a potential offender doing the work necessary to grasp the intricacies of this sentencing regime.

The consequences of offending, even on the least serious basis, will be a long minimum sentence. For example, if someone is charged with producing six marijuana plants "for the purpose of trafficking," the penalty is a minimum of six months. The maximum sentence has also been increased to fourteen years. Production for the purpose of trafficking can be a serious organized crime offence, of course. However, someone who is growing six plants in his or her basement is not likely to be connected to organized crime. He or she is more likely to be someone who intends to share some marijuana with a friend at a party, or is growing it for pain relief, or plans to share it with a friend for pain relief.

The legislation goes further. If the person is growing six plants and there is a health or safety factor involved, the minimum sentence increases to nine months. Health and safety factors include using "real property that belongs to a third party to commit the offence." This could include leasing a house to create a grow-op. It would include, for example, a large grow-op of the kind located in the former Molsons Brewery building in Barrie, Ontario. It can also mean growing six plants in someone else's house. Such situations can be prosecuted, and they will be.

If the production of the marijuana constitutes "a potential security, health or safety hazard to children who were in the location where the offence was committed or in the immediate area," then another health and safety factor is triggered. This factor is vague and could have an unlimited application, as could "the production constituted a potential public safety hazard in a residential area." The only health and safety factor that is well-defined is "the accused placed or set a trap."

That is the regime for *producing* marijuana. Sentences for *possession for the purpose of trafficking* or for *trafficking in marijuana* will also now depend upon a number of factors. The mandatory penalties apply only if the quantity of marijuana exceeds three kilograms. If there are no aggravating factors, there is no minimum sentence. This seems strangely out of proportion to the production regime. An offender can sell up to three kilograms of marijuana and walk out of court with a fine, whereas a person growing six plants to share will automatically go to jail for six months.

However, with respect to *trafficking* and *possession for the purpose* charges, if there are aggravating factors, everything changes. Any of the factors on List A will attract a minimum sentence of one year. Thus, if the offence is committed "for the benefit of organized crime," it will attract at least a one-year sentence. If the offence involves the use or even a threat of violence, that attracts at least a year in jail. If it involves the use or even the threat of the use of a weapon, the offender gets at least one year. If the offender has already been convicted of a designated drug offence, or served time for one in the past ten years, he or she gets at least one year (this factor will cover a lot of offenders). The final factor is too convoluted to summarize: if the offence is committed "through the abuse of authority of position or by abusing access to restricted area to commit the offence of importation/exportation and possession to export," the offender will serve at least one year.

That is just List A. The List B aggravating factors will up the ante by attracting a minimum sentence of two years. These include having or trafficking three or more kilograms of marijuana in a prison. This factor at least has the elegance of simplicity and definability. The others are a minefield of vagueness.

For example, an offender committing the offence "in or near a school, in or near an area normally frequented by youth or in the presence of youth," will serve the minimum sentence of two years. It is fair to suggest that if the government is planning to incarcerate individuals for two years or more, it should be precise about how to determine that the sentence is warranted. "Near a school" would cover just about every location in some cities. "Near an area normally frequented by youth" could mean anything from a church basement to a road hockey site to a park. "In the presence of youth" is extremely broad and, depending on how it is defined, could apply in many instances whether or not the offender knows a youth is present.

Another List B factor is committing the offence "in concert with a youth." What does this phrase mean? Does it mean the offender must have involved the youth in the offence? Or that the youth was there at the time the offence was committed? Or that the youth must have participated in the offence? Does the offender have to know the person was a "youth"?

The final aggravating factor on List B is committing the offence "in relation to a youth (e.g. selling to a youth)." What else besides selling to a youth would be included in this? What if the offender is trafficking so as to have the money to be able to take care of a youth? Would that qualify for the two-year minimum? If not, why not?

There are yet more complications with respect to sentencing for marijuana offences. If an offender is charged with producing between 201 and 500 plants, the minimum is one year, or eighteen months with health and safety factors. If he produces more than 500 plants, it is two years, or three years with these factors. Someone will have to count all the plants, harvest them, keep them in a secure location, and produce them for court if required. And for any amount of oil or resin the sentence is a minimum of one year, or eighteen months with these factors.

Another anomaly of the minimum sentencing regime for drugs was pointed out by Professor Neil Boyd in his testimony before the Standing Senate Committee on Legal and Constitutional Affairs.[10] Looking at the chart, he shows that the *distributors* of more dangerous drugs (heroin, cocaine, methamphetamine, and so on) would be treated less harshly than *producers* of the less dangerous drug (marijuana), irrespective of the actual amounts to be distributed. This is because, in order to attract the one-year minimum sentence for *distributing* dangerous drugs, an offender must also attract one of the aggravating factors listed in List A. (Note that column 1 of the chart is blank in respect to *trafficking* and *possession for the purpose of trafficking*.)

Figure 10. The Chart Setting Out New Sentences for More Serious Drugs.

Annex A:
Proposed New Mandatory Sentences for Serious Drug Offences
Schedule 1 drugs (cocaine, heroin, methamphetamine, etc.)

	OFFENCE		MANDATORY PENALTY			NOTES
			w/Aggravating Factors – List A[1]	w/Aggravating Factors – List B[2]	w/Health and Safety Factors[3]	
[1]	Production	2 YEARS	n/a	n/a	3 YEARS	
[2]	Trafficking		1 YEAR	2 YEARS	n/a	
[3]	Possession for the Purpose of Trafficking		1 YEAR	2 YEARS	n/a	
[4]	Importing/ Exporting	1 YEAR 2 YEARS (if more than 1 kg of Schedule 1 substances)	n/a	n/a	n/a	Offence is committed for the purpose of trafficking
[5]	Possession for the Purpose of Exporting	1 YEAR 2 YEARS (if more than 1 kg of Schedule 1 substances)	n/a	n/a	n/a	Offence is committed for the purpose of trafficking.

Source: Backgrounder: Penalties for organized drug crime act (Ottawa: Department of Justice, May 2010).

In other words, if someone *distributes* heroin but does so without any of the aggravating factors present, there is no minimum sentence. *Producers* of marijuana, on the other hand, do serve a minimum sentence even when no aggravating factor has been triggered. This cannot be the result that was intended by the drafters of the legislation.

At the risk of repetition, this shows how impossible it will be for a potential offender to know what the sentence would be, even if he or she did try to find out before committing the crime. And organized crime gangsters are not likely to be deterred by the justice department's grid for sentences. Eugene Oscapella, a drug policy analyst, calls the legislation a "wonderful gift to organized crime. We're going to drive some of the smaller players out of the business and they'll be replaced by people who do not respond to law enforcement initiatives."[11]

Violence is continually referred to by Conservatives as the reason for harsh drug sentences. Yet the evidence often does not support the fear of violence. For example, an RCMP study of 25,000 files on marijuana cultivation shows that violence or the threat of violence among cultivators is rare.[12] Yet the Canadian justice system is now planning to spend millions of dollars incarcerating people who represent no threat to the public.

The violence associated with illicit drugs relates to turf wars fought by cartels and gangs who are trying to control the trade. If the drugs were legal (or decriminalized), the cartels would move on to some other illicit business, and the violence associated with the drugs would evaporate. The trade would be carried on by government-regulated businesses, and organized crime would not be attracted to this area of activity. Expert Benedikt Fischer says:[13]

> [Bill S-10] will likely make illicit drug markets more appealing and lucrative to those who run, control and benefit from it the most—international drug production and importation syndicates, organized crime, and gangs. In fact, every politician supporting [Bill S-10] and the prohibition apparatus at its base should expect appreciation from these entrepreneurs for maintaining and protecting these exceptionally lucrative markets.
>
> As has been aptly stated, "Drug prohibition laws are state sponsoring laws for organized crime." While making illicit drug markets even more lucrative, they have the potential to become more volatile and violent.

Professor Fischer says that "a regulated and state controlled cannabis supply model...would quickly eliminate much of the economic lucrativeness for organized crime of currently illicit cannabis markets and hence reduce related volatility and violence."

Justice Minister Nicholson, though, resolutely sticks to what he has decided the public wants. He believes his legislation is a smart response to a public outcry to crack down on the growing "scourge" of drugs: "I can tell you there is support for this bill from many ordinary Canadians who are quite concerned about drug abuse."

TOWARD A NEW MODEL

The Conservative government believes it knows what the public wants, but public opinion on the subject has been investigated by a number of pollsters and the results are unequivocal. An Ekos survey published on March 18, 2010, found that 50 per cent of respondents thought that possession of small amounts of marijuana for personal use should not be a crime.[14] This was, unfortunately, reported inaccurately by CBC News. Its report said Canadians' opinions were "split on pot." In fact, only 30 per cent of those polled disagreed with the proposition, while 20 per cent were neutral. This indicates that far fewer people were opposed to the decriminalization of marijuana than were in support of it.

A similar result was obtained by an Angus Reid poll in November 2010. Reports said that "half of Canadians" support "legalization" of marijuana. In fact 50 per cent said they did, but only 44 per cent said they did not.[15] We do not know what the other 6 per cent thought, but clearly fewer Canadians are opposed to legalization than support it. Similarly, 33 per cent would scrap the "decriminalization" law proposed by the Martin Liberal government, while 47 per cent would not. Again, more Canadians want to see a relaxation of the laws than do not.

Thus it is puzzling to hear Justice Minister Nicholson thunder, "We are absolutely convinced in our consultation with Canadians that this [crackdown on drugs] is welcomed across the country."[16]

Canadians have been voting informally for years on the marijuana issue. They have been using the drug in convincing numbers. Statistics from 2004 showed that 44.5 per cent of Canadians were prepared to admit using marijuana at least once.[17] Some 14.1 per cent said they had used it in the previous twelve months (up from 7.4 per cent in 1994—so about double the number in ten years). And 45.7 per cent of users reported using it just twice or less in the past three months. It is reliably estimated that two million Canadians use marijuana recreationally.[18] What social purpose is served by criminalizing all of these Canadians?

The Justice Minister insists that people who sell or grow marijuana belong in jail because pot is used as a "currency" to bring harder drugs into the country. He offers no evidence for this proposition. He says, "This lubricates the business and that makes me nervous."[19] Making the Minister of Justice nervous is an interesting new criterion for sending countless pot-smokers to jail.[20]

Marijuana is demonstrably less dangerous than tobacco and alcohol. These latter drugs send thousands every year to hospitals and to their deaths.[21] As well, alcohol is known to fuel much physical violence. Marijuana, on the other hand, causes its users to become passive rather than violent. As far as we know, any harm that might be caused by marijuana relates only to the fact that the drug is generally, although not always, smoked.[22] Because no clinical trials have ever been performed on marijuana, many authorities (when asked to prescribe marijuana for medical use) are still reluctant to recommend its use.

It is suggested that we need to be more worried about dangerous drugs like methamphetamine, and it is true that meth is a dangerous drug. Because, however, it is used much less frequently than alcohol, cannabis, or cocaine, it should not be the prime driver for such sweeping public policies on substance abuse as Bill S-10.

The Canadian Centre on Substance Abuse has published a research study called "The Costs of Substance Abuse in Canada 2002."[23] It concluded that in 2002 tobacco cost the Canadian economy $17 billion (42.7 per cent of total substance abuse costs). Alcohol cost $14.6 billion (36.6 per cent) and all illegal drugs together 8.2 per cent (20.7 per cent). Clearly, legal drugs are much more of a financial drain on society than illegal ones.

Mortality rates were also tabulated for 2002. Again, tobacco headed the list at 37,209 deaths (16.6 per cent of all deaths for the year), alcohol was next at 4,258 (1.9 per cent), and illegal drugs last of the three at 1,695 (0.8 per cent). Just as important, leading causes of death for those abusing illegal drugs were overdose (958), drug-related suicide (295), drug-related hepatitis C (165), and drug-related HIV (87). Proper regulation and treatment would have eliminated virtually all of these.

MP Keith Martin, a medical doctor, has been putting forward private members bills since 2002 in an effort to have fines substituted for prison for anyone caught with less than thirty grams of marijuana or with one or two marijuana plants.[24] He maintains that decriminalizing simple possession will sever ties between casual drug users and organized crime. His idea of decriminalizing possession of two plants (at most) is designed to ensure that users would no longer have to get their pot from dealers.

Some argue that we must go much further and completely legalize and regulate marijuana if we are to eliminate gang control of the industry.[25] Certainly, there is a century of evidence that prohibition does not operate to reduce the trade or the violence. On the other hand, in the case of tobacco, which has become more available than ever over the past forty years, its use has fallen dramatically.[26] This has been occasioned by aggressive public health education and widespread support for non-smokers rights. As a result, while 60 per cent of Canadians smoked in the mid-60s, only 25 per cent do now. Prohibition was not part of the strategy. There is every reason to believe that the legalize-and-regulate approach would also succeed with respect to marijuana.

Not only the Conservatives' own party faithful (such as Mr. Flanagan), but also authorities on drugs and drug use have weighed in on the side of decriminalization or legalization. In addition to Canada's own experts, there have been international pleas for a change of direction. The Vienna Declaration, adopted as the Official Declaration of the XVIII International AIDS Conference,[27] states that the war on drugs has been a costly failure and denounces the "severe negative consequences" of the policy on both public health and crime rates. It urges a move away from the war and toward regulation and harm reduction.

A push to decriminalize cocaine and heroin as well as marijuana is coming from serious, credible sources.[28] Among those supporting such an approach are the outgoing president of the Royal College of Physicians, the chair of the Bar Council of England and Wales, and a study in the *British Medical Journal*—all of these in the United Kingdom.

Mexico, where some 35,000 people have been murdered since 2006 because of the war on drugs, is beginning to think about changing its approach.[29] It recently decriminalized the possession of small amounts of marijuana, cocaine, methamphetamine, and other drugs.[30] And President Felipe Calderón has recently called for a debate on legalization.[31]

Supporters of strict laws and long sentences believe they will drive drug use down, but the evidence is to the contrary. A 2008 World Health Organization study found that "countries with stringent user-level illegal drug policies did not have lower levels of use than countries with liberal ones."[32] In fact, the *British Medical Journal* article points out that, when drugs were decriminalized in Portugal, there was a decrease in their use, especially among school-age young people. Since Portugal decriminalized the use of marijuana in 2001, its rates of use have been among the lowest in the European Union.[33] Meanwhile the rate of use in the United States, where marijuana is outlawed, is almost twice that in the Netherlands, where it is sold in licensed cafés.

Prime Minister Harper is emphatic that he does not want his young children to be able to get their hands on illicit drugs.[34] Yet it is clear that their illegality makes it easy. As one observer notes, "Try buying a bottle of scotch after midnight, or a pack of cigarettes without photo ID. Meanwhile, cannabis transactions can happen at any time, anywhere (no shoes, no shirt, so what?)." [35] For children, regulated sales would make it virtually impossible to obtain these drugs.

There is another misperception about marijuana—that it is a "gateway" drug, leading users to move on to harder drugs. This is contrary to the evidence. For example, in the Netherlands, where marijuana "coffee shops" abound, there is less of a drug problem than in other European countries, and "the estimated prevalence of problem users of hard drugs...is the lowest per thousand inhabitants in Western Europe."[36]

That the war on drugs also contributes significantly to serious public health problems cannot be denied. Outside sub-Saharan Africa, injection drug use now accounts for about one in three new cases of HIV. Sir Ian Gilmore, the former president of the Royal College of Physicians, says that the war on drugs is failing, and that it is time to treat heroin addiction as a health problem rather than as a criminal problem. HIV and hepatitis C are ailments that commonly result from intravenous drug use. The problem of dirty needles can be easily remedied, but only if governments will swear off arresting everybody who engages in the practice of intravenous injection.

Still in Britain, the former drugs minister in the Home Office, Labour MP Bob Ainsworth, recently surprised many when he declared that the war on drugs has been "nothing short of a disaster."[37] He recommended studying other options, like decriminalizing possession of drugs and legally regulating their production and supply. When he was defence secretary with responsibilities in Afghanistan, Mr. Ainsworth saw that the war on drugs "creates the very conditions that perpetuate the illegal trade, while undermining international development security." He wants to take the trade away from organized criminals and hand control of it to doctors and pharmacists.

The appearance of Asa Hutchinson at Canada's House of Commons public safety committee should also command the Conservative government's attention.[38] Mr. Hutchinson, who headed the United States Drug Enforcement Agency under President George W. Bush, says Canada should avoid the mistakes that made US incarceration rates soar. Mr. Hutchinson is a former prosecutor who advocated a tough-on-crime approach, but is now advocating a revision of harsh American justice policies.

Asa Hutchinson has signed on to the "Right on Crime" initiative spearheaded by Newt Gingrich and other high-profile Republicans who are advocating a re-evaluation of incarceration policies. Mr. Hutchinson said to the committee, "We have made some mistakes and I hope you can learn from those mistakes." The two biggest mistakes, he says, were a failure to put resources into rehabilitation, and the implementation of mandatory minimum sentences.

Federal United States anti-drug expenditures increased 600 per cent to more than $18 billion in 2002. Estimates say that national regulation of marijuana would result in savings of more than $44 billion a year in US enforcement expenditures alone. The United States also spends $12 billion a year to keep 500,000 people behind bars because of their drug use.[39] Lacking any evidence that this has been money well spent, eight states have repealed most of their mandatory minimum sentences for drug offences. As well, the federal *National Criminal Justice Commission Act of 2010* seeks to reform the "war on drugs" by recognizing that "mass incarceration of illegal drug users has not curtailed illegal drug usage" but has resulted in "disproportionate impacts on minority communities." It urges a public-health approach to drug dependence. This was approved by the House of Representatives in July 2010.

There was a flurry of activity in the United States as a result of the November 2010 congressional elections, in which many medical marijuana operations were approved, and incremental steps were taken toward legalization in some places. Many cities now tax local marijuana establishments, and California voted overwhelmingly in November to tax and regulate marijuana.[40] They voted down Proposition 19, which would have decriminalized the drug, but nine cities voted to tax marijuana dispensaries. Given that California has lately been spending more money on prisons than on higher education, and that a lot of that money is spent to warehouse drug users, it is beginning to make sense to relax the laws, tax the product, and pay down the budget deficit.

Marijuana is California's top cash crop, worth about $14 billion per year.[41] It is also the top cash crop in a dozen states, and one of the top five in thirty-nine more, valued at anywhere from $36 billion to $100 billion. That is a gift to the black market and to organized crime. If it were taxed similarly to alcohol and tobacco, it would yield about $6 billion in revenue annually.

Little by little, individual states are beginning to move in the direction of legalization. Twelve states and the District of Columbia have decriminalized possession of small quantities of marijuana. Seventeen states allow its medical use. California just made marijuana possession a civil infraction, meaning prison is not a possible penalty, and that a $100 fine will be imposed for possession of an ounce or less.[42]

Newly elected Georgia Governor Nathan Deal, a Republican, said in his inaugural address that putting drug addicts in jail was placing an unsustainable financial and civic burden on his state.[43] He said that the state would instead begin providing Drug, Driving Under the Influence and Mental Health Courts, Day Reporting Centers, and expanded probation and treatment options. "We cannot afford to have so many of our citizens waste their lives because of addictions," he said. "It is draining our State Treasury and depleting our workforce."

The Lone Star State has redirected money saved by reducing incarceration into community treatment for the mentally ill and low-level drug addicts. For the first time, there is now no waiting list for drug treatment in Texas (and crime dropped 10 per cent from 2004 to 2009, its lowest annual rate since 1973).

In Montana it is reported that people are refusing to sit on juries trying drug offences.[44] In one case, the accused was a drug dealer with a long record who was being tried for distributing a small amount of marijuana. One after the other, prospective jurors refused to serve, saying things like, "I'm not going to convict someone of a sale with two or three buds," or "I can't do it. I was convicted of marijuana possession a few years ago, and it ruined my life."

Montana is one of fifteen states that permit medical marijuana use. Montana's new Republican government, however, is planning to repeal the six-year-old statute permitting it.[45] Some fear that, in the process, the Montana economy will be wrecked. This is because the growing of medical marijuana has helped Montana survive the hard times created by the collapse of the construction industry and the second-home market.

Fully legal, taxable revenues are now being collected in Montana from the new class of entrepreneurs who are building the indoor marijuana factories. The economic ripple effect has been astonishing. Gardening supply companies are selling equipment to the growers, the state's biggest utility is selling vast amounts of electricity to supply grow-ops, and bakeries are even buying marijuana for use in their pastries.

An industry group formed by the marijuana growers estimates that they spend $12 million annually in Montana, and have created 1,400 jobs in one year—no small accomplishment in a state of only 975,000 people. The marijuana-growing business is also one of the few industries in Montana that is year-round.

Montana appears to be the outlier in its planned repeal of laws that allow medical marijuana use. The trend in the United States is more toward reassessment of hard-line enforcement.

One aspect of that enforcement that points to a need for change is the high level of racial discrimination involved in enforcing the current laws. For example, according the Drug Policy Alliance, African-Americans are two to four times as likely to be arrested as Caucasians in every major county of California.[46] This is despite the fact that young African-Americans actually smoke marijuana less than young Caucasians. The National Association for the Advancement of Coloured People feels these laws are the "latest tool for imposing Jim Crow justice on poor African-Americans."

With cocaine, the discrimination is even more egregious. Conrad Black, referring to the twenty-eight months he spent "as a guest of the U.S. government," remarked on the racist aspect to the cocaine war:[47]

I had seen at close range the injustice of sentences one hundred

times more severe for crack cocaine than for powder cocaine,
a straight act of discrimination against African-Americans,
that even the first black president and attorney general have
only ameliorated with tepid support for a measure, still being
debated, to reduce the disparity of sentence from 100 to one to
18 to one.

PUBLIC HEALTH ISSUES

One unexpected aspect of the war on drugs that will have a serious impact upon public health has just come to light.[48] It seems that large marijuana grow-ops are leaving behind huge cesspools of toxic waste, including herbicides, pesticides, fertilizers, and diesel fuel. One observer reported a cesspool so toxic that it would not freeze at twenty degrees below zero. If the industry were decriminalized or legalized, it would consequently be required to obey environmental regulations. A hazard like toxic cesspools would not be permitted.

There is a further public health advantage to allowing the regulation of drugs. As long as the drugs are sold on the black market, buyers have no idea about either the potency of the drugs or the level of adulteration (or by what substance the drug has been adulterated). Thus, users can overdose if the potency of a new shipment of, say, heroin is appreciably higher than the user is accustomed to.[49] Health problems can also result from the ingestion of unknown adulteration products.

Some of the most significant advances are being made in the area of medical marijuana. In the name of compassion, many have championed the legalization of the drug for purposes of pain relief and the treatment of other symptoms. MP Carolyn Bennett, a medical doctor, is a proponent of marijuana for relief from pain and the nausea attributed to cancer treatments and some medical initiatives.[50] She says marijuana can also restore appetite, relieve constipation associated with other treatments, and allow patients to sleep and gain weight back because of the relief from pain. It is estimated that the 10,000 people currently licensed to use the drug represent only a tiny fraction of those who need it.[51]

One of the main drawbacks of the Canadian medical marijuana licensing system is that there is a gap of eight to ten months for renewal of one's licence to use the drug. During the gap between licences, people are being raided and arrested for getting the drug somewhere other than from Health Canada sources. This is insupportable, and appears to be the result of a lack of resources. Health Canada says that it is overwhelmed with applications, and the Conservative government does not seem inclined to increase funding for that purpose.

There is a simple solution for the delay issue, which would cost nothing and which has already been implemented in Oregon. After a thirty-day wait, if the medical marijuana licence still has not been renewed, there is a "deeming" provision that deems that the licence has been renewed. Since 90 per cent of Canadians are in favour of the use of marijuana for medical purposes, this could and should be easily fixed.

Another drawback is that someone wishing to use marijuana for medical purposes requires the signature of a medical doctor. Because there have been no clinical trials, doctors are reluctant to prescribe the drug. Some sufferers have been turned down by as many as thirty doctors.[52] Based on this kind of evidence, a decision of the Ontario Superior Court recently found that Canada's medical marijuana program is failing to provide access to the drug for those who need it.[53] At the same time, Mr. Justice Donald Taliano ruled that the offences of simple possession of marijuana and cultivating marijuana are unconstitutional, because these charges are used to criminally convict people who have not been able to obtain approval for medical reasons. The federal government has appealed the ruling.

The Conservative government exhibits "extreme queasiness" about all aspects of drug questions,[54] even those aspects that have to do with the saving of human lives and the protection of public health. The government has been trying for five years to shut down the InSite program in Vancouver, which is a supervised injection program based upon a harm-reduction model. Yet InSite has been shown to save money, save lives, and reduce diseases.[55] The respected medical journal the *Lancet* recently reported that overdose deaths dropped 35 per cent over the first two years of InSite's operation.[56] Lest the government claim that the public would never support programs that "make it easy" for addicts to get and use their drugs, the polls suggest otherwise. Angus Reid Strategies conducted a poll in April 2010 in which only 36 per cent of respondents said they would scrap harm reduction programs.[57] The poll does not report how many said they would support such programs. Then in November 2010 the pollster asked respondents if they thought harm reduction programs should be maintained. Forty-nine per cent said they agreed they should. That is convincing proof of public support for programs that seek to deal with drug addiction as a public health problem.[58]

The Conservative government's queasiness ramps up at the suggestion that there should be needle exchange programs in prisons. According to Dr. Thomas Kerr, incarceration of injection drug users is a key factor driving Canada's worsening HIV epidemic.[59] The number of cases in prisons has risen by 35 per cent over five years. A Vancouver study showed that incarceration more than doubled the risk of HIV infection among people who use illegal drugs. And a Correctional Service of Canada study found that almost 40 per cent of inmates in federal prisons reported having used drugs in their institutions.

The Correctional Service admits that there is intravenous drug use within the system, and has gone so far as to provide bleach for inmates to clean their needles.[60] Unfortunately, bleach is not very effective at killing viruses. But the Correctional Service and the Harper government cannot bring themselves to provide clean needles, offering all sorts of reasons it would cause problems.

Evaluations of the sixty worldwide needle exchange programs in prisons show that the fears are unjustified.[61] The programs do not lead to an increase in drug use, do not lead to syringes being used as weapons, and do not result in an increase in accidental needle-stick injuries. Canada's Correctional Investigator has also recommended needle and syringe programs in the prisons, but the Correctional Service has flatly refused to provide these.[62]

Voices are likely to be raised, saying, "Who cares whether a few junkies get a deadly disease in prison?" First of all, prisoners deserve to be accorded the same human rights as any citizen, including the right to equivalent health care. Second, many of those addicted prisoners will also be suffering from mental health issues or from being sexually victimized. These are people whom the public would normally to want to help. Third, these sick prisoners will eventually be released to the community, where they will spread their diseases to their family, friends, and community. The expense of treatment alone should give us pause.

André Picard says, "Clean needles cost a few pennies. An open mind is priceless." It would be helpful, and healthful, if the government could open its mind to implement programs that have been shown to save the lives and health of citizens. Some of these are canvassed in the final chapter, and they include drug treatment courts which are diverting offenders away from prison in favour of counselling and treatment.

Knowledgeable people continue trying to convince the Conservative government to rethink its position on drugs. On February 6, 2011, an open letter to the Prime Minister signed by over 500 doctors, scientists, and academics called for the withdrawal of Bill S-10.[63] They asked the government to be "smart on crime," and noted that a single case of HIV infection costs the health-care system, on average, $250,000. They urged Mr. Harper to withdraw the legislation for four reasons: there is no evidence that mandatory minimum sentences reduce drug use or deter crime, mandatory minimum sentences have a disproportionate negative impact on youth and Aboriginal persons, over-emphasis on drug enforcement has a negative impact on public health and rates of HIV, and mandatory minimum sentences are expensive and ineffective.

This "war on drugs" being waged by the Conservative government is largely a war on young people, the ill, and the addicted. It has failed spectacularly everywhere else it has been tried. Yet no amount of expert evidence or experience has so far swayed Mr. Harper or his government. There appears to be no justification for Bill S-10 other than moralistic and judgemental ideology. Neither of these provides a suitable basis for public policy. The damage such legislation will cause is beyond reckoning, and it is our children who will pay the price.

Bill S-10 died on the order paper in March 2011. Opposition leaders were all opposed to the legislation. The Conservatives have promised to resurrect it as part of the omnibus bill in the first 100 days of their new administration.

6: THE FINANCIAL COSTS

Canadians have a right to know what the heavy emphasis on crime is going to cost. When asked, Public Safety Minister Vic Toews initially said, "We're not exactly sure how much it will cost us,"[1] but it would not be more than $90 million.[2] He later implied that he did have an estimate but said, coyly, "I'd rather not share that."[3] Later he claimed the costs of the legislation would not exceed $2 billion. After much prevarication, the Harper government fell in 2011, largely because of its refusal to provide estimates for the costs of its tough-on-crime agenda.

It is confounding that with a historically high structural deficit and in a shaky economic recovery the Harper government has continued to pursue its very expensive crime laws. These bills will result in the lengthy incarceration of thousands of additional offenders under harsh conditions and, once implemented, will create huge pressure on the Treasury. There will be high costs not only in financial terms, but in social and human terms as well.

Public Safety Minister Toews maintains that crime costs Canadians $70 billion per year, and that his government is prepared to pay whatever it costs to put dangerous repeat offenders in prison.[4] He does not, however, explain how the proposed legislation will achieve that. He refuses to provide any serious estimates to justify the expenses that will be incurred. And he ignores cost-benefits analyses that show that huge savings in criminal justice costs can be obtained by well-placed dollars spent on prevention, treatment, and diversion.

Back in 2004, federal bureaucrats did an analysis of the Conservative election platform, and concluded that their law-and-order agenda would come in at $11.5 billion over five years.[5] Today's plan is likely to cost much more than this, if we look at preliminary calculations from the Parliamentary Budget Office, and the fact that many more crime bills have been introduced than were imagined in 2004.[6]

THE PARLIAMENTARY BUDGET OFFICER'S REPORT

When the Parliamentary Budget Officer reported that just one piece of legislation (Bill C-25) would cost $5.1 billion over five years,[7] Mr. Toews replied testily that in his opinion Kevin Page, the Parliamentary Budget Officer, had been wrong in most of his projections.[8] Thus he dismissed, arbitrarily, the only serious attempt to estimate the costs of the abolition of 2-for-1 credit for remand time, and did so without offering his own numbers.

The Parliamentary Budget Officer made it clear that his estimates were on the low side. He was not able to include the effects of certain additional factors like the increased costs of programming for inmates who would be spending more time in sentenced custody.[9] His estimates also excluded the extra costs of *Charter* challenges and the increased numbers of appeals. They also did not include the costs of new applications for enhanced credit under Bill C-25. No one who has challenged Mr. Page's conclusions has provided contrary information.

The 2-for-1 legislation was passed without parliamentarians having the least idea of the likely costs. This one bill alone will cause the total budget for Canadian corrections to increase by a factor of 2.15 over five years.[10] Never one to mince words, *Globe and Mail* columnist Jeffrey Simpson says of the Bill C-25 fiasco, "There's a difference between being 'tough on crime,' as the federal Conservatives profess to be, and being stupid about crime, which is what they are."[11]

In discussing the likely financial costs, it is important to keep certain numbers in mind. Even excluding the cost of land acquisition and development charges, the cost of adding cells to the federal system is high. Commissioner Don Head says that a single cell in a low security institution costs $260,000 to build. Medium security cells cost $400,000, and maximum security cells cost $600,000.[12] The Correctional Service is expecting to receive funding increases "unheard of" in its history, due to the cost of the tough-on-crime agenda.[13]

The Parliamentary Budget Office estimates that Bill C-25 will result in a need for 4,189 more cells.[14] Federal inmates will spend, on average, 159 more days in custody under the new law. Assuming distribution as at present, this would mean 745 new low security cells, 2,346 medium security cells, and 1,131 high security and multi-level security cells. The grand total to construct all of these new cells is $1.813 billion. The Correctional Service will have to build two new low security facilities, six more medium security facilities, four high security facilities and one multi-level security facility—thirteen new prisons. All will have to be built on existing Correctional Service of Canada land, or the price will go up accordingly.[15]

Mr. Page points out that if the Correctional Service decides instead to double-bunk inmates, then such construction costs will not be required. However, the consequences of double- and triple-bunking are so serious that the influx of new inmates can clearly not be safely accommodated in this way.

Public Safety Minister Vic Toews says that double-bunking is "not a big deal."[16] People who work in prisons say that it is a very big deal. It leads to violence and instability. Pierre Mallette, president of the Union of Canadian Correctional Officers, testified before members of Parliament on February 15, 2011, saying that prison guards are already experiencing the effects of overcrowded cells (Bill C-25 had been in force for about a year).[17] Close to 30 per cent of prison cells now house two inmates. Mr. Mallette said it is impossible to determine accurately which offenders can safely share a cell. Consequently, double-bunked inmates are attacking each other, creating dangerous conditions for both inmates and guards. Since the federal inmate population is expected to grow by close to 30 per cent in the next two to three years, guards have reason to be concerned.

Howard Sapers, the prison ombudsman, says that double-bunking has increased 50 per cent since the Conservatives took office, so some prisoners are sleeping in bunk beds, or on cots, or on mattresses on the floor.[18] He says, "As population pressures increase, we are likely to see increased incidents of institutional violence." According to Corrections data, "the number of major institutional incidents increased during [2009]—including preventable deaths in custody, violent assaults, serious bodily injury and use of force."[19]

Canada has international obligations for the proper housing of inmates. The First United Nations Congress on the Prevention of Crime and Treatment of Offenders states: [20]

> *Where sleeping accommodation is in individual cells or rooms, each prisoner shall occupy by night a cell or room by himself. If for special reasons, such as temporary overcrowding, it becomes necessary for the central prison administration to make an exception to this rule, it is not desirable to have two prisoners in a cell or room.*

Yet the Conservative government's solution to the overcrowding problem will be to double-bunk. And plans are underway to hire more than five thousand new employees at the Correctional Service of Canada—one of the only departments in the federal government on a hiring spree.[21]

GOVERNMENT ESTIMATES

The government's estimates show that capital expenditures (essentially the building fund) for the prison system will increase 33 per cent from $246.8 million in 2009–2010 to $329.4 million in 2010–2011.[22] Recent estimates project an increase in capital spending to $505.959 million in 2011–2012.[23] This represents a whopping 105 per cent increase in just two years.

Meanwhile, Public Safety Minister Vic Toews has admitted that capital expenditures will have to be increased even more significantly. He now says there is a plan to spend $9 billion on new prisons. This is in addition to $2 billion over five years to increase capacity within existing prisons.[24] He offers no justification for these numbers, which, we note in passing, exceed the government's estimate of the cost of new fighter jets. His new figures do, however, contradict the government's own estimates as quoted above.

There is also the cost of operating and maintaining all these new facilities. The Parliamentary Budget Office calculates that the average cost per inmate per cell is $84,225 in the provincial/territorial system, and $147,467 in the federal system.[25] The numbers are even more startling, however, when we look at different security classifications.[26] Maximum security male inmates cost the system $223,687 per year—almost a quarter of a million dollars per year. For women in maximum security, the number is even higher—$343,810 per year.

Combining capital costs with operations and maintenance, the increases in expenditures since the Conservatives took office are already very high. Between 2005–2006 and 2009–2010, the increase for the Correctional Service of Canada's total annual appropriations was in the order of 32 per cent (from $1.704 billion to $2.245 billion).[27] Estimates released in early 2011 show that the total expenditures in 2011–2012 are expected to be $3 billion, an increase over 2010–2011 (the adjusted figure of $2.5 billion) of 21 per cent.[28] That is a 21 per cent increase in one year.

Recent statistics confirm that increased capital expenditures are coming at the expense of programming for offenders. The Correctional Service of Canada provides some excellent rehabilitation programs, but no one pretends that these are adequate. The prison ombudsman says that only about 25 per cent of federal inmates are engaged in programs at any one time. Only about 2 per cent of Correctional Service's overall budget is dedicated to programs, which include violence prevention, substance abuse, family violence prevention, and sex offender programs.

Program spending for these four programs has declined since the Conservative government took office. One estimate puts the decline in funding of all prison rehabilitation programs at 47 per cent since 2006.[29] With the exception of violence prevention, program spending is expected to flat-line from 2009–2010 to 2015.[30]

Correctional Services estimates show that violence prevention program funding will increase to about $12,500,000 in 2011–2012, and will continue at this level until 2015. Substance abuse program funding, on the other hand, has dropped from about $11,000,000 in 2007–2008 to $8,000,000 in 2009–2010, and is not expected to increase. Similarly, funding available for sex offender programming dropped from $6,000,000 in 2006–2007 to $5,000,000 in 2009–2010, while funding for the family violence prevention program fell from $3,000,000 in 2006–2007 to less than $2,000,000 in 2009–2010.

The federal correctional service now houses approximately 13,500 inmates. Altogether, in 2011–2012 there will be $27,500,000 available for programs for all federal inmates, a total of about $2,000 per year per inmate or $5.58 per day. These figures will not increase until at least 2015, although the number of inmates is expected to rise by about 30 per cent as a result of the "Truth in Sentencing" law alone, and will rise much higher as more tough-on-crime bills come on stream. The already meagre funding for programming is inadequate. As funds become scarcer for each inmate, it is likely that offenders will be released having received no help at all, with the result that recidivism will increase.

Federal estimates tabled on March 1, 2011, show a $7.4 million decrease in funding for community programs focusing on youth gangs.[31] Some $13.1 million will be cut from other efforts that help Canadians build safe communities. There is 30 per cent less money for the Victims of Crime Initiative, and 55 per cent less in grants and 49 per cent less in contributions for the Youth Justice Fund.[32]

Marjean Fichtenberg, of the Canadian Resource Centre for Victims of Crime, deplores the emphasis on an agenda that emphasizes building new prison cells. She lost her son to murder by a parolee. She says that one way to protect victims is through preventive measures, such as giving offenders the programs they need while in prison.[33] She is discouraged at the government's emphasis on building new prison cells, saying, "This law-and-order agenda, where they're building more prisons, is still leaving the victim out because it's still focusing only on the offender." Victims are trying to overcome an "image of victims as being vengeful and waiting for nothing more than punishment for the offender."

COSTS TO PROVINCES AND TERRITORIES

Provincial and territorial governments will also incur extraordinary costs. They are already engaged in a huge expansion of prison infrastructure in the order of $2.8 billion, but this expansion was undertaken before the new federal tough-on-crime agenda.[34] Consequently, it is expected that the provinces will find themselves in a serious financial shortfall.

According to the Parliamentary Budget Office, the provinces will bear the brunt of the increases under Bill C-25. Whereas today the provinces and territories shoulder about 49 per cent of the total burden for corrections across the nation, Bill C-25 will raise this proportion to 56 per cent. The Parliamentary Budget Office estimates provincial and territorial costs (including construction, operations, and maintenance) will come in at $6.5 billion in the first year, continuing to rise each year thereafter.[35]

Provinces and territories are largely responsible for the costs of administering criminal justice. They provide staff, security, stenographers, clerks, court time, sheriffs, judges, provincial prosecutors, courthouses, and jails. Under Bill C-25, more offenders will also be serving longer sentences in provincial institutions, where the provinces will foot the bill for capital and operating costs. Other new legislation, including the drugs bill and young offender legislation, will put pressure on provincial budgets as well.

The provinces appear to be wakening to the consequences of the new legislation. Although it was the attorneys general of some provinces who initiated Bill C-25, they are now appealing to the federal government for financial help.[36] Federal government officers have recently travelled to select provinces, offering financial assistance in building more prison cells.

The provinces recently requested that the federal penitentiary system be allowed to house their longest-serving provincial prisoners, to ease pressure on provincial treasuries.[37] They argued that, because most offenders in the provincial system are serving less than six months, there is no real programming available to any of the offenders in that system, even those serving longer sentences (which can be as much as two years less a day). If those serving more than six months were housed in federal institutions, there would be programs available for them. Public Safety Minister Vic Toews has refused to help, saying it is a jurisdictional matter that would require a constitutional change.

As Anthony Doob succinctly and correctly points out, "He's wrong." Nothing—certainly nothing constitutional—is stopping the federal correctional system from accepting prisoners from the provincial system. However, this would play havoc with the federal budget deficit, something the Harper government wishes to avoid.

COSTS OF OTHER CRIME LAWS

Bill C-25 is not the only piece of legislation that will put a strain on the government's coffers. The new mandatory minimum sentence regime for drugs offences, destined to be part of the new omnibus bill, will send thousands of additional offenders to prison. Professor Neil Boyd, an expert in the field, estimates that the new laws dealing with marijuana cultivation alone will result in an additional five hundred growers going to jail for six months each year—just in British Columbia.[38] He estimates that, at an estimated $57,000 per year per inmate, it will cost an additional $30 million to house marijuana growers in British Columbia prisons.[39] It is also likely that a new prison would have to be built for the purpose.

There are ten provinces and three territories, with marijuana being grown in all of them. The financial implications of this single aspect of the drug legislation are self-evident. More mandatory minimums for firearms offences and property crimes will add to the expense. The addition of dozens of new offences to the list of those not qualified for conditional sentences will also stretch the budget. The amendments to the *Youth Criminal Justice Act* will consign many more young people to jail.[40] Many other new laws will add to the prison populations. Taken together, their effect upon the federal budget will make the cost of Bill C-25 pale by comparison.

Bill C-49 is already costing the Treasury a huge amount of money, and it has not even become law. This bill was launched shortly after the arrival of several hundred Tamil migrants in August 2010 by way of the Thai cargo ship *MV Sun Sea*.[41] The bill was introduced a scant two months after the arrival of the ship, and has been roundly criticized by the opposition and by human rights advocates because it proposes holding such migrants in custody for a full year without a right to judicial review. As of February 2011, the detention of the Tamil migrants had cost Canada $18 million, even though most of them were released long ago and only five have been linked even remotely with the Tamil Tiger fighters.

These are just some of the examples of very expensive legislative changes by the Conservative government that will not deliver improved public safety. But there are a number of additional costs associated with the new legislation. For example, Statistics Canada reported in 2009 that the number of police officers in Canada has been steadily increasing over the past decade.[42] The number of officers is 9 per cent higher than it was a decade ago, and the 1.5 per cent increase from 2008 to 2009 was the third-highest annual increase in thirty years. At the end of 2009, there were 67,000 police officers across the country.

This level of policing comes at a cost. After adjusting for inflation, police expenditures rose for the twelfth consecutive year in 2008.[43] The total amount spent on policing was $11 billion, or 6 per cent more in constant dollars than in the previous year. This was the largest annual increase since 1990. At a time when the crime rate is dropping, these are significant increases, even allowing for inflation and the increased costs of salaries. Adding dozens of new laws can only send policing costs soaring.

A distinction needs to be made between simply funding hundreds of additional police positions and funding the sophisticated mechanisms necessary for the police to do their work. Charles Momy, president of the 41,000-member Canadian Police Association, complains that municipal police are being saddled with national issues on top of day-to-day crime, but are getting no extra funding.[44] He cites cyber crime, including child pornography, financial fraud, and cyber-bullying, along with organized crime, emergency preparedness, and national security as areas that devour police budgets. The resources to combat sophisticated Internet and nation-wide crime issues are not being made available. The latest government estimates also show that no more funding will be made available for the Money Laundering Initiative.[45] Mr. Momy says, "We hope to persuade the federal government that they need to be much more sensitive to the impact of their decisions and the financial burden they place on local governments and police organizations."

Statistics on hiring in the civil service also tell a tale. The percentage increase in employees in 2008–2009 was highest in the Department of National Defence, at 8.2 per cent.[46] But the Correctional Service of Canada and Canada Border Services were tied for second place, and each increased by 6.7 per cent. Next was the new organization called "Public Prosecution," which was expected to make 783 new hires. Meanwhile, Commissioner Don Head announced in February 2011 that the Correctional Service of Canada plans to hire five thousand new staff to handle its increased work load.[47]

There are other significant new costs associated with the administration of justice and not always taken into account when the increased pressure on budgets is calculated.

Wherever there is a mandatory minimum sentence, or a lengthy potential sentence, accused persons will fight their charges fiercely. Hundreds of new trials, bail hearings, appeals, and *Charter* challenges will be added to court dockets, requiring the building of courts and the hiring of new personnel. Sheriffs will be needed to escort prisoners. More court clerks and support staff will be required. Additional Crown Attorneys and more judges will have to be appointed to handle the new cases. There will be a need for more correctional officers, classification officers, and parole officers. Legal Aid funding will have to increase significantly. There will be a need for more programs providing alternatives for those seeking bail. John Howard and Elizabeth Fry Societies and community alternative programs will be stretched and will need more funding.

COSTS AND BENEFITS OF ALTERNATIVES

One other area must be considered. Programs designed to keep offenders out of the very expensive prison system are an important piece of the financial puzzle. Many of these programs are described in more detail in the final chapters, but the brief summary here shows that alternatives to prison bring significant financial benefits.

As noted above, according to the Parliamentary Budget Office, the cost of maintaining an inmate for one year in a provincial/territorial prison is, on average, $84,225. The cost for a federal inmate is, on average, $147,467.

By contrast, the Drug Treatment Court in Toronto costs $12,000 to $20,000 per offender per year. Of the offenders who go to Drug Treatment Court, 52 per cent "graduate," meaning they never go to jail.[48] Instead, they are placed in the community and supervised by the John Howard Society and others. Drug treatment courts are also a feature of the American justice system. There, it is estimated that for every dollar spent, the courts produce $2.21 in benefits (reduced crime and costs of incarceration).[49] Such courts provide intensive treatment to offenders, save money, and reduce recidivism rates to boot. The Urban Institute estimates that if the program were made available to all such offenders, the level of benefits would be $3.36 per $1 spent.

A program called the Perry Preschool Program (conducted in Michigan) estimated a savings of $250,000 per child for a program of preschool care offered between 1962 and 1967 to 123 children (including a control group) from low-income families. The savings were identified by following up on the subjects until they turned forty. The savings per dollar spent on the program amounted to $12.90, mostly because the benefiting males committed fewer crimes.[50]

A program at Hollow Water, Manitoba, which diverted a large proportion of the reserve population away from prison, reports that for every dollar spent, $3.75 in expenditures were avoided that would otherwise have been spent on provincial costs like pre-incarceration, prison, and probation.[51] Also, for every dollar spent, two dollars to twelve dollars were saved that would have been spent on incarceration and parole federally. For every two dollars spent by the government on the program, the community also received six to fifteen dollars' worth of services and value-added benefits. Public Safety Canada called this a "cost-effective alternative."

Prison Justice in British Columbia reports that alternatives to incarceration like probation, bail supervision, and community supervision cost five to twenty-five dollar's per day per offender.[52] The calculations provided by Prison Justice show that the comparable rate to imprison these offenders would be $259.05 per day federally and $141.78 per day provincially.

Savings are achieved through all kinds of alternative programs.[53] For example, a program that sent nurses to work with first-time mothers saved two dollars for every dollar spent. An American program called the Seattle Social Development Project sent people into classrooms to work with the children. For one dollar spent, four dollars were estimated to be saved.

Anti-gang programs in Winnipeg called New Directions and Oasis (which deals with youth from war-torn African countries) are also finding success. They cost about $13,000 per year per youth. They are among many cost-effective alternatives likely to lose funding as the Conservative government cuts programs.

This short summary shows there are significant savings to be had. There is no reason such proven programs could not be replicated across the country, reducing the need for new prisons, saving money, and helping people pay their debts to society and succeed in their communities without experiencing incarceration.

The Harper government's refusal to provide firm estimates of the cost of its tough-on-crime agenda has caught the attention of the media, as well as that of opposition parliamentarians. Citing the many statistics that show Canadians are really not interested in prosecuting marijuana offences, a recent *Globe and Mail* editorial said the government's refusal to release estimates of the costs of charging, prosecuting, and incarcerating users is "untenable."[54] "Billions are at stake for an unclear social purpose." The writer wonders how Mr. Harper can expect taxpayers to give him a blank cheque on crime legislation while "stressing fiscal rectitude and the promotion of financial literacy." The *Globe* later reiterated warnings issued by Kevin Page and said, "To the extent Canada allows for untrammelled (and unnecessary) growth of the prisons, it will have less money available to invest in people and productivity."[55]

The *Toronto Star* has also pointed out that the government's estimates are "absolutely unbelievable."[56] The latest number the government had provided for estimated costs of the crime crackdown was $650 million over five years. The *Star* calculated that, since the government spent $330 million on prison infrastructure alone last year, expenditures would have to *decrease* by 60 per cent annually to arrive at a figure of $650 million over five years. Meanwhile, the government used "every excuse conceivable" to withhold actual information.

The Conservative tough-on-crime agenda has the potential to plunge Canada into a more serious structural deficit in the immediate future. Canadians might be willing to bear such a cost if the government could show that it would produce results in an even lower crime rate. The effect of its new legislation, however, will be the opposite.

7: THE HUMAN COSTS

PRISON CONDITIONS AND HUMAN RIGHTS

The Conservative plan to revert to an old and discredited model of criminal justice will produce another kind of cost. This is the cost in human misery, not just for offenders, but also for their families, friends, and communities. Longer sentences and harsher conditions bring increased human costs.

It is one of the more persistent myths in Canada that its prisons provide a soft landing for offenders, a "Club Fed" for criminals. On the contrary, while new and more progressive approaches to the treatment of prisoners over the past couple of decades have improved conditions somewhat, prisons are still dangerous, violent, soul-destroying places, whether they are remand cells or maximum-security penitentiaries.

The treatment of one female offender serves as an illustration. According to the Correctional Investigator, this woman had engaged in a number of self-harming incidents that increased in both severity and duration.[1] Despite documented mental health concerns, she spends most of her time in segregation.

> On almost every occasion of self-harm, her behaviour is met with overly restrictive, punitive, and security-based interventions that often necessitate use of force, including the adoption of the standing control restraint technique to manage her. (This technique requires the offender to stand, in leg irons

and high profile rear wrist locks, until self-injurious behaviour ceases, which can be hours.) In this case, pressure was applied to the rear wrist locks to induce discomfort when she was not compliant or had attempted to drop to the floor...Significantly, the challenging "adjustment" behaviours that this offender presented while in custody have virtually ceased since her conditional release into the community.

In another case, a search was conducted at a maximum security penitentiary over a ten-day period, generating 379 separate "uses of force" incidents.[2]

During the search, members of the Emergency Response Team and a Tactical team wearing ballistic protection [were] deployed to conduct inmate counts, security patrols, cell extractions and strip searches. Compliant inmates were frequently searched at gunpoint...By the end of the 10 day search inmates were "visibly agitated" due to a reported lack of hygiene—some had not showered in days nor been provided with soap or even toilet paper in their cells.

This is the kind of humiliating treatment that was practised in penitentiaries thirty years ago. Inmates came to interviews apologizing for the fact that they had not been allowed to shower for a week, or that their false teeth had been taken away from them. Personal appearance and hygiene are generally highly valued by prison inmates, both to make life inside bearable and for them to retain their sense of dignity. Access to showers, soap, and so on was being purposely removed.

Mr. Sapers's recent annual report said that "unprecedented legislative and policy activity" by the Conservative government is causing rising offender populations and surging correctional costs.[3] The result has been an increase in violent incidents and a decrease in inmate programs. He said, "My message today is that conditions are undermining corrections."[4] Correctional Service data show that the number of major institutional incidents increased during 2009, including preventable deaths in custody, violent assaults, serious bodily injury, and use-of-force incidents (which alone increased by more than 25 per cent over 2008).[5] At the same time, less than 25 per cent of the prison population was engaged in "core" correctional programs—the programs directed toward reducing recidivism, without which obtaining parole is impossible.[6]

Mr. Sapers warns that adopting simple solutions for complex problems would produce unintended consequences. He says that as a result of increased overcrowding, "the climate is increasingly harsh, tense and stressed and it's undermining the rehabilitation efforts. Current conditions inside our federal penitentiaries are...challenging the ability of our correctional authority to deliver a correctional service that is fair, safe and humane."[7]

He describes the conditions in one Pacific Region medium-security institution.[8] Built in the 1960s, it has no running water in 75 per cent of the individual cells, meaning there are no toilets or sinks. Inmates use a centralized washroom facility on the range, which presents a problem during lockdown situations. In the case of a recent lockdown, inmates waited up to three hours to use the washrooms. They were issued plastic bottles for urination, but for bowel movements, they were reduced to defecating into plastic bags. These were thrown out of their windows. It was not possible to do hand-washing and other basic hygiene. Meals were served in these cells and sanitary wipes were provided. This is no "Club Fed." This is a Canadian prison in 2010.

Aside from the physical conditions, there are serious psychological effects of spending years in prison. One inmate who had spent every day of seven years in either maximum security or the Special Handling Unit (super-maximum) was asked what effect this had on a prisoner:[9]

> You become accustomed to a violent and volatile atmosphere. The Special Handling Unit is a much more intense place where you have to fortify yourself. You have to train yourself to be mentally strong in order to survive. When you go out into a common room with other prisoners if you make a mistake you could be dead.

Conditions in the Special Handling Unit or SHU (called "the shoe" by inmates) appear not to have changed much in thirty years. In the early 1980s, for a short period of time, there was a murder every week in the Special Handling Unit at Millhaven Penitentiary. It was rumoured that the inmates had made a pact to kill each other one at a time until the last one took his own life. Whether true or not, the fact that such a rumour had any credence at all speaks volumes about the living conditions in the prison at the time.

Despite the appalling conditions in many of Canada's prisons, progress has been made in the way correctional work is conducted. One of the progressive approaches adopted in the wake of the damning 1977 MacGuigan Report[10] was "dynamic security." This means "meaningful and constructive interactions between offenders and front-line staff."[11] As a result, guards and inmates began to treat each other more like fellow human beings. Dynamic security produced a less volatile atmosphere in the prisons, which became safer and more humane.

Turning the clock back to a time when there was little such interaction will reverse these gains. The *Roadmap*'s recommendations will lead to such a regression. Less interaction means inmates spend more time locked in their cells, with more control and regulation than usual, and more restrictions on access to yards, to recreation and hobby crafts. There are more "exceptional" searches and restricted routines. Access to Case Management officers is more restricted, and there are protracted interruptions in education and other programs. Correctional officers are withdrawn from inmates and posted in observation towers or behind electronic barriers.

These changes threaten the safety and health of inmates and staff alike. The dual mandate of the Correctional Service of Canada is to exercise reasonable and effective control while at the same time assisting offenders in their rehabilitation and reintegration. The latter part of the mandate will fail if there is little interaction and a consequent deterioration of mutual respect between staff and offenders.

The Conservative government's punishment-oriented approach and adherence to the *Roadmap* recommendations means it prefers to put billions of dollars into building more prison cells rather than into providing programs and treatment. But, as Mr. Sapers says, "There is no jurisdiction in the world that has ever built its way to a crime-free society."[12] The money being poured into prison construction is being removed from programs which have been shown to work.

One interested party calls the Conservative government's prison expansion plans a "moral and political catastrophe."[13] Conrad Black was scarcely able to believe the recommendations made by the *Roadmap*, or that the government he supports was planning to implement them. He insists that you do not reform people by caging them behind barbed wire and doing nothing to deal with their problems. Longer, more severe sentences, he says, will produce people who are more embittered and less qualified to re-enter normal law-abiding life.

Authors Graham Stewart and Michael Jackson eviscerate the *Roadmap* in their critique, *A Flawed Compass: A Human Rights Analysis of the Roadmap to Strengthening Public Safety*.[14] They point out that the *Roadmap*'s recommendations fly in the face of the *Charter of Rights and Freedoms*, and will undo years of progress. They assert that it is a myth to suggest that prisoners' human rights are somehow at odds with public safety. The decent treatment of prisoners will produce less risk to the public, not more. Comparing Canada's record to that of the United States, it is clear that Canada, by attempting to honour the human rights of offenders, has held the line on crime and got better results at a fraction of the cost.

The approach to corrections adopted in the wake of the MacGuigan Report reduced violence in prisons.[15] The approach recommended by the *Roadmap* will return prisons to the pre-dynamic-security days, when guards and prisoners operated under an "us vs. them" code. Then, there was persistent and pervasive violence. This will become the norm again, as the screws are tightened on the inmate population. Family visits will become arduous for both inmates and families because of extra surveillance to keep out illicit drugs. Programs like the prison farms, which inmates looked forward to and learned from, will be abolished. Instead, prisoners will now be trained in other jobs, but only if employers (and funding) can be found. Any funding will come from other programs that have been proven to work, but that will now be cut.

Program shortages within the prison system are now so severe they have become a threat to public safety, according to Howard Sapers.[16] Yet the government is increasing spending on new prison cells at twice the rate it spends on programming. Approximately 2 to 2.7 per cent of the total corrections budget is allocated to programs. This amounts to $500 to $675 million per year for all programming, a plainly insufficient amount for more than 13,500 federal inmates. The lack of programs is producing violence and despair. One of the more obvious results is that inmates will be ineligible for parole because they have not participated in programming.

The *Roadmap* calls for prisoners to have only basic rights, with all additional "privileges" to be "earned."[17] How, ask Stewart and Jackson, is this to be achieved by inmates who suffer from mental illness, drug addiction, illiteracy, and all manner of dysfunction?[18] And how are these offenders to benefit from work programs if other remedial programs (education, mental health, addiction, anger management, life skills) are curtailed to fund the new work programs?

Roadmap recommendations are plainly designed to exact further punishment from people who have already paid with their freedom. Conrad Black calls it a "bad plan to take Canada to a destination it should not wish to reach."[19] As he points out, treatment of prisoners has been recognized for centuries as one of the hallmarks of civilized society. Efforts to make visiting privileges more difficult are "just a pretext to assist in the destruction of families and friendships." Concentrating on generating employment skills at the expense of other programs (general education, substance abuse avoidance, behavioural adaptation) is a mistake.

"I am no hemophiliac bleeding heart," he says, "but non-violent people can sometimes be helped to abandon illicit practices by some of these programs. No useful purposes will be served by cranking back into the world unreconstructed sociopaths who can fix an air conditioner or unclog a drain."

The Correctional Service would appear to be in agreement. It talks about continuing with the "evidence-based programs that are designed to make offenders accountable for changing their criminal behaviour and attitudes, thereby significantly reducing the risks they present to Canadians when they are returned to the community."[20]

The Correctional Service points out that the effectiveness of any work or employment programs, as recommended by the *Roadmap*, will be circumscribed by the downturn in the economy. Specifically, "the Federal Government deficit, contraction in the economy, limited affordable housing, and rising unemployment rates could have a negative impact on the safe transition of offenders to the community."[21] The Correctional Service thus recognizes the value of the existing evidence-based programs while expressing reservations about the planned work programs.

The Correctional Service is very concerned that funding for social programs and employment may also not be available to help offenders once they are released:

> *There is a risk that there may be fewer community resources and supports available to the returning offender because of pressures on funding to social programs. Also, securing affordable housing and financial support may become more difficult for released offenders, which may contribute to less than favourable correctional results. There is also a risk that offenders may not be able to find meaningful work upon release because of higher rates of unemployment.*

Thus the Correctional Service of Canada gently reminds the Conservative government that the rehabilitation of offenders rests largely upon the social programs available outside the prison as well as inside it.

THE MENTALLY ILL

Mental illness in prisons is one of the most important issues the Correctional Investigator identifies. He highlights something that most Canadians do not know: federal offenders are excluded from *The Canada Health Act* and are not covered by Health Canada or provincial health care systems.[22] The federal system of corrections has only $190 million per year to deal with the health concerns (including mental health) of some 13,500 inmates. At approximately $14,000 per inmate per year, this is woefully inadequate. The mental and physical health problems presented by large numbers of inmates are complex.

The percentage of mentally ill offenders is growing by five to ten per cent per year in both provincial and federal systems.[23] At least 25 per cent of new admissions to federal prisons have a mental illness. Many of these are in prison because there are no available hospital beds, or because it is easier for police officers to place an offender into custody than to spend hours waiting with him in a hospital emergency room. In addition to those with mental illnesses are those who are developmentally handicapped or of low intelligence. There is no intervention at all in many cases, as "the system is simply under-resourced," according to Joe Wright, legal counsel to the Ontario Review Board.[24] Some refer to this trend as "the criminalization of mental illness."[25]

One source notes that "nearly 35 per cent of the 13,300 inmates in federal penitentiaries have a mental impairment requiring treatment—triple the estimated total as recently as 2004, and far higher than the incidence of mental illness in the general population."[26] Yet less than 15 per cent of mental-health patients ever commit a criminal offence of any kind.[27]

The recidivism rate for those found not to be criminally responsible for their offences due to mental disorder is under 10 per cent, according to a Justice Department study.[28] This is as compared to about 60 per cent recidivism for those in the regular system who are between the ages of eighteen and twenty-five, says a Statistics Canada report for 2002. Those who are released by way of absolute discharge (when a provincial review board deems them stable enough to release) go back to their normal lives with no supervision at all. They are, however, released only if it is decided that the offenders do not pose a "significant or real risk to the community."

Fully 35 per cent of the male offender population in the Atlantic region receives some mental health service.[29] In the Pacific region, the number is 37 per cent, which includes those with a cognitive deficit. Female offenders present even higher numbers: in the Pacific region, at least 50 per cent have a mental illness. These are numbers that warrant a vastly increased infusion of resources and programs.

The House of Commons Standing Committee on Public Safety and National Security recently presented its report on the subject of mental illness and drug and alcohol addiction in prisons.[30] It concluded that not nearly enough is being done to deal with these issues, and that offenders who do not receive adequate treatment are more likely to commit crimes after release.[31]

The committee's seventy-one thoughtful recommendations were rejected out of hand by Conservative members, who penned a dissenting opinion: "We feel obliged...to make known...how we disagree with what this opposition dominated committee has put forward, and what we propose as an appropriate way forward."[32] Their "way forward" included five recommendations, three of them dealing with drug interdiction (not treatment). The others recommended fixing aging infrastructure and continuing to implement the Mental Health Strategy.

The committee noted that a substantial increase in program funding would be needed to deal with the pervasive issues of inmates with drug and alcohol addiction and mental illness. The 2 to 2.7 per cent of the Correctional Service's budget allocated to correctional programming is expected to cover all the costs of training, quality control, management, and administration. Yet waiting lists are long for the programming that is currently available, and much more programming is required to deal with the special problems of this segment—everything from diversion programs and cultural accommodation for Aboriginal people to mother-child interventions and more halfway houses.

Prisons should not be a backup system for mental health care in the community, yet more and more patients are being housed in jails. The consequences for the mentally ill themselves are extremely negative, as jail conditions tend to exacerbate the problems they have. The consequences for the rest of the jail population are also serious. Mentally ill inmates contribute to high tension and violence in prisons, and they become the target of violence themselves. Any aberrant behaviour or peculiar habits in a prison population upsets the delicate balance maintained among inmates. Placing two or sometimes three inmates in a cell only makes worse what is already an intractable problem.

Much of the problem of over-incarceration of the mentally ill can be traced to the de-institutionalization of psychiatric patients over the past thirty years. While de-institutionalization was arguably the right policy, it needed to be followed up with an organized and funded plan: housing, clinics, crisis support, and so on. But instead of putting resources into assisting former patients to cope with life in the community, governments largely abandoned them to their own devices, or to the admirable but often inadequate efforts of volunteers. The predictable result has been that untreated mental illness has led to conflict with the law, and the prison system is scrambling to deal with offenders it is ill-equipped to manage.

Young people with mental illness are particularly vulnerable to getting caught up in the justice system. The Canadian Mental Health Association estimates that up to 20 per cent of Canadian youth are affected by a mental health disorder, and only 20 per cent of those are getting the help they need in their communities.[33] Keli Anderson, Executive Director of The F.O.R.C.E. Society for Kids' Mental Health in British Columbia, says that in every classroom with thirty children there are likely to be four or five who have mental health problems, yet only about 20 per cent receive treatment.[34] Though the *Youth Criminal Justice Act* specifically states that criminal law is not to be used as a way of providing access to mental health services, that is exactly what is happening. Criminalization of mental illness, particularly among youth, is becoming a disturbing trend.

The situation is unlikely to improve when there are numbers of mentally ill people who are also homeless and who commit crimes just to survive, often unaware they are breaking the law.[35] Many offenders are languishing in jail waiting for psychiatric beds after being found not criminally responsible for their offences. And, in Ontario at least, there is a standoff between hospitals and jails over whose job it is to house such offenders, so they stay in police holding cells.

Janet Gauthier, deputy superintendent of Maplehurst Correctional Complex, says that 200 of its 1,200 inmates have serious mental impairments, including schizophrenia, bipolar disorder, brain injuries, and the effects of fetal alcohol spectrum disorder.[36] There are also many with dementia, low intelligence, a lack of coping skills, and full-blown psychosis. She says that at one time these offenders would all have been in psychiatric facilities. "That day is gone. Now, we have incarceration."

So Canada's prison system has turned into a holding tank for the mentally ill. But there are insufficient numbers of trained staff and psychologists, and long waiting lists for whatever programs are available. Prison psychologists say they spend more time conducting risk assessments than in delivering clinical treatment and rehabilitation services.[37] As a result, offenders rarely qualify for parole and must serve longer sentences.[38] They are also at a higher risk for reoffending because they have not received adequate treatment. The circle is vicious, counterproductive, and unsustainable.

Most mentally ill offenders spend their days heavily medicated. Segregation is used on a regular basis, although "international human rights standards recognize that solitary confinement should only be used in very exceptional cases, for as short a time as possible and only as a last resort."[39] The number and duration of instances of segregation is increasing in Canadian federal prisons. In some maximum security institutions, up to a third of the population can be in segregation at any one time. Every day, there are over nine hundred offenders in segregation in the system. These include offenders at risk for suicide or serious self-injury, even though segregation worsens underlying mental health issues.

Putting resources into the right kinds of facilities can alleviate the over-incarceration of these offenders in the regular penitentiary system. Thanks largely to the efforts of Senator Robert Runciman, former Ontario minister of correctional and community services, the St. Lawrence Valley Correctional and Treatment Centre in Brockville, Ontario, provides 100 beds for male prisoners with mental illnesses.[40] A pact between the Royal Ottawa Hospital and the Ontario government was reached despite opposition from Mr. Runciman's Conservative cabinet colleagues.

In this facility, 70 per cent of the staff are health-care workers, and 30 per cent are security—the reverse of most correctional health-care units. The average inmate stays about four months and participates in a selection from thirty programs, including programs on anger management, self-esteem enhancement, yoga, psychotherapy, relaxation therapy, medication management, and group therapy for sex offenders and domestic abusers.

Less than half of the ex-patients at the St. Lawrence facility reoffend, compared with 92 per cent at other institutions that house similarly sick offenders. Its fine track record is drawing international attention.

The difference between such a facility and a normal secure prison is palpable, and the importance of dealing with these offenders in less secure settings with more treatment cannot be over-emphasized. The Standing Committee on Public Safety and National Security had this to say:[41]

We must stop regarding imprisonment as a free resource,

while associating costs with crime prevention. On the contrary, research has shown that imprisonment is an expensive measure that is generally not suited to the care of people suffering from mental disorders. Imprisonment can facilitate the appearance of mental disorders, or contribute to their recurrence and the aggravation of symptoms, particularly as a result of the stress generated by the danger of intimidation and violence within institutions, separation from family and loved ones, and concerns related to eventual release.

The issue of intimidation and violence is no small consideration. As one forensic psychiatrist at Maplehurst said, these offenders are "very vulnerable. Some of them can be annoying. There is so little stimulation for them in the jails that they have temper tantrums. And if they do, it is going to get them hurt."[42] In fact, it can get them killed. The dynamics of a maximum-security setting, for example, are so delicate that any behaviour out of the ordinary can prompt other inmates to eliminate the source of the irritation and disruption.

An example from the Special Handling Unit at Millhaven Institution seems apt. Two inmates were charged with the attempted murder of two others. The victims suffered from mental illness and constantly displayed annoying and disruptive habits. When the matter came to trial, an inmate took the stand to swear that he had tried to kill these victims. He explained himself to the jury by saying that "bugs" (inmate jargon for mentally ill inmates) could not be tolerated in the prison. Their strange habits disrupt the balance within that artificial and violent environment. The only solution for the smooth running of the population in the SHU is to eliminate the source of the disruption. He was acting in the best interests of the other inmates and of the staff who worked in the unit.

THE ADDICTED

Another segment of Canadian society over-represented in our prison populations are people addicted to drugs and alcohol. Fully 80 per cent of offenders entering the federal prison system identify themselves as having a substance abuse problem.[43] Many of these also suffer from a mental illness.

The lines are drawn between those who feel that a zero tolerance, interdiction approach to the presence of drugs in prison is mandatory, and those who feel that a public health treatment and harm reduction approach, in addition to interdiction, would be more effective, as well as more humane. The proponents of zero tolerance are determined to eliminate all illicit drugs from prison. The latter groups acknowledges the unpleasant truth that this is not realistic, and argues that it is important to deal with the public health effects of the drugs.

Drug addicts often arrive in the system because they have resorted to illegal activities to obtain money to buy the drugs they need. Upon admission to prison, they find that drugs are readily available, but that the conditions under which they can be administered are worse than they were on the street. Thus, the incidence of HIV/AIDS is shockingly high in the system. The Correctional Service of Canada has gone only as far as to make bleach available, although bleach does not adequately sterilize the needles.

The public safety committee considered evidence on this subject, noting that the Correctional Service approach to drug use was to control it rather than treat it. Committee members reported that $122 million had recently been provided to the system. The funds were supposed to be used for substance abuse programs as well as for control, but all of the money went to control (sniffer dogs, ion scans, x-rays, and so on) "to the detriment of substance abuse programs and harm reduction initiatives."[44]

The committee noted that the goal of eliminating all drugs from the system is unrealistic. Once this has been recognized, it seems logical that the system should provide treatment, prevention, and harm reduction programs to help those addicts whose health is unquestionably in jeopardy. The Corrections Service has refused to do so despite recommendations by the Correctional Investigator, who has repeatedly said that this is a public health and a human rights concern. He says that the Correctional Service is required to act to alleviate the harm, and "denying prisoners access to the same harm reduction measures available in the community that do not present an unmanageable security risk raises human rights concerns."[45]

Security risks and safety of staff are cited as the reason for a strict interdiction approach. Yet, as already noted, studies show that the concerns are unfounded. The Correctional Service's own Health Care Advisory

Committee has in fact recommended needle and syringe exchange programs, but Corrections has declined to act. A safer-tattooing program piloted in 2005 was also cancelled by the Conservative government, meaning that even more dirty needles are now spreading even more deadly disease throughout the prisons, and thence to the public. This is despite the fact that tattooing is perfectly legal.

The public safety committee made recommendations requiring more funding for programs to reduce the incidence of HIV/AIDS, provide for drug treatment units, give special attention to offenders with both drug addiction and mental health problems, and also to provide for better interdiction. As already noted, the Conservative members of the committee wrote that they "strongly disagree[d]" with these recommendations. The three recommendations they made on drug policies were all to tighten interdiction.[46] In doing so, they reiterated the government's zero-tolerance strategy and, contrary to the best evidence, insisted that providing needles would put a "potential weapon in the hands of convicted criminals."

Substance abuse is the main reason that many offenders commit crime. It brings them into the prison system, and it will bring them back after release if nothing is done to deal with their addiction. It makes them sick with diseases that they spread to the community, causing no end of misery and high health costs. Interdiction has limited effectiveness when ingenious means can always be found by the desperate to get their hands on the drugs they are addicted to. A sensible approach would be to combine reasonable interdiction efforts with a public health strategy that would ameliorate the harm done. But there seems to be a moral impediment in Conservative government members that will not allow them to act humanely when it comes to illicit drugs.

ABORIGINAL PEOPLE

In addition to the addicted and the mentally ill, another constituency is over-represented in Canadian prisons: Aboriginal people. The Supreme Court of Canada noted this in its landmark decision in *R. v. Gladue*.[47] In the mid-1980s, Aboriginal people comprised 2 per cent of the general population but 10 per cent of the penitentiary population. By 1997, the numbers were 3 per cent and 12 per cent. By 2006–2007, the numbers were 4 per cent and 24 per cent (including both provincial and federal prisons).[48] In the federal system, the number today has risen to 20 per cent of the prison population.[49] Mr. Sapers points out that for women the number is 33 per cent, and that the female Aboriginal offender population has grown by almost 90 per cent in the last ten years. Aboriginal women comprise the fastest-growing segment in federal prisons.

The proportions are truly shocking in the prairie provinces. At a time when Manitoba and Saskatchewan had an Aboriginal population of about 7 per cent, Manitoba's jails housed 46 per cent Aboriginal people, while Saskatchewan's housed 60 per cent. Today, 69 per cent of the Manitoba prison population is Aboriginal, compared with 12 per cent of the general population. Saskatchewan's numbers are 81 per cent to 11 per cent; Alberta's 35 per cent to 3 per cent; and British Columbia's 21 per cent to 4 per cent.[50] The current government's law-and-order approach will only exacerbate the problem, and is part of what Jeffrey Simpson calls being "stupid about crime" rather than "tough on crime." Today, Aboriginal young people are more likely to go to jail than to finish Grade 12.[51]

The Supreme Court of Canada in the *Gladue* case noted these disparities and set down a regime for sentencing Aboriginal people that was supposed to reduce the numbers in custody. As Mr. Justice Melvyn Green of Ontario said, "We had to get the numbers down because they were ridiculous. But ten years later, my God, we are even deeper in the jungle. This is really the horror."[52]

For those who work with Aboriginal people in the system, the biases against them are obvious. In Ontario, twice as many Aboriginal youth are being jailed as non-Aboriginal youth who commit the same offence.[53] As well, they will serve more of their sentences than non-Aboriginal offenders. Jonathan Rudin, program director for Aboriginal Legal Services of Toronto, says, "racism is real, and one of the places it exists is in jail. Aboriginal people have less access to parole and rehabilitation programs."

A study by Michelle Mann showed that Aboriginal offenders, compared to the non-Aboriginal inmate population, tended to be released later in their sentence; over-represented in segregation units; more likely to be released on statutory release (because they were not granted parole) or at warrant expiry (the very last day of their sentence); and more likely to be classified as higher risk and in higher need in categories such as employment, community reintegration, and family supports.[54]

Jane McMillan, an Aboriginal legal scholar at St. Francis Xavier University, says there is "a sort of compassion fatigue—not just in the judiciary, but the justice system in general." She says that many judges do not seem to understand how Aboriginal people have been affected by marginalization and by becoming aware of the destruction of their culture over the centuries. *Gladue* offered a great opportunity for "empowerment and sovereignty and community-building, [but]...what we are seeing instead are harsher, more conservative sentences."

Funding for alternatives to custody for Aboriginal people is tightening. Substance abuse treatment, Aboriginal spirituality centres, and community sentencing circles are all becoming things of the past.[55]

The Correctional Investigator, too, concludes that *Gladue* has not made the impact hoped for.[56] Aboriginal offenders in the federal system still tend to be younger, incarcerated for more violent offences, with higher needs, and from backgrounds of domestic abuse, physical abuse, substance abuse, or all three. While the Correctional Service has recently revised its policy to allow for a consideration of these kinds of factors, there has still been no progress. The prison ombudsman's recommendation for the appointment of a Deputy Commissioner for Aboriginal Corrections has fallen on deaf ears.

WOMEN

Another category over-represented in the federal prison system comprises women, both Aboriginal and non-Aboriginal. [57] This increasingly complex and diverse population has grown by almost 40 per cent over the past ten years. Of the total number of women offenders, 33 per cent are Aboriginal. This number has increased by nearly 90 per cent over ten years (compared to a 17.4 per cent increase for Aboriginal men).

According to the prison ombudsman, two-thirds of all female offenders suffer from a substance-related abuse or disorder. Women are almost twice as likely to be serving a sentence for a drug offence as men. In 2007–2008, 80 per cent of female offenders (compared to 14.5 per cent of men) had also previously been hospitalized for psychiatric reasons, and 25 per cent have a mental health diagnosis. Even these estimates are deemed to be low by some researchers. Kelly Hannah-Moffatt, chair of the sociology department at the University of Toronto, said close to 100 per cent of women offenders suffer from a debilitating mental problem such as psychosis, clinical depression, schizophrenia, or coping strategies that involve self-harm.[58]

Within the federal prison system there are no stand-alone minimum-security institutions for women, meaning that they must be released from medium- or maximum-security institutions directly to the street. This makes their reintegration into the community that much more difficult. Living behind razor wire is not conducive to re-establishing a more normal lifestyle in readiness for release. There is no facility like the St. Lawrence Valley Correctional and Treatment Centre for women with mental illnesses.

The prison ombudsman notes that the much-vaunted efforts of the current government to train prisoners for "real" jobs on the outside have produced an anomalous result in the case of women. Women offenders tend to need education, employment, substance abuse counselling, and family dysfunction assistance. Instead, they are being offered training in food preparation, cooking, cleaning, and laundry services—in other words, "domestic" work. These kinds of programs are clearly inadequate in the twenty-first century.

Mr. Sapers cites the government's redesign of the Mother-Child program as an example of a regressive step in rehabilitating women offenders. Prisons for women are often far from their homes. The Mother-Child program allows them to keep their young children and infants with them in the facility. In 2008, the Minister of Public Safety changed the eligibility criteria for this program, making large portions of the female offender population ineligible. Women no longer qualify if they have been convicted of a serious violent crime. Since 50 per cent of women are serving sentences for violent crime, this automatically eliminates 50 per cent of the population. The maximum age of a child who can participate has been reduced from twelve to six, thus reducing eligibility further. And Child and Family services must support the offender before her participation can be approved, adding another hurdle. As a result of these changes, the number of participants in the program has been reduced by more than 60 per cent.

VICTIMS OF CRIME

There is one other major and vocal constituency that is ill-served by the Conservative approach to corrections. These are people who have suffered at the hands of offenders. Victims have a large stake in how the government deals with crime. They have already paid a high price because of the offence that made them victims. They do not want to pay even more in human costs because of a system that does little or nothing to address their needs or to rehabilitate their victimizers.

Mr. Harper and his ministers have attempted to usurp the voice of victims, insisting that the tough-on-crime agenda is designed to offer relief and comfort to them. In doing so, the government maintains that defending offenders' human rights somehow derogates the rights of victims. It uses this argument to justify harsher treatment of offenders from the moment they come into custody until they leave. This is the politics of "the other," in which one group is set against another group to the detriment of both.

Prime Minister Harper justifies his crime legislation and the financial cost it will exact by saying, "Canadians want to be able to feel safe in their homes and communities, and that means that the bad guys need to be taken out of circulation. Does that cost money? Yes. Is it worth it? Just ask a victim."[59] Some victims are content with his tough-on-crime approach, but many are not.

Heidi Illingworth is Executive Director of the Canadian Resource Centre for Victims of Crime, which has been in operation since 1993. She says, "We must measure how justice is done in this country by how we treat persons harmed by crime—instead of by the sentence an offender receives."[60] Steven Sullivan, former federal Victims Ombudsman, confirms that the tough-on-crime agenda is about nothing but sentencing, and says that sentencing will not make much, if any difference, to the situation of victims.[61] Victims' advocates want more than lip service given to their needs.

Victims know what works to make their communities safe. The Church Council on Justice and Corrections recently spoke out clearly against the tough-on-crime agenda. This is significant because Christians are among the constituencies that form a strong base for the Conservative government's ascendance.

"We are trying to educate the public and the people in our churches about this," says Lorraine Berzins of the Church Council.[62] Ms. Berzins worked in federal penitentiaries for fourteen years. She has been a victim of serious crime, including a hostage-taking. She speaks with other victims all the time.[63] She is one of the very few who have seen the criminal justice system from many perspectives. She says, "[The Conservative crime agenda] goes so much against all the evidence about what keeps communities safe, and it does so much harm, and they are going to spend so much money, that it's really surprising that there isn't more opposition."

The Church Council pleaded with the government to put money into communities rather than into prisons. It pointed out that "increasing levels of incarceration of marginalized people is counter-productive and under-mines human dignity in our society." It asked the government to fund measures that are well-established and have been shown to work: well-supervised probation or release, bail options, reporting centres, practical assistance, supportive housing, and programs that promote accountability, respect, and reparation.

Victims are alarmed at the direction the government is taking, and believe it will make them less safe. In an eloquent submission, Ms. Berzins told the government what victims want:[64]

> We want to be safe, we want emotional support, we want assis-
> tance and whatever care required to heal and recover, we want
> information about many aspects of what happened; we want
> the offender to be held accountable, but even better we wish
> that person would take responsibility, realize the harm that was
> done, the wrongness of it, try to do something to repair or make
> up for it, show remorse and some desire to compensate in some
> way; and we want to know what kind of a person would do
> such a thing, and what can be done so it doesn't happen again.
> Many victims are concerned about prevention, they want us to
> learn something from their experience that can help us all go
> on with life in great peace, they need to believe again that life
> can be good and safe and worth living despite everything. This
> is what many victims tell us, in the most unexpected circum-
> stances. Real life goes on after court, and these are the things
> that become important for survival.

She says that these needs are hard to meet because the justice system is adversarial, and often does not allow offenders to admit anything even if they want to. The victim, too, is a pawn of the system. The system is so overloaded that plea bargaining happens without addressing any of the stated needs. With this, she says, people get slotted into one of two extremes and these are set up to oppose one another, even though the process is not helpful to anybody affected by the crime—the victim, the offender, or the community.

Arlène Gaudreault is President of the Association Québécoise Plaidoyer-Victimes and an internationally recognized victims' advocate. Appearing before the House of Commons Standing Committee on Justice and Human Rights, she spoke in opposition to harsher sentences for young offenders.[65] "We do not believe that calling for a more enforcement-oriented justice system will automatically translate into greater protection for society in general, and victims in particular," she said. She also referred to research by Allan Young,[66] which shows that "there is no evidence to support the hypothesis that victims want harsher sentencing. In fact, studies show the opposite...Victims are not excessively punitive, any more than people who are not victims. That is also the case among victims of violent crime."

Steve Sullivan agreed that calling for more enforcement would not automatically translate into greater protection for society, or for victims of crime.[67] On the subject of prison conditions and rehabilitation, he had this to say:

> Victims understand, better than most, that nearly all offenders will eventually be released from prison. Given their personal experiences, they know the impact violence can have, which is why many victims sincerely hope that offenders will be rehabilitated while in prison. The best protection victims, their families, and the community will have is if the offender can learn to modify negative behaviour before he or she is released.

Ms. Gaudreault also said that the confidence of victims and the public would not be restored so much by enforcement as by other means. These would include programs to reduce poverty and inequality, many of which are being cut by the Conservative government. She was emphatic that harsher sentencing is a placebo, and that the government would be better to attack the risk factors for crime:

> *By trying to toughen sentences for some categories of offenders,*
> *the reassuring message is supposed to be that victims are being*
> *taken care of and what becomes of them is a matter of concern,*
> *but in reality neither the root problems nor the solutions are*
> *being tackled. It is a way of salving [the politicians'] conscience.*
>
> *Initiatives for victims and offenders must be based on*
> *a long-term vision and must not be developed for political*
> *gain. It is easier to amend legislation than to fund services.*
>
> *The Association Québécoise Plaidoyer-Victimes submits*
> *that measures to help parents and families reduce poverty and*
> *inequality are essential to combat and reduce criminal victim-*
> *ization. We can restore confidence on the part of victims and*
> *the public in general by other means, by other solutions, than*
> *enforcement.*

In very strong language, highly critical of the government, Ms. Gaudreault called upon politicians to stop exploiting victims for their own partisan purposes:

> *[The] victims' cause is increasingly exploited and used as a tool*
> *for partisan purposes by political parties of all stripes. Victims'*
> *rights are used to legitimize more crime control, but that dis-*
> *course does not express the position of all victims, with the*
> *nuances that must be recognized. It does not serve the cause*
> *of victims, and we reject Canada's decision to take this path...*

Steve Sullivan also deplored the Conservative government's treatment of victims and its approach to criminal justice:[68]

> *Granted, if asked, the ministers would argue that their get-*
> *tough-on-crime agenda is for victims; that tougher sentences*
> *and more prisons are what victims need and want. They don't*
> *have any evidence of this, of course, but as the government has*
> *made clear on a number of fronts, evidence and stats don't*
> *really factor into their policy development approach.*

> *What do tougher sentences have to do with the sexual assault victims who do not report their crimes that Minister Day talked about? Not much. Their decision not to report their victimization has less to do with lenient sentencing and more to do with the criminal justice system that revictimizes them. There are a fair number of cops and Crowns in this country who would tell you they would not want their own daughters to report a sexual assault.*

While pretending to speak on behalf of victims, the government's estimates identify a decrease of $8.9 million which reflects the sunset of the Victims of Crime Initiative in 2010–11.[69] Mr. Sullivan suggests that the government should change its priorities:

> *I believe the ministers when they say they care about victims. These are decent men and women who have families. But they need to walk the walk, not just talk the talk, so here is what they should do—at the next cabinet meeting, tell the Prime Minister he should abandon his crime agenda and put the bulk of those resources into programs for victims and prevention. When the Prime Minister says no, and we all know he will, then they should stand up for victims and walk out.*

And so it comes full circle: victim, offender, the community—inextricably linked. The public policies chosen affect them all. In the mix are large numbers of very disadvantaged Canadians, whether mentally ill, drug addicted, Aboriginal, women, sexually abused, or some combination of these. Canadian communities would benefit from a nuanced, intelligent approach to criminal justice that puts human rights first. Unless something changes, this is not what we can expect from a Harper government.

8: CRIME PREVENTION AND ALTERNATIVES TO PRISON

The Conservative government's solution to crime is imprisonment. That is an easy solution, but it is also wrong and cruel and counterproductive. We have known this for a long time. As the MacGuigan Report said: "Imprisonment in Canada, where it is not simply inhumane, is the most individually destructive, psychologically crippling and socially alienating experience that could conceivably exist within the borders of the country."[1]

Canadians have had nearly two centuries to forge a workable and effective justice system. But, as one experienced judge said, "the whole system has been so hung up on punishment for so long that to let go of it would be to admit we have been wrong for hundreds of years. It is easier to continue to make the error than to admit the error."[2]

Incarceration is destructive. We know this. It should be reserved for those very dangerous offenders who must be removed from the community to preserve public safety. Canadian prisons are full of people who are not "very dangerous." There are myriad ways of dealing with most offenders that do not require imprisonment, and many more ways of preventing crime in the first place.

What follows is by no means a comprehensive overview of programs that work, but a description of some representative programs will perhaps demonstrate the high success rates and fiscal economies of alternative approaches, as well as many Canadians' determination to establish community-oriented solutions and reject the easy, expensive "tough-on-crime" approach.

BEFORE THE CRIME

Crime will never be completely eliminated, but we should first try to keep crime to a minimum. This requires that governments and communities alleviate the risk factors.

An important caveat: to say that poverty is a risk factor for crime is not to blame crime on the poor, or to say that poverty necessarily leads to crime. If the correlation were that straightforward, then the poverty-stricken province of Newfoundland three or four decades ago should have been a hotbed of crime, and it was not. Poverty is simply a risk factor in the same way that mental illness, drug addiction, and sexual abuse are risk factors. Without interventions and assistance, these can, alone or in combination, foster conditions where crime can result.

There are hundreds of programs designed to prevent crime. In a 2003 *Compendium of Promising Crime Prevention Practices in Canada*, Wanda Jamieson and Liz Hart chose three or four of the most promising programs in each province and territory, and described their objectives and processes.[3] Such a compendium, updated to include new programs, would be a useful resource for any government.

Some features are common to many crime prevention programs: they are largely aimed at youth, and they target local issues in sensitive and culturally appropriate ways. Many of the programs offer basic literacy, education, and training. They are set up to help parents be better parents and to create healthy, functional families. They target substance abuse and other public health issues. They reclaim cultures and languages. They send children into after-school recreation programs with their peers and, where appropriate, out on the trap line with elders.

Some programs are directed toward specific crimes such as arson and sexual exploitation. Women and girls are taught how to make themselves safe, and how to defend themselves. Men and boys are taught how to respect women and girls, and how to manage their anger. Program managers find creative ways to teach and learn, whether by performing theatre, making music, or in any number of ways that might appeal to their targeted group.

These programs are aimed at reducing crime, but they become community-building programs in the process. They add a healthy, proactive element to the neighbourhoods. It is hard to imagine tax dollars better spent.

Mr. Harper's Conservative approach to criminal justice has already been tested in Ontario, and many of the architects of Mike Harris's "common sense revolution" are now working for Mr. Harper. Harris's cuts to after-school programs, prevention programs, and community supports are blamed by some for the fact that crime rates have not fallen for young men aged twenty-five to thirty-three in Ontario, even though crime rates are otherwise down.[4] Those programs were providing recreation, assistance, and guidance to this demographic. When they were removed, the risk factors reasserted themselves.

There are many risk factors for crime, but one easily identified is fetal alcohol spectrum disorder. It produces anti-social behaviour that can lead to criminal activity. Preventing it, and modifying the behaviour associated with it, would go far to lowering the crime rate, but there has been little or no government funding.

MP Keith Martin points out that fetal alcohol spectrum disorder is the leading cause of preventable brain damage in babies.[5] It is a "silent scourge" in Canada, and an estimated 40 per cent to 50 per cent of those in prison suffer from it. That should command the government's attention. The government's response so far? It has produced posters informing the public about the disorder and encouraging pregnant women not to drink. This is wholly inadequate. Strategically targeted funding could be used to educate women about refraining from drinking during pregnancy and could also be used to help those who suffer from the disorder. The government is ignoring its obligation to provide treatment to as much as half of the prison population.

Pre-school programs have an excellent track record for reducing risk factors. In Ypsilanti, Michigan, the Perry Preschool Program worked with children at risk and followed them to age forty.[6] By ensuring the children received good preschool attention, the program ensured that they were more able to complete school. Their lives were better in many ways. They depended less on welfare, and their incomes as adults were much higher. As Keith Martin said:[7]

This is an important study because it proves that if we ensure children grow up in an environment that is loving, caring, free of being subjected to violence, sexual abuse and other horrific situations, those neurologic connections develop well. As a result of that, there is a profound impact in preventing and reducing crime and ensuring that children have the best outcomes in their lives.

Dr. Martin pointed out that for an investment of just $15,166 in this program, there was a saving to taxpayers of $250,000. That is a 17:1 saving.

Dr. Fraser Mustard, a Toronto-based early childhood development expert, says early childhood development programs can cut future anti-social or criminal behaviour by half.[8] To our shame, an OECD (Organisation for Economic Co-operation and Development) study from 2006 shows that Canada ranks dead last among fourteen industrialized countries in early childhood education and care.

The *Globe and Mail*'s editorial board has come up with a new and interesting idea.[9] Taking the Parliamentary Budget Office's figure of $5.1 billion over five years as the cost of the 2-for-1 law, the editorial suggests using the money instead to establish a kind of "birth bond." The suggestion is that Canada could afford to seed a $13,783 education account for each newborn. Or perhaps the country could offer "Free in University" instead of "Truth in Sentencing." There would be money left over, since net tuition paid by all students is only $3.5 billion per year. Or Canada could fund more research with the money. "If Canada has money for an expansion of the jails, which is doubtful, it should think instead about ambitious ways of investing in productivity and people."

SOME SUCCESSFUL PREVENTATIVE PROGRAMS

Pathways to Education is one program the Conservative government *is* funding. It was devised by a community health centre in Toronto's inner city.[10] For $5 million per year, it provides mandatory tutoring, support workers, financial aid (free transit tickets or lunches), and $1,000 a year toward postsecondary education for high-schoolers who might otherwise fall through the cracks. The results have been more than encouraging. The dropout rate fell from 56 per cent to 12 per cent, and the rate of attendance at college or university rose to 80 per cent from 20 per cent. An assessment of the program found a $600,000 lifetime benefit to society for each student enrolled in the program. This type of investment will pay off in far lower prison costs, and will produce expanding benefits over time. It is hoped that the new majority government will continue the program and expand it across Canada.

Immigrants to Canada, too, are vulnerable to risk factors and deserve continued attention.[11] Sage Youth is a program in Toronto developed by Tamba Dhar, herself an immigrant to Canada. The program is designed to work with higher-risk refugees to ensure that the children have a mentor and an early program in which there is a caring environment where their basic needs are met. Ms. Dhar does this through the prism of literacy, and she does it on a shoe-string budget. Such a program, which has been shown to be effective, should be encouraged and funded. It should not have to rely upon the donations of individual Canadians. If the government is serious about preventing crime, this is the type of program which could be made broadly available.

A neighbourhood office in the immigrant community of Thorncliffe Park provides English classes, job training, child care, and a youth drop-in centre with computers and social clubs designed to keep restless teenagers occupied. While this neighbourhood fits the police profile for a high crime area (poverty, density, high numbers of teenagers), the worst youth offence that one police officer could come up with was loitering.

Some unsung community programs are prize-winning successes. In Sarnia, Ontario, Rebound has been running since 1984, and has provided community-based programs to thirteen thousand young people. Concentrating on life skills, education, and cognitive skills for youth, it has won the prestigious Donner Canadian Foundation Award for Excellence twelve years in a row. Among other programs, there are Youth Justice Forums, substance abuse programs, programs for girls who show violent tendencies, and programs which help young people learn how to stop and think before acting. The latter is a simple concept, but crucial to reducing the impulsive behaviour that often gets youngsters into trouble. Like many of the community programs, Rebound deals with young people who have been in trouble with the law as well as those who are at risk for problems in the future.

Lack of affordable housing has been on the table for decades, with governments continually repeating the mantra that it is a private sector concern. When that argument fails, they claim it is somebody else's constitutional obligation—the tried-and-true Canadian method of avoiding responsibility. Housing has become serious for both potential and past offenders, and could easily be addressed by government.

The John Howard Society of Toronto recently interviewed 363 inmates in the provincial prison system and found that 22.9 per cent had no fixed address before going to jail;[12] 32.2 per cent said they had no home to return to; and 12.4 per cent had no idea where they would go upon release. Cost-benefit studies have shown it is cheaper to provide supports and affordable housing than to deal with the "homeless prisoner."

With no address, and often no identification, the homeless do not qualify for social benefits. It takes little imagination to see how they are compelled to obtain the resources to live. It takes even less imagination to understand why they end up returning to jail for a simple breach of the condition that they provide a fixed address. This is one of the reasons for the revolving door that Messrs. Harper, Nicholson, and Toews continually refer to, and could be easily fixed through a judicious application of resources to provide more housing.

Crime prevention is the stated objective of the federal National Crime Prevention Centre, and former Victims Ombudsman Steve Sullivan demands to know why the Conservative government is not putting more funding into it. This organization has a mandate to implement the National Crime Prevention Strategy.[13] That strategy states as its priorities the government's top three crime priorities: guns, gangs, and drugs.

The National Crime Prevention Centre does fund community groups in their efforts to prevent crime. However, the funding is inadequate. As Mr. Sullivan puts it, why is the Centre not funding programs "to get youths off the street so they are no longer selling their bodies for a hot meal and a safe place to sleep at night?"

The 2011–12 *Estimates* show that the Harper government will provide 49 to 55 per cent less funding in grants and contributions for the Youth Justice Fund.[14] The Youth Justice Fund has as its mandate, among other things, to increase the use of community-based sentences for less serious offences by young offenders, to increase the use of means outside the formal court process, and to improve the justice system's ability to rehabilitate and reintegrate.[15] It is unlikely that the fund will be able to provide these services with its funding cut by half.

According to MP Mark Holland, the annual amount of funding dedicated to crime prevention by the Conservative government has been reduced from $120 million in 2006 to $30 million today.[16] Yet the police, too, have been asking for money to be put into building community capacity, dealing with addictions and mental health issues. Police chiefs across the country have been speaking out.[17] They say Canada is incarcerating too many people and the wrong people. They need an alternative to the lock-up for many of the people they deal with every day.

According to the Program Activities Planned Spending published by Public Safety Canada, by far the majority of program funding is still destined to enforcement and emergency management.[18] In 2010–2011, Crime Prevention programs are expected to receive $64,770,000, which will be reduced to $57,591,600 for the next two years. By contrast, Emergency Management will receive nearly three times as much ($168,898,000) this year, and Law Enforcement will receive four times as much ($272,124,000). The cart has been placed firmly before the horse.

To see how preventive programs actually work, it is useful to look at one or two in depth.

Since the Conservative government's preoccupation is with "guns, gangs, and drugs," a good place to start is in the North End of Winnipeg, where Aboriginal street gangs are a continuing problem.

To get to the bottom of the gang problem in the North End, Aboriginal gang members have been meeting with a group of academic experts and the director of the Ogijita Pimatiswin Kinamatwin (OPK) program to talk about what might reduce crime in that neighbourhood.[19]

So far, the official response has been ramped-up policing. Policing has been intensified to the point where, according to those who live there, "it's like the military in the North End now" and anyone who "fits the description" is being targeted.[20] "It's like we're under siege," said one gang member.[21] SWAT teams even turn up at funerals. Winnipeg gang members say flooding the streets with police is likely only to aggravate the problem.

While most inner city residents do want a greater police presence, they want community policing where police are a positive presence, where police get to know the residents and particularly the children. More cruisers are not a positive step and provoke anger and more disrespect. One scientific trial in the United States evaluated the prevention value of random police patrols by increasing patrols in some areas and reducing them in others.[22] The study concluded that "the level of preventive police patrol had no impact on crime levels—that is, it did not prevent crime."

While intensive policing initiatives are expensive, they are not effective.[23] At most they temporarily move gang activity elsewhere, and it inevitably returns as soon as the pressure is off. Increased police presence can even increase crime by driving it further underground, where the stakes become higher and the violence more serious.

North End gang members themselves astutely identified the usual risk factors: addictions, violence, family disintegration, neglect, hunger, abuse, racism, poverty. They then identified the prescription for change. In the words of the report:

> *Building pride and self-esteem through the provision of the right kinds of jobs and investing in more community recreation and drop-in centres for kids and families in the North End would be important steps in that direction. We know that this strategy will work because there are successful, small-scale examples— such OPK and BUILD—now operating in Winnipeg's North End.*

OPK is a community-based program that works with Aboriginal street gang members. They are taught construction skills in the course of renovating North End houses. OPK also importantly provides immersion in Aboriginal culture. The paid work gives gang members a sense of pride and dignity. The organization has 9.5 employees and a budget of about $450,000 per year. There are at least thirty more young street gang members who would join OPK if there were sufficient funding.

Other young people are working with the BUILD program (Building Urban Industries through Local Development). It is a non-profit that combines environmental stewardship with poverty reduction. It trains people with limited experience to retrofit existing buildings. In this way, houses in poor areas are insulated and their heating bills are reduced in a program called Warm Up Winnipeg. At the same time, young people obtain training.

The Winnipeg gang members said they wanted to work, even at low rates of pay. As one said, "What we never had was that sense of belonging. That sense of—I don't know how you say it—you feel good about yourself because you accomplished something. You make a legitimate pay cheque because you worked and you're learning something."[24]

The greatest fear that these tough street gang members expressed was that the next generation would follow in their footsteps. They all have nieces and nephews, and many of them have children.

> These are the ones you have to help to slow the violence. I don't want to see them in ten years doing the exact same thing that I just finished f'ing learning from. I went to jail for a long time. I don't need them to go to jail, doing the exact same thing that I learned...You need to help those little kids get off the street.

Oasis (run by New Directions in Winnipeg) targets youth who come from war-torn African countries. They are easy prey for recruitment by street gangs like the African Mafia and MadCowz, which compete for control of the city's crack cocaine trade. The thirty-five boys in the program receive counselling, access to educational resources, and help for their families. It costs $13,000 per year per boy, about a tenth of what it would cost to keep him in prison.

Justice Minister Nicholson says that longer sentences keep gang members behind bars long enough to disrupt their gangs.[25] This is at odds with the experience of prison staff and those who work with gang members. Prison is in fact a prime locus for recruitment, and street gangs tend to replace members as fast as the system can incarcerate.[26]

Early in 2011 it became apparent that federal funding for Winnipeg's anti-gang programs was in jeopardy.[27] Crime prevention programs being run by New Directions, the Spence Neighbourhood Association, and Ndinawe may be forced to close if they are unable to replace the withdrawn federal contributions. Removing federal funding from these kinds of programs is short-sighted. The cost in prison cells will far out-weigh any small investment made now in preventing these youth from becoming offenders.

Far to the south of us, an intriguing effort has been made to combat a similar scourge. Mayor Enrique Peñalosa of Bogotá, Colombia, was faced with a daunting task.[28] With a population of eight million, Bogotá in 1997 was a city at war—the centre of a vast drug trade, rampant corruption, and one of the highest murder and kidnapping rates in the world. There was also a high rate of conventional crime, spawned by the usual socio-economic risk factors.

Peñalosa knew that fear of "the other" is bred by urban spaces that divide communities by income, race, and status. In the spirit of Jane Jacobs, he attacked this by creating a huge downtown pedestrian space—evidence, as he said, of "true democracy at work." He built miles of bicycle paths, hun-dreds of new parks, new schools and libraries, and a decent public transit system. Making spaces liveable for the poor as well as the rich and filling the streets with pedestrians made those spaces safer for everyone.

He established a permanent office for violence prevention, which cre-ated an information system on trends and causes of violence.[29] The office coordinated police, health care, and other helping agencies in tackling the risk factors that incubate crime. This office worked to control drug and alco-hol consumption, remove handguns, and assist victims to respond to their victimizers without further violence. It imposed an occasional curfew to keep men off the streets so that women and children could do their shop-ping and enjoy the space without fear.

As a result, the city is now safer than Caracas, Rio de Janeiro, and yes, Washington, DC, and Baltimore.[30] In 1994, there were 4,457 homicides in Bogotá. In 2003, there were 1,607. That is a rate of 80 per 100,000 reduced to 23.4—a 71 per cent decrease in ten years.[31] While this is still very high compared to Canadian homicide rates (two per 100,000), the success of the experiment can hardly be denied.

Peñalosa also had opinions about the way crime and criminals should be treated. He was accustomed to hearing the people of Bogotá dis-miss the high murder rate by saying that most of the victims were just *narcotraficantes*—drug dealers. Nobody cared how many of them died. But Peñalosa insisted that each life was worth the same as any other life, and that international human rights law demanded that cartel members be arrested, prosecuted, defended, and imprisoned the same way as anyone else in society.[32] Once people stopped thinking about criminals as "the other," they were able to begin working to prevent the crime.

A different type of program was adopted in Boston, Massachusetts, from 1994 to 1996, to control youth gang violence.[33] While there was a targeted police effort, there were also street social workers mediating gang disputes and helping youth and families gain access to social services. There were increased services for runaways, efforts to reduce the number of school dropouts, and an emphasis on job training and providing jobs. The result: youth homicides dropped from forty-four per year (each year from 1991 to 1995) to fifteen (in 1998); 66 per cent in just three years. Irvin Waller reports that the numbers have started creeping up since 1998, and attributes this to the reduction in funding for community services that were so instrumental in the original success of the program. This becomes a recurring theme. Mr. Waller also reports on programs in Canada that have involved more than one sector of the public service and that have shown real progress in crime prevention.[34] Winnipeg made a concerted effort to reduce its high auto theft rate by concentrating on the most prolific offenders (getting them back to school and providing mentors), and by putting money into making cars harder to steal (with the help of the public auto insurance company, the Manitoba Public Insurance Corporation). The city soon reported more than a 75 per cent drop in auto theft.

The province of Alberta recently set up a task force to identify the causes of crime and suggest solutions. It has produced a secretariat of nine ministries, including the usual law enforcement sector, but also the health sector (especially for mental illness issues), and youth and schools. Working together, they are tackling the causes of crime and reducing the number of victims. They estimate that for every dollar spent on prevention they will save $7 on policing and prisons.

Lawyer James Morton makes an eloquent case for directing funding toward prevention.[35] As he says, "Crime is largely a reflection of underlying social failings." It is hard for some to accept that we are all to some extent responsible for the conditions that produce crime, largely through our failure to assist those who are in need.

Entire communities are in trouble, and many of them are First Nations. One in two hundred non-Aboriginal children is cared for by the state, compared to one in ten First Nations children. Yet First Nations child welfare agencies typically receive about 20 per cent less funding than provincial agencies. Again, the federal and provincial/territorial governments wrangle endlessly about who is responsible. The result is enhanced misery for thousands of children.

Poverty, addiction, abuse, and neglect are rampant in some First Nations communities. Social programs that focus on systemic problems are badly needed. The Aboriginal population is growing by leaps and bounds. Urgent attention and funding is needed if Aboriginal young people are to grow up crime-free, healthy, and productive.

"Real crime control," says Morton, "requires a social safety net." This is unlikely to materialize under a Conservative government that does not believe in government-funded social programs. It has reduced or cut funding for many, and appears to believe in less spending on all fronts other than defence, corrections, and law enforcement.

INSTEAD OF PRISON

What alternatives are there, without resorting to incarceration, when all efforts have failed to prevent crime? Every government must consider alternatives, since it is simply not possible, or wise, to imprison every offender.

While Conservatives prefer to send offenders to prison and keep them there, it is more sensible to provide programs and treatment outside prison walls as long as the risk to public safety can be managed. It costs a fraction of the price, and has a much higher likelihood of success. The government in any event is failing to provide programs for 75 per cent of those incarcerated federally, and there is little available in provincial institutions. For the 25 per cent of the prison population that is lucky enough to get signed up, taking programs under the harsh conditions of incarceration is less likely to produce good results. As well, communities are more likely than correctional facilities to know what programs will succeed for an individual offender from their midst.

RESTORATIVE JUSTICE

One well-known alternative approach is restorative justice.[36] The Public Safety Canada website describes restorative justice as "an alternative to standard criminal justice processes, with roots in traditional and indigenous forms of justice. It focuses on repairing the harm caused by crime, within the context of relationships and communities."[37] Canada played a key role in establishing the principles of restorative justice adopted by the United Nations Economic and Social Council in 2002.

Allan Manson describes restorative justice as a way of producing reparation and the restoration of equilibrium.[38] Unlike the retributive model, this approach "is intended to reconcile and repair the harm caused by an offence. Its beneficiaries include the offender, the victim, and the community at large." Many types of programs are restorative: family group counselling, reintegrative shaming, victim-offender reconciliation, and so on.

The Supreme Court of Canada has described restorative justice principles this way:[39]

> In general terms, restorative justice may be described as an approach to remedying crime in which it is understood that all things are interrelated and that crime disrupts the harmony which existed prior to its occurrence, or at least which it is felt should exist. The appropriateness of a particular sanction is largely determined by the needs of the victims, and the community, as well as the offender. The focus is on the human beings closely affected by the crime.

The Court then endorsed the use of conditional sentences as a useful vehicle for promoting these objectives.

What does the public think about the idea of using restorative justice rather than imprisonment? According to a January 2007 survey, "the strongest public support lay with the restorative justice objectives of promoting a sense of responsibility in the offender and securing reparation for the crime victim."[40] The authors found there was less public support for the principles of deterrence and incapacitation.

One model of restorative justice, the sentencing circle, has been used in Aboriginal communities to great effect. This approach, like others, has the advantage of increasing the resources available beyond what the justice system could normally provide. It has produced good results both for individuals and for the empowerment of the community. With some effort, such cultural approaches can also be adapted to the urban context, as with the Aboriginal Legal Services diversion project in Toronto. These programs are not without problems, but the direction is a healthy one. Experienced facilitators are crucial to success.

HOLLOW WATER, MANITOBA

Some restorative programs will deal only with non-violent crime, while others tackle serious violent crime as well, with good results. The Community Holistic Circle Healing Program at Hollow Water in Manitoba is a case in point.[41] In the 1980s, this Aboriginal community had a record of nearly 100 per cent alcohol abuse, unemployment was at 70 per cent, there was a severe shortage of housing, and it was suffering from three generations of sexual abuse. It was estimated that 66 to 80 per cent of the community were victims of abuse, and 35 to 50 per cent were victimizers. All of the victimizers were previous victims. The community rated its collective health on a scale of zero to ten at zero.

In the circumstances, it was imperative to find an alternative to the normal justice system. Otherwise, a large proportion of the community would have been sent to prison, and the destruction of the community would have been assured. In conjunction with the justice authorities, it was agreed to try Community Holistic Circle Healing. This involved the intervention of highly trained workers, who counselled all of the parties, and then encouraged the victimizer to tell his or her story, to confess to the workers and then to the family, and then to participate in a Healing Contract (which was the sentence handed down by a Manitoba judge). Workers also helped the victim through the process.

The program enjoyed great success until the late 1990s, when attitudes changed, hierarchies reasserted themselves, funding was insufficient, and a poor relationship developed between the program and the Band Council and Child and Family Services. However, throughout the process, old traditions and ceremonies had been recovered, and more recently the program was concentrating on wilderness therapy and the reestablishment of the special role of women and children in the community. Staff are receiving ongoing training, and the program is fighting for adequate funding to continue its work.

An evaluation in 2001 indicated that of the 107 offenders dealt with by the program, only two had reoffended. This is six times less than the national average for sex abuse offenders. It is not clear whether this excellent record held up over time, but it is clear that the new program was initially seeing good results, and that it was therefore worth sustaining with an appropriate level of commitment.

Funding for this program has not increased since 1993. Yet for every two dollars spent, it is estimated that six to fifteen dollars were saved in direct costs. There were also huge benefits to the community, which courageously faced up to its past and to its problems. It tried to keep its offenders in the circle while working to heal its victims. Community Holistic Circle Healing was a serious effort to restore the equilibrium so cruelly interrupted by the effects of colonialization, socio-economic deprivation, and hopelessness. A community that could have been dispersed to prisons across the country is still struggling with its past, but determined to succeed. But, again, a lack of funding has played a part in unravelling the early success.

VANCOUVER'S DOWNTOWN COMMUNITY COURT

British Columbia has just created a new program that is being studied by other justice systems in Australia, the United States, Russia, China, and elsewhere in Canada. It is called the Vancouver Downtown Community Court, and is a unique partnership between the justice system and social and health services agencies. Located in the courthouse are the usual justice officials, but also forensic liaison workers, a forensic psychiatrist, a nurse, health-justice liaison workers, employment assistance workers, a victim services worker, a British Columbia Housing support worker, and a native court worker.

Together, these collaborating agents have produced great successes in their first year. From September 2008 to July 2009, nearly two thousand cases (involving about a thousand individual offenders) have been resolved. Crime has been reduced accordingly. Offenders receive help with addictions, employment, housing, and other issues. They contribute thousands of hours to community service. Over a dozen local organizations are involved with the court as partners.

Attorney General Michael de John, QC, said of the court, "We are encouraged by the impact the community court is making in reducing criminal activity through addressing both the crime and its underlying causes."[42] Solicitor General Kash Heed was also pleased with the results:

> *Policing smarter means moving beyond old-style approaches like locking offenders away with little consideration for why they committed the crime in the first place. The community court gets to the root cause of crime with solutions to help offenders deal with their problems in a meaningful way and thereby reduce the chance of them re-offending.*

Sgt. Matt Clark, who works in the downtown east side of Vancouver, said the police like this court, too.[43] He said it is demoralizing to arrest the same people over and over. The downtown court is actually dealing with their problems and helping them stay out of trouble.

The final recidivism statistics from this program will not be known until 2012, but in the meantime much useful work has been done to divert offenders and restore them to healthy, contributing lives. Former prosecutor Mark Rowan says, "People do not understand that the *Criminal Code* is the last resort in our society. People should not be rushing to brand people as criminal when they are going through a rough patch in life and are redeemable."[44]

Jail sentences are used in 45 per cent of the cases in this court compared to the higher numbers in Vancouver Provincial Court (56 per cent). Of the non-sentence outcomes, 80 per cent are "stayed" by the Crown, who recommends alternative measures rather than proceeding with charges (compared to 53 per cent in Vancouver Provincial Court and 42 per cent in the rest of the province).

According to one of the presiding judges, Thomas Gove, 20 per cent of all offenders are sent to alternative measures, in which case they receive no criminal conviction.[45] The court is a less adversarial venue, and offenders get help with housing, psychiatric issues, and drug addictions. Judge Gove says that if you can deal with these, you will enjoy much success. He says that he is by no means naïve, but that even those who fail make some progress, and access to social services makes the difference.

Judge Gove gives one example of the work they are doing:

> Perhaps the best way to talk about Downtown Community Court is to talk about one of our cases. "Tim" is addicted to crack cocaine and has one of the longest records for theft in Vancouver.
>
> He is usually sentenced to months, if not years, in jail. We decided to try him on the Case Management Team. After a couple of slips—such as breaching his curfew—he got the message that along with being offered assistance, he was being closely monitored. He could accept the help offered or he would be on his way back to jail.
>
> His parents, from whom he had been estranged for many years, were contacted.
>
> Through the work of his case managers, Tim is now living with his parents, on his way to completing his education and—most important—not using drugs and therefore not stealing.

It took Tim a while to get the message, but it appears the effort was worth it. The court is moving in the right direction, away from incarceration and toward a more holistic way of dealing with crime in the poorest postal code in the country.

An encouraging note is offered by those who set up a similar court in Brooklyn, upon which the Vancouver court is modelled. Officials there said in 2008 that crime had dropped 70 per cent since the inception of the program in 2000.[46]

DRUG TREATMENT COURTS

A passionate argument for secure detoxification facilities as an alternative to prison is being made by Calgary Police Chief Rick Hansen.[47] He says we are sending too many of the wrong people to jail, and are wasting resources rearresting the same people over and over, all because they are addicted or mentally ill, undiagnosed, and often self-medicating. There would be lots of room in prisons for the serious criminals if we were to divert the others to treatment. Mr. Hansen says that jail guards are also in favour of this, and that it would save a lot of money over time.

A drug treatment court has been in operation in Toronto for years.[48] The court is presided over by Justice Paul Bentley, who works closely with the John Howard Society to release willing offenders to clean, safe, monitored housing where they can receive treatment for their addictions. The intention is to break the cycle through treatment. Participants submit to a barrage of weekly urine tests, medical appointments, Narcotics Anonymous meetings, and classes on parenting and criminal addictive behaviour.[49]

Justice Bentley says that 52 per cent of those who go to treatment remain in treatment and thus are never sent to jail. He travels the world talking about this drug treatment court and advising others how it works. It costs about $12,000 to $20,000 per year per inmate. Justice Bentley says that doing what we have been doing in the past (sending these offenders to prison) is a "terrible failure." It is a waste of money, and it makes society, in his words, "not safer."

Drug treatment courts have produced "dramatic reductions in criminal behaviour" and a "significant reduction in drug use."[50] Such courts in the United States have a high success rate in which only a very small percentage of program graduates reoffend.[51] There are about 2,500 of these courts in the United States, where participants undergo intensive treatment instead of prison.[52]

The state of Georgia has twenty-eight drug treatment courts, and its statistics show that the two-year recidivism rate among participants was only 7 per cent, compared to 15 per cent for offenders on probation alone, and 29 per cent for offenders who went to prison. This is typical of drug courts around the country. One Georgia county boasts that 98 per cent of its participants are employed. A drug court sentence in Georgia costs at least $10,000 less than a prison sentence.

The total cost to the federal government for six drug treatment courts across Canada is $3.4 million per year. Seven other communities want to introduce similar programs. Nevertheless, Justice Minister Rob Nicholson refused to commit to funding beyond March 2010.

TEEN COURTS

Teen courts have also been shown to produce remarkable results in the United States.[53] These are courts in which youth who commit crimes are judged by their peers. Young offenders dealt with in this way are far less likely to reoffend. Teen courts are more cost-effective than the regular court system, and they have been shown to sharply reduce recidivism.

This assessment of the effectiveness of teen courts is glowing:[54]

> American teen court programs continue to demonstrate phenomenal success, all at a miniscule cost. Peer courts not only appear to reduce repeat crime by youth, they are dynamic programs that promote volunteerism and community service, build a range of interpersonal skills in their participants and interactively teach youth about law and justice in partnership with adults. Though letting youth cooperatively handle their own problems is a simple concept, it has turned out to be an uncommonly effective one—one that is fast becoming an integral part of youth justice in America.

MP Bill Siksay refers to the Burnaby youth restorative justice program in his own community in British Columbia. Its shoplifting program has had great success in helping young people appreciate how serious this crime is. It also ensures that the relationships damaged by shoplifting are restored. When a similar approach was taken in Britain in the 1990s (educating young offenders about the consequences of their crimes), the program reduced the rate of recidivism among shoplifters from 35 per cent to 3 per cent.[55]

COMMUNITY SERVICE ORDERS

Community service orders are also a sensible response to crime. In The Netherlands, these have become a popular alternative to prison sentences of less than six months. In a recent study, two groups of offender were compared.[56] The groups were identical except that half went to prison and half did community service. Only offenders who had never been previously sentenced at all were included in the study. The offenders were checked for recidivism at one, three, five, and eight years after their sentences expired.

Those who were sentenced to prison had higher recidivism rates at each of the four time intervals. This was true for all crime, including both property and violent crimes. The report concluded that sending offenders to prison for the first time for periods of up to six months *increases* the likelihood of subsequent offending.

The Canadian government can save millions of dollars in incarceration costs by allowing community service orders in more cases. These orders not only help lower the recidivism rate, but also contribute to the community through the work done by offenders, and help them learn the value of work and of doing something positive for their communities.

OTHER COUNTRIES, OTHER CONCEPTS

A system of "day fines" has been adopted by Germany and Finland. It is based upon the seriousness of the offence.[57] The fine is generally levied according to the amount of money the offender earns on a given day and is meted out over a specified number of days.

More radically, some Scandinavian countries all but eliminated prison sentences for young people since the 1990s, without negative effects on their crime rates. Norway abolished its youth prison system altogether in 1975.[58] Finland had only ten boys under the age of eighteen in prison in 1997. Finland's population at the time was over five million. The Finnish Director General of Prisons said, of the notion of imprisoning youth:

> *The biggest problem, I think, is early recruitment to a prison career. You should never put a young person in prison during his teens...In the age from perhaps 12, 14 to 19, we are shaping the part of the population which is staying with the criminal justice system to the end of their life."*

New Zealand has been handling young offenders in Family Group Conferences since 1989. The offenders are made to face their victims and make amends. The results have again been remarkable. Even in the worst cases, offenders who are steered clear of custody and complete their conditions rarely come back to the justice system on new charges. In its first year, out of a hundred offenders, only two were incarcerated. In Canada, at that time, the number would have been closer to thirty.

A program called Transformative Justice Australia teaches an alternative process based on the healing circle used by the Maori in New Zealand.[59] Judge John Reilly of Alberta said his experience of the program was "mind altering and life changing. For the first time, I saw a possibility of a justice system that would do more than just lock people up until they got tired of going to jail."

Judge Reilly talks about his education in restorative justice. He said that formerly, in his Eurocentric world view, restorative justice meant that "if you break a window, you pay for the repair of the window." He came to see that it was much more complicated than that: "If you break a window, you damage your relationship with the owner of the window and with everyone who is upset by your conduct. The real meaning of restorative justice is the repair of those relationships."

The Aboriginal people Judge Reilly worked with in Alberta taught him a lot about justice. Eurocentric justice sees wrongdoing as something that needs to be punished, whereas the Aboriginal people he knew saw it "as illness in need of healing and as ignorance in need of teaching." He also saw the great need expressed in *Gladue* of paying especial attention to the circumstances of Aboriginal offenders. He says, of the typical Aboriginal offender, "he came from a community that was dysfunctional from top to bottom, and...to punish him for being dysfunctional wasn't fair." Judge Reilly recognized that if nothing were done to correct the community dysfunction, then punishing offenders would accomplish nothing.

He refers to the general success of sentencing circles, and cites the remarkable case of one victim who had been very severely injured by an offender. Before taking part in the sentencing circle, the victim had asked the court to imprison the offender for one to two years. After the ceremony was complete, however, he forgave the offender and asked that he be allowed to go free. This victim's injuries would remain with him for the rest of his life, but his life "may be far better because he has been able to let go of his bitterness." Judge Reilly says, "This must have been a huge step forward in the healing process for him." As often occurs, the healing effect was experienced by both parties.

In the United States, Jerry Miller became famous when he took over the management of the youth corrections system in Massachusetts in the 1970s.[60] He closed down virtually all of the large reform schools, choosing instead to place each young offender in a community-based program. Within four years, the 1,000 offenders in custody had been reduced to forty. Follow-up research done by Harvard University showed that there was no new crime wave. There was less repeat offending and a decline in the percentage of adult prisoners coming up through the juvenile system. Twenty years later, Massachusetts tried only twelve youths in adult court, compared with more than four thousand in the state of Florida. At the time, Florida's population was only about twice that of Massachusetts.[61] Remarkably, in that same year, 1989, Massachusetts had dropped to forty-sixth out of the fifty states in number of reported juvenile crimes.

Miller went on to work at the prison at Camp Hill in Pennsylvania, where the only available options for juveniles were prison or probation. Under that system, the panel responsible for deciding the fate of these youths had been finding consistently that 95 per cent needed to be in secure custody. Miller then presented the panel with a third option. He proposed the creation of an individualized plan for each one. The panel was soon deciding that only 10 per cent required incarceration.

Miller had innovative ways of enforcing more humanizing policies. In Massachusetts, children had been known to be stripped naked and held for days in dark concrete cells, made to drink from toilets, or made to kneel for hours on a stone floor with pencils under their knees. There was also an overuse of segregation. Miller abolished these practices, and ruled that the person who ordered a youngster into isolation had to sit with the offender in the cell until release. "The rule effectively stopped use of isolation," Miller said.

There is a common theme to all of this. Alternatives to prison for both non-violent and violent offences, and for young people in particular, pay real dividends in social and financial terms. Even serious violent crimes can be dealt with in such a way that the community is able to move forward even though the offender may not go to prison.

The Conservative government's approach is that all violent offenders must go to prison, preferably for long sentences. Many non-violent offenders must also go to prison, especially if they have committed what is regarded as a serious property crime. Mr. Harper's government has never seriously considered diversion or alternatives to prison. The savings in human and financial terms do not appear to figure in its development of criminal justice policy.

9: REHABILITATION AND THE FINNISH MODEL

IN PRISON

What if all else fails, and offenders find themselves in a prison? What programs and treatments work to help rehabilitate them and make their reintegration into society more likely to succeed? How *do* we keep violent offenders from reoffending?

Much has already been said about the conditions of prisons and the special needs of prisoners. It thus goes without saying, and the Correctional Service of Canada agrees, that to ensure a minimum of recidivism, appropriate programming must be in place and properly funded. As well, the atmosphere of the prison must be conducive to learning, working, and healing, and human rights must be respected.

The special needs of today's prison population have been enumerated. They include mental illness, drug and alcohol addiction, illiteracy, and the many effects of poverty, abuse, gang affiliation, sexual abuse, and cultural deprivation. All of these have known solutions. It only remains for the government to find the will and the resources to provide appropriate supports and treatment.

In addition to correctional programs, there are successful community justice programs in the prisons. These can produce good results not only for the offender but also for the victim. Like restorative justice programs on the outside, restorative programs in prison require that trained professionals prepare the parties to meet with each other, then set up and mediate a meeting, which may be face-to-face or through another means of communication.

FEARMONGER

The Correctional Service's Restorative Opportunities Program has been operating since 2004. It provides the opportunity for people affected by serious, traumatic crime to communicate with the offender and try to address the harms caused. Professional mediators spend considerable time preparing the parties for dialogue, and then facilitate the meetings, which take place only if all parties are in agreement. The program is based upon a Victim-Offender Mediation Program in British Columbia that was evaluated in 1995 and showed a high degree of success.

British Columbia's Community Justice Initiatives Association in Langley is the prototype in Canada.[1] In operation for twenty-five years, it is one of the few programs that addresses serious violent crime through victim-offender mediation.[2] Since an offender fears nothing more than his victim, it is often the victim who holds the key to resolving the effects of such crimes for both parties. This is an example from the Langley project:

> *A victim of a masked rapist was so emotionally damaged by her attacker that she eventually decided to meet with him in prison in the hope of resolving some of the worst effects. She had been attacked at four a.m. and her clock radio was accidentally turned on in the struggle...For nine years she had been unable to sleep between the hours of three and five a.m., or to enjoy any kind of music.*
>
> *After meeting the offender, the "monster of her nightmares was no more." She was immediately able to sleep through the night, enjoy music and get on with her life. The offender too acknowledged that he had received a gift through her courage.*

A pilot project called MOVE in Moncton, New Brunswick, employed similar methods. This is one of the examples of successful mediation in that program:[3]

> *A female victim had been the clerk at a convenience store when she was robbed and terrorized at knife-point. The robber said he would come back and get her if she talked to the police. She was not able afterwards to get over the fear. She suffered bulimia*

and insomnia, had nightmares, her marriage broke down. The robber got five years.

When the offender was told of this, he was amazed at the victim's fear. He thought she would know that every robber says, "If you call the cops, I'll come back and get you." The offender was living every day in fear in the prison. He had no idea that the same was true for his victim on the outside.

When the two met in the prison, they shared their stories. The victim got all of the answers she needed. She knew that the offender was genuinely sorry for what he had done. They struck an agreement about how they would greet each other when they met in the streets of their small town upon his release.

For the victim, the fear was gone. The nightmares were gone. She said, "The matter is over. I'm healed."

There are many, many stories like these, about how both parties benefit.

As important for the offender, though, is the underlying atmosphere of respect for human rights that must be part of any prison setting. The MacGuigan Report issued an excoriating condemnation of the system in 1977. It said:[4]

The persistent recidivist statistic can be related to the fact that so many in prison have been irreversibly damaged by the system by the time they reach the final storehouse of the Criminal Justice System—the penitentiary...It was compounded in schools, foster homes, group homes, orphanages, the juvenile justice system, the courts, the police stations, provincial jails, and finally in the "university" of the system, the penitentiary.

Most of those in prison are not dangerous. However, cruel lock-ups, isolation, the injustices and harassment deliberately inflicted on prisoners unable to fight back, make non-violent inmates violent, and those already dangerous more dangerous. Society has spent millions of dollars over the years to create and maintain the proven failure of prisons. Incarceration has failed in its two essential purposes—correcting the offender and providing permanent protection to society.

FEARMONGER

SOME CORRECTIONAL OFFICERS' VIEWS

The MacGuigan Report was a serious indictment of the system, and it is encouraging that the treatment of prisoners has come a long way since then. According to long-time correctional officers, there was a sea change in the way staff and inmates related to each other after MacGuigan, and it has been a change for the better:[5]

> [Formerly], at the Pen the ability for officers to walk amongst the inmates, to walk into the exercise yards, wasn't there. Staff were as frightened of the most violent inmates as the other inmates were. They hid in cages up above them. So the inter-action amongst the inmates and the guards was very poor... The con code in those days was almost a code of silence with staff. You told staff nothing. You imparted nothing. If you were friendly with staff it wasn't even a verbal gesture, it was sort of a nod as you walk by, like "you're alive, I'm alive"...I know that the prisons when I first walked in the door at B.C. Pen were so damn dangerous that you were glad to be home any given day. I know now when I walk in the door I expect to be home... We've learned to do things better and it is paying a dividend to us now. Possibly there are some people that are saying there are too many rights for inmates, but if they lose those rights then possibly we lose the same rights. Because when they take away their rights, they take away our rights.

That is an affecting description of the old and the new way of dealing with prison inmates, and it comes from someone with many years of experience in both. This officer is saying there is no room in prison for the concept of "the other." Both guards and inmates have rights. The exercise of rights by inmates does not derogate from the rights of guards. Everyone is better off if there is a degree of mutual respect.

Another long-time correctional officer agreed that the new approach has produced a difference in the way staff think about the inmates. He said that today staff are talking about what programs will help inmates, how to deal with attitude problems, and so on. People didn't talk that way in the old days. Then he noted, "A lot of people complain about the *Charter of Rights*, how it has relaxed the rules and allowed the inmates to get more things. Well, true, it has, but it has made our job easier in ways, too."

Doug Cassin is described by Professor Michael Jackson as a "hard-rock officer." He was asked what he thought of the media's opinion that prisons are Club Fed, with televisions and Nintendo games and videos and private family visits. Did Mr. Cassin think that these changes were "coddling prisoners"?[6]

> *I think I've said the same thing in my day, too, but when I take a realistic view, we don't have as many hostage-takings or smash-ups and assaults. But it is still a maximum security prison, and if an inmate causes too many problems he is still segregated...I wouldn't want to be living here having my meals delivered on a cart and locked up for twenty-three hours a day. I've been through my share of the ruckus in prison, and I think for the most part it is a safer place for an officer to work now because of a lot of these things.*
>
> *The other part of my answer is that one of our mandates is to protect society. Protecting society, a lot of people think, is just keeping the inmates in the fence, but 99 per cent of these inmates are going back to the street. Now I'm not guaranteeing that because you let him watch television he's going to be a model citizen, but if you've got a guy where you've had him chained to a bed or locked up or you are fighting with him every day and you send him out on the street in that condition, and we've seen instances like that, you are not actually protecting anybody.*

Another officer remarked upon the changing attitude to human rights in the prison:[7]

> *There is also an evolving understanding on the part of staff. They understand much better that the Rule of Law is not an impediment to running the prison. The feeling in the past was*

179

*that if prisoners have rights then we won't be able to do any-
thing and all hell will break loose. That's not the fact.*

The retired warden of Alouette Correctional Centre in British
Columbia, Ms. Brenda Tole, disagreed strongly with the idea that the
more restrictive the prison conditions, the safer it is for correctional
staff.[8] She said:

*It is a fallacy that the more structured the environment, the
safer it is. It isn't. The more confined, structured, and authori-
tarian the environment is, the more difficulty they [inmates]
have in living within that environment, and they tend to
produce much more in the way of management problems. As
a result, it's not a safe environment. It's unfortunate when
institutions move more and more towards that—more technol-
ogy, more security, more restrictive movement—because what
you actually generate is a very dysfunctional population that
presents a threat to the staff.*

Correctional officers in Canada's prison system are in a highly stressful
occupation. One American study showed that correctional officers take
their own lives at a rate 39 per cent higher than the rest of the working age
population.[9] Under the tense and violent atmosphere of thirty years ago,
prison was brutalizing for both inmates and guards. This will be alleviated
by continuing to provide for a safer and more humane workplace. As the
atmosphere improves, officer security will also improve, and the suicide
numbers will fall.

SOME INMATES VIEWS
One long-time inmate identified another factor. He said that there was
genuine compassion among some members of staff, and that it encouraged
him to do better, particularly when he was in the Violent Offender Program.
"Compassion was not a quality he had seen much of in his early days of
imprisonment, but it had given him an additional reason to try to succeed,
he said, so as not to let down those who had extended themselves for him."[10]

Former inmate Amber-Anne Christie talked about how the environment and physical design of correctional facilities are significant factors in rehabilitation.[11] She had been in many prisons before, but until she went to the Alouette Correctional Centre in British Columbia she had shown no signs of being able to function in society. She says of Alouette that "this exact prison changed my life...This prison treated me like I was a person and not a number." Her description of life in that prison is instructive:

> The way the prison [Alouette] was being run was more like a rehabilitation centre than a prison. It was amazing. Not only was there a library and a gym there, there was a native elder there to talk to. As well, there was drumming and dancing every Tuesday night. As a mother myself, I have to say that it helped me to remember the things I was giving up, and I know that the other inmates dealt with their problems and reacted differently because there was a baby there.

This shows a distinct improvement from when the Honourable Louise Arbour reported on the Kingston Prison for Women in 1996. She concluded that the Correctional Service of Canada had developed a culture with little respect for the rule of law and the rights of prisoners.[12] Dynamic security still had not been fully adopted by the system. Clearly, if the above inmate testimonials can be believed, the following decade or so saw improvement.

One positive change has been the hiring of women as correctional officers.[13] Although the push was initially an effort to achieve gender equality in the workplace, it actually changed the nature of the interaction between prisoners and staff for the better. The atmosphere was more normal, more like the outside world, with women present. Communication was more meaningful. "Verbal abuse that parades as communication" was toned down. Women now occupy positions from line staff to warden.

FEARMONGER

REVERSING THE IMPROVEMENTS

Given the positive changes over the past couple of decades, it is especially alarming to see the Harper government adopting the *Roadmap to Strengthening Public Safety*. This document does not mention human rights or the Charter of Rights in its more than two hundred pages, but it does seek to roll back human rights on many fronts.

Ignoring the Supreme Court of Canada, the *Roadmap* takes the position that restricting the rights of inmates does not require justification. The authors conclude that inmates have a right only to their "basic" rights (food and shelter, for example), and that anything else has to be "earned."[14] The *Roadmap* ignores the extensive history and experience that produced the Charter and the *Corrections and Conditional Release Act*. The latter was expressly drafted to make it clear that offenders retain their rights and privileges "except those removed or restricted as a consequence of sentence." Under current legislation, the Correctional Service is required to apply the "least restrictive measures" to the treatment of inmates. The *Roadmap* recommends that this be amended to "appropriate measures," thus effectively weakening the influence of human rights law in the system.

There is a moralistic tone to the *Roadmap*, which emerges in the details. Its insistence that inmates "earn" parole, for example, is based upon the inappropriate premise that offenders' parole release depends upon whether they *deserve* to be released. On the contrary, parole boards are charged with releasing offenders only according to an assessment of the risk they pose to the community. Making them "earn" release will ensure that most never achieve parole, for reasons already explained.

The *Roadmap* also supports "an approach that links conditions of confinement to an offender's responsibilities and accountabilities."[15] This is an unsubtle way of saying that an offender will be punished with harsher conditions if it is decided that he or she is not acting the way staff would like. The areas which would be affected are enumerated: movement around the penitentiary, private family visits, leisure activity, personal clothing and property, searches, pay levels and access to money, access to employment, and access to programs—virtually everything that brings a measure of human dignity to the unnatural situation prisoners find themselves in.

This is a list of what *Roadmap* authors consider to be privileges, that can be taken away by the administration. The dynamic between staff and inmates will thus be distorted, with the exercise of power and control over every aspect of the inmate's life reinstated, just as it was in the days of routine hostage-takings and riots.

Searches for drugs, which are already relentless, will be stepped up.[16] Visits will be disrupted or prevented altogether by more sniffer dogs and ion scans and x-rays. Proven successful programs like the prison farms have already been abolished in favour of "work" programs, which are unproven, very expensive, and hard to administer because of the shortage of willing employers.

Education is seen only as an avenue to work, without any other intrinsic value. In the 1970s and 1980s, prisoners could attend university to take courses, and some completed degrees. In 1993, access to university courses was cancelled, even though the acquisition of a university degree has a greater impact on recidivism than earlier-year education.[17] Now offenders have to do everything by distance education, thus losing the important social component. They also have to pay for the courses themselves, an impossibility for most.

There are many examples of success deriving from the education received in prison. One inmate served more than eighteen years for murder. He was allowed to attend university while in the penitentiary and obtained a degree. He was finally released, continued his education, and is now a respected criminologist with a PhD.

Overcrowding in prison has already been described as a recipe for violence, unrest, the transmission of communicable diseases, and many other negative consequences. It should be noted that it also contributes directly to the inability to prepare an inmate for reintegration upon release. This is because the penitentiary system relies upon a system of "cascading" to ready its inmates. An inmate held in maximum security is expected to move to medium security and then to minimum security over time. Thus, when he is ready to be released, he will be accustomed to a less secure environment, and to more contact with others both inside and outside of the walls. This system is disrupted when there is overcrowding in medium security, as there is now. Inmates from maximum security are not able to benefit from cascading because there is no room for them in medium. Thus, they end up being released directly from the most secure prison setting straight into the community, with the predictable result that they are unable easily to cope with their new freedom. This is a recipe for recidivism.

One female inmate commented about the overcrowding in women's facilities, where her institution was designed for 60 but was holding 130 women.[18] She said that the cottages meant for family visits were often commandeered to house extra inmates. Family visits were curtailed, and so was this aspect of the inmate's reintegration plan.

The *Roadmap* ignores the fact that visits have become a valued and rehabilitative experience for inmates, helping them maintain contact with their families and communities, and facilitating their reintegration into society upon release. A study conducted by Florida State University in 2008 showed that the more visits an offender receives, the less the likelihood that he will reoffend.[19] Former inmate Conrad Black points out that "the authors of the *Roadmap* want all visits to be glass-segregated, no physical contact. This is just a pretext to assist in the destruction of families and friendships."[20] If the concern is the importation of illegal drugs, then he suggests that the staff conduct strip-searches of inmates as they leave the visiting area (as they do in Florida), rather than harass the visitors.

It goes without saying that rehabilitative programming in prison is essential. Correctional Investigator Howard Sapers is quick to acknowledge the Correctional Service's expertise. He says the department has "some of the most innovative and effective correctional programs in the world, with a proven ability to reduce recidivism."[21] He notes that participation in such programs is associated with "a greater likelihood of conditional release, reduction in readmissions and decreased violent, general and sexual re-offending." But the resources and the will to continue providing these programs are not there.

The Conservatives are cancelling programs that have stood the test of time and have contributed both to the improved conditions of prison life and to the rehabilitation of prisoners. The abolition of the prison farm program is a prime example. This program, which had been in place for 150 years, has given thousands of prisoners a reason to get up in the morning, and has taught them essential skills for a life of employment upon release. These skills are directly transferable to labour markets in the community. They include punctuality, self-discipline, self-respect, responsibility, dependability, problem-solving, and an ability to organize and communicate, to say nothing of empathy for other sentient beings. All of these will have been lacking in the lives of many inmates, and the prison farm program gave them an opportunity to get them.

Public Safety Minister Toews says that the prison farm program was cancelled because only 1 per cent of prisoners ever went into farm work upon release, and because the program was losing money. The Correctional Service, though, was glowing in its assessment of the value of the Frontenac Institution farm in Kingston, describing the "positive changes it makes in inmates' lives."[22] The farm bragged that its dairy herds were winning awards and that the farm operations provided concrete training opportunities for almost 20 per cent of male offenders.

In calculating the cost of the program, it appears, the government again failed to do its sums. In fact, its spokesperson had "no estimate of the net cost or savings of ending the program."[23] One estimate claims the cost of the program was $4 million per year, but does not take into account that it provided food in large quantities for the prisons and surplus that went to local food banks. Once the farms are gone, the bill for milk in just three Ontario prisons will be in the order of $1 million.[24] Nobody knows what the other produce, such as eggs, will now cost. It is highly likely that the program was paying for itself all along.

Illiteracy also needs addressing among Canada's prison population. Research by the Correctional Service on the effectiveness of the Adult Basic Education (ABE) Program shows that the program "appeared to have the greatest impact on offenders who were initially defined as higher risks for re-offending."[25] In 1998, a follow-up study on federal offenders who had participated in the ABE program, which offers upgrading in reading, writing, and mathematics,[26] found that

> ABE participants show measurable re-integration gains from participating [in] educational programs. Overall, the study sample was a higher than average risk group, being somewhat younger, and more likely first term with a violent conviction. "For those who complete their program, improvements in their

185

rate of re-admission ranges from 5–30 per cent, which are
modest but significant."

Among the most serious of negative prison conditions is the threat to public health from intravenous drug use and tattooing. Prevalence of both HIV and hepatitis C (HCV) are much higher in the prison population than in the general public. Seven to ten times as many prisoners have HIV as the general population, and thirty to forty times as many have HCV. Between 2000 and 2008, Hepatitis C rates increased by 50 per cent. Dirty needles are a major problem, and harm reduction could be easily accomplished through needle exchanges.

As already noted, even though such a program would greatly reduce the spread of HIV and HCV in the prisons, and thus would reduce the risk of transmission to the community, the government refuses to move forward. And, there will be no increase in funds for substance abuse programs for the next three years.

It is even more difficult to understand why the government in 2006 cancelled a safer tattooing program that had operated as a pilot the year before. This too is an issue of public health, since inmates are using dirty needles to create tattoos in unhygienic conditions. It is a serious problem in an era when tattoos are not only a badge of honour for prison inmates, but have become generally-accepted personal adornments for both men and women. Once again, the pilot was cancelled despite the evidence. A largely positive evaluation had concluded that the program had the potential to reduce harm and risk while enhancing the health and safety of staff, inmates, and the general public.

The demographic in federal prisons has been changing, with more older inmates than in previous years. Nothing of note is being done to enable these inmates to survive a system designed for the young, the strong, and the fearless. Issues specific to the needs of the elderly are no longer even being tracked. Special needs of Aboriginal peoples, special requirements for women inmates, the needs of the ill-educated and illiterate—all of these need to be addressed with targeted programs that reach every inmate in a timely fashion.

Conrad Black describes the *Roadmap* as encouraging a "Manichean process of baiting, dehumanization and stigmatization."[27] He says that the purpose of imprisonment is to "discourage law-breaking and persuade offenders to avoid recidivism, not to reenact Dante's Inferno for a demarcated category of the damned."[28] The *Roadmap* "turns the humane traditions of Canada upside down":

> *The objective of the penal system must be to return those capable of functioning licitly in society as quickly as practical, allowing also for straight punitive or retributive penalties, but not for mindless vengeance. The whole system must be guided by the fact that the treatment of the accused and confined has been recognized by ethicists and cultural historians for centuries as one of the hallmarks of civilized society.*

More radically, Mr. Black recommends that "the whole concept of prison should be terminated, except for violent criminals and chronic non-violent recidivists..." He calls the *Roadmap* a "garrotte of a blueprint," and says that the government is "flirting with moral and political catastrophe." In language that seems at odds with Mr. Black's known conservative leanings, he says Canada should reject the *Roadmap* and "again be a model of the innovative public policy pursuit of institutionalized decency and social reform."

AFTER PRISON

There is one last area of treatment that enables offenders stay to out of trouble with the law and to contribute to society. This has to do with the programs available to them upon release. Many of the programs already described also help ex-inmates reintegrate, but many others are exclusively designed to help offenders when they reach the street.

At the moment, virtually all prisoners are released under some form of supervision. This will change if the Conservative government decides to adopt one of the central recommendations of the *Roadmap*: the recommendation to abolish statutory release. The government has so far seen the perils of adopting this recommendation, wherein the most high-risk inmates would be released to the community without conditions. But

Justice Minister Nicholson has lately mused about reforming parole and release laws, and it is probable that the elimination of statutory release is what he has in mind.

Offenders are released today under conditions supervised by the parole board. This is a way of encouraging lawful behaviour, and is also meant to assist offenders in finding schools, jobs, housing, non-governmental helping organizations—whatever they need to function with dignity in society.

If there were any doubt as to the urgency of providing assistance for inmates upon release, it is contained in research conducted by Dr. Binswanger of the University of Colorado. His study produced an alarming statistic. Newly released inmates were almost thirteen times more likely to die during the first two weeks after their release than their counterparts in the general public.[29]

Other research by Visher and Travis in 2003 shows that for successful reintegration and reduced recidivism, a number of needs are fundamental: the re-establishment of family roles and support networks, emotional support, access to programming, and housing assistance. Recent research shows that providing services in the neighbourhoods where released offenders live (within two miles of the offenders' homes) can reduce future reoffending.[30]

Factors associated with reoffending are, predictably, identified as educational deficiencies, unemployment, poverty, homelessness, and so on. Among former inmates with none of these problems, only 22 per cent reoffended. Among those with all of them, 88 per cent reoffended. Recidivism rates increase with the addition of each deficit. There is every reason to believe that this American research would apply with few adjustments to the Canadian case.

The John Howard Society and Elizabeth Fry Society are long-standing organizations that help offenders at all stages of their contact with the justice system. They are particularly effective in helping ex-inmates readjust after serving a sentence. In Kingston, where there are still eight penitentiaries in operation, the John Howard Society offers reintegration counselling, practical support, referrals, assistance with Ontario Works, and access to emergency shelters, meal programs, food banks, clothing, bedding, furniture, and other sundry items of daily living.[31]

The Elizabeth Fry office in Ottawa is one of many across the country providing assistance to women offenders. Among the programs for released offenders are Anger Management, Group Counselling, Individual Counselling, Healthy Choices, Relapse Prevention (addictions), and Community Reintegration.

In the United States, there are programs as well. A study by the Center for Impact Research in the United States found that mandatory addiction treatment, education programs, and employment services were effective in preventing recidivism.[32] It pointed to New York's Community and Law Enforcement Together program, which has cut recidivism to 17 per cent among participants, compared to 41 per cent of other inmates.

In Newark, New Jersey, 25 per cent of the residents have been involved with the criminal justice system.[33] In an effort to reverse this, the mayor and the Manhattan Institute have set up the Office of Re-Entry. It focuses on work. Former inmates can walk into City Hall and ask for help getting a job. Since 2008, when the program began, 60 per cent of those who participated found work. Only 10 per cent have reoffended.

ComAlert (Community and Law Enforcement Resources Together) was created in Brooklyn in 1999 by a district attorney. It also acts as a bridge between prison and the community for returning parolees. The program's founder says, "We welcome people home, and we want to keep them there," in conjunction with the Doe Fund's "Ready, Willing and Able" program, which provides jobs like street cleaning. Later, ex-inmates can train in other types of jobs like food preparation. A Harvard study showed that ComAlert parolees were 30 per cent less likely to be rearrested than parolees who had not been in the program. ComAlert also provides drug treatment and counselling. Rearrest rates dropped 64 per cent for those who completed at least ninety days of court-ordered drug treatment.

In Hawaii, a program called HOPE (Honest Opportunity Probation with Enforcement) also focuses on drug treatment. Those who take part are 55 per cent less likely to be arrested for a new crime.

Arizona simply offers probationers twenty days off supervision for every thirty days they are compliant with their conditions. The number of probationers returning to prison has fallen by 28 per cent since 2008. The number with a new felony conviction has fallen by 31 per cent. This has saved Arizona $35.9 million in 2010, and up to $3 billion in new prisons.

An interesting and successful program has also been developed by retired businessman Mark Goldsmith in New York.[34] GOSO (Getting Out and Staying Out) is dedicated to drastically reducing the recidivism rate for eighteen- to twenty-year-old men through purposeful education and directed employment. It is aimed at inmates at Rikers Island and in upstate New York. When an offender attends at the GOSO office upon release from prison, the staff determine his housing, counselling, and treatment needs. These could be mental health, drug treatment, anger management, and emergency housing. When he leaves the GOSO office he has an alarm clock, a note pad, pens, a weekly planner, condoms, a metro card, and a professional resume. These are meant to help him be on time, be prepared, and be safe. Most importantly, the offender leaves with a plan for the immediate future.

This pragmatic and down-to-earth approach has produced excellent results. Of the more than four hundred who have been part of the GOSO program, 85 per cent have stayed out of prison. This is compared to the Riker's Island average of 33 per cent. Most of the participants are either working or pursuing college or both.

In Canada, in addition to John Howard and Elizabeth Fry, countless other programs are equally pragmatic and are producing real successes. As one more example, the Eastern Ontario Youth Justice Agency provides a number of programs, including A Different Street, which works with young men sixteen to twenty who are recently released and homeless.[35] They are provided with counselling and helped to overcome systemic barriers when accessing services. Community Support Teams are also provided to both boys and girls between ages twelve and seventeen.

Statistics showing the success of these after-prison programs are impressive. The way to reducing the revolving-door syndrome is clear.

THE FINNISH MODEL

The Finnish experience included all four stages of alternatives—prevention, alternatives to prison, treatment within prison, and assistance on release. Dan Gardner has written extensively on Finland's efforts to develop its justice system, and the lessons are clear. An effort to pursue such a model and modify it for our own circumstances would hold great promise for a wholesale reform of Canada's system.[36]

The backstory: Finland was under the sphere of influence of the Soviet Union for most of the last century. As such, it adopted the Russian approach to criminal justice, which was strictly punishment-oriented. In the 1950s, Finland's incarceration rate was two hundred prisoners per hundred thousand people—normal for Eastern Bloc countries, but four times the rate in Sweden, Norway, and Denmark.

In the 1960s, a conscious decision was made to change the system by reducing the rate of imprisonment. More conditional sentences were used, parole could be achieved after fourteen days in prison, and those who violated parole were eligible again after one month. All first-time offenders are let out after serving half their sentence; others serve two-thirds. Mediation is used broadly to help victims and offenders decide how best to set things right. Children under fifteen cannot be charged with a crime, and offenders between fifteen and twenty-one can be imprisoned only for extraordinary reasons (and are released after one-third of their sentence).[37] Life sentences for serious crimes are routinely commuted, with offenders serving between ten and fifteen to sixteen years and no more. There is dangerous offender legislation, which allows for the unlimited incarceration of repeat, serious, violent offenders. There were eighty of those in custody in 2002.

An especially important change was that sentencing guidelines were introduced that set shorter norms. Unlike the guidelines used in the United States, or the mandatory minimums adopted in Canada, judges may rule outside the guidelines if they feel it is appropriate, thus respecting judicial discretion.

Prisoners have contact with people both inside and outside of the walls, with frequent visits from family and friends, including conjugal visits. Male and female prisoners live together. They can work or study at any education level. After serving six months, prisoners can apply for a "home leave" to return to their home towns for up to six days every four months. Although the home leave program has been controversial, 90 per cent of these leaves occur without even minor difficulties. Volunteers can come into the prison and visit offenders, even in their cells. The goal is that offenders have a close connection with someone: "It is very important that everybody should have somebody waiting for him." Jobs and homes are on the list of requirements that the authorities help secure for the offenders. Violence is rare in the prisons.

Statistics bear out the efficacy of this approach. Finland's incarceration rate in 2002 was fifty-two per hundred thousand people, less than half of Canada's and a fraction of that of the United States. The director general of Finland's prisons, Markku Salminen, was a police officer for thirty years. He says that in Finland, "We don't have this idea that 'hard crimes deserve hard punishment'." It would be hard to find a view more diametrically opposed to that of the Harper Conservatives.

The best evidence of the success of this approach is a comparison with Finland's close neighbour, Russia. The St. Petersburg region, with 5.9 million people, had 72,000 police officers in 2002. The five million people in Finland employed 8,500, just 12 per cent of the Russian city's force. In 2001, Russia was incarcerating 644 people per 100,000 of population, compared with fifty-two in Finland the following year,[38] and Russian offenders were more likely to be incarcerated for longer and in far worse conditions. Meanwhile, the murder rate in Russia was ten times that of Finland. As Gardner says, "If a nation wishes, it can send few offenders to prison, and make those prisons humane, without sacrificing the public's safety."

Pursuing a more sensible approach to crime in Canada will require a fundamental shifting of philosophy. The Conservative government responds to crime by being reactive, reactionary, and repressive.[39] What actually works to drive crime down and rehabilitate offenders is proactive, progressive, and humanitarian.

CONCLUSION

The Canadian criminal justice system is headed for a crisis under the Harper government. For ideological reasons, the government is legislating more incarceration across the board, despite conclusive evidence that this will have no positive effect upon the crime rate. It is doing so at a time when the crime rate has been dropping for years. There will be no effective impediment to the government's agenda, now that it has a majority.

This headlong drive to a Harper version of being tough on crime consists, simplistically, of more and longer prison sentences. It will not increase public safety. It will not help victims. It will bankrupt the treasuries of federal and provincial and territorial governments, as similar approaches have done in the United States. Worst of all, it will destroy lives, ruin families, and damage communities.

What is driving such a highly punitive agenda, one that is not supported by research, evidence, or experience? Canada already imprisons more people per capita than most comparable Western democracies, and incarceration rates do not affect crime rates anyway. There must be some other motivation.[1]

Everything from the personality of the Prime Minister to the ideological and religious background of his caucus has been suggested as among the reasons for the focus on this agenda, but no convincing explanation has been given. The Prime Minister and his government believe that they know what Canadians want with respect to criminal justice. This belief appears largely to drive an agenda in which the government ignores even the advice of its own supporters.

Don Gardner is an expert on how Finland has cut its incarceration rates without experiencing an increase in crime rates. He is convinced that it is the "beliefs" of the Harper government that are most influential in all matters of public policy:[2]

> *The government "believes." And, as every man of faith knows, belief can conquer even the mightiest army of facts. But for those of us in the reality-based community—the famously dismissive phrase of a Bush official—belief isn't good enough. We expect policy to be supported by facts and research. Perhaps that makes us lesser men and women, but we can't accept something as true simply because it's been given Stephen Harper's benediction. So where's the evidence that the government's radical, US-style approach to criminal justice will make us safer? You won't find it on its website. There are lots of bold claims, of course. But in the press release and background information, there isn't a word about evidence.*
>
> *Not that any of this will bother Mr. Harper or his ministers. They've got faith. And they've made it clear they have no intention of changing their minds, no matter what the research says. It's the rest of us—those who still value evidence and reason—who should be concerned.*

Craig Jones takes another tack. He suggests that the tough-on-crime approach is driven by "the raw retail politics of penal populism." This would imply a political pragmatism that precludes anything that does not appeal directly to the voter. Most of what the Harper government is proposing rejects the research and expertise on criminal justice, but the agenda still appears to be popular with some members of the public. Mr. Jones suggests that the government is anxious to be seen "doing something" about crime. Hence, at a time when even the United States is rejecting mandatory minimum sentences and closing prisons, Canada is moving in the opposite direction.

The Conservatives' tough-on-crime legislation has the political advantage of producing immediate, visible results. Harper and his ministers can point to longer sentences, new offences, and harsher prison conditions. Preventive and rehabilitative programs, on the other hand, although they cost less and produce better outcomes, take more time to show results. In a world of four-year election cycles, recently reduced to about two, the choice is clear for any government wishing to make an immediate impact with the public.

The idea that tough-on-crime is popular with voters also helps to explain the impotence of the opposition in resisting the agenda. No one wants to be seen as "soft on crime," which was Mr. Harper's characterization of the Paul Martin Liberal government. And, keeping in mind the brief election cycle, no one wants to take the time necessary to educate a mainly uninformed public as to what a responsible approach to crime should look like. But research shows that when the information is provided, people arrive at a progressive view of what works in criminal justice.[3]

The Conservative approach to criminal justice appears to be one piece of an overall strategy by Conservatives to move Canadians away from their natural moderate, centrist, more liberal philosophy and toward more conservative ideals.[4] Calling this "incrementalism," Conservative strategist Tom Flanagan says:

> Some have argued recently that Canadian conservatives have to build for the long term, trying to affect public opinion so that conservatism becomes an entrenched public philosophy... Who would deny that Canada's present climate of opinion has been fostered by the Liberal Party's long-term dominance of federal institutions? If you control the government, you choose judges, appoint the senior civil service, fund or de-fund advocacy groups, and do many other things that gradually influence the climate of opinion.

In addition to this general philosophy, Mr. Flanagan says that the Harper government directs its efforts first and foremost to "strategic purposes."[5] He maintains that the party is a "garrison party...focused on election readiness rather than policy development," thus confirming that political pragmatism and voter appeal are at the centre of the government's activities.

Statistics and evidence-based policy development have been stoutly ignored by the Harper government. Faced with the fact of a dropping crime rate and the evidence against mandatory minimum sentences, Justice Minister Nicholson dismissed concerns and disparaged what he called "trying to govern by statistics."[6] Ian Brodie, former chief of staff to Prime Minister Harper, famously rejected evidence-based criminal justice policy-making in these words:[7]

> *Every time we proposed amendments to the Criminal Code, sociologists, criminologists, defence lawyers and Liberals attacked us for proposing measures that the evidence apparently showed did not work. That was a good thing for us politically, in that sociologists, criminologists and defence lawyers were and are all held in lower repute than Conservative politicians by the voting public. Politically it helped us tremendously to be attacked by this coalition of university types.*

Among the pieces of evidence dismissed by the Harper government are those provided by previous Conservative governments. To take just one example, in 1990, a study prepared for the Department of Justice under Prime Minister Brian Mulroney concluded that long sentences are counter-productive.[8] It said that "the evidence shows that long periods served in prison increase the chance that the offender will offend again...In the end, public security is diminished, rather than increased, if we 'throw away the key'." These few words hold the key to a responsible approach to criminal justice.

The Harper government employs the fear factor. By repeating its position that violent crime is on the rise, that repeat offenders are getting a slap on the wrist from judges, and that guns, gangs, and drugs are a growing threat, the government has been able to convince the public to accept its harsh measures. At the same time, it is able to distract the public from areas in which the government has stumbled, whether they be climate change, our failure to win a seat on the United Nations Security Council, the Afghan detainees, or the millions spent on the G8 and G20 meetings. Virtually unopposed by the mainstream media, the Conservatives have succeeded in convincing many that we are losing the fight against crime, and that this is the all-important issue.

Overwhelming evidence shows that the billions of dollars being spent on prisons would be better spent on attacking the risk factors for crime. Proven treatment programs in prevention, alternatives to prison, humane treatment in custody, and support for ex-inmates should be properly funded. This is achievable, and would produce improved public safety.

Such a change will require a slow and difficult adjustment of the entrenched culture. Police and prosecutors must be encouraged to divert offenders out of the criminal courts. Judges must be encouraged once again to tailor sentences to individual cases, to use non-custodial sentences wherever it is safe to do so, and to reduce the length of custodial sentences across the board. A generous system of release from custody must be initiated. Proven successful programs must be adequately funded at every step of this process. Research must be funded to monitor the success of the system and to provide new ideas for improvement.

The federal government could begin to change the culture by overhauling the *Criminal Code of Canada*. Rather than simply having new offences and new sentences added, as the government is doing now, the entire *Code* needs to be streamlined and brought up to date. This will be a huge project, but one that will bear fruit in more predictable, consistent, and just results. It is a job for the Law Reform Commission, which was disbanded at the beginning of the Harper mandate. A Commission on Sentencing would be a further important undertaking, if it were aimed at redesigning the criminal justice system in the interests of all Canadians. These are not simple solutions to complex problems. They will be as complex as the project demands. It is the twenty-first century, and Canada must be up to this task.

The public must be educated about the importance and efficacy of these changes. It is likely that people are already beginning to see the current system as unsustainable, now that the extraordinary financial costs are becoming apparent. People want to see positive results for their hard-earned tax dollars. It is clear that the incarceration model does not produce those results. Canadians are capable of understanding alternative models, and of understanding that the current system is not sacred. The more the Conservative government insists upon its discredited retributive model, the more Canadians will begin to demand a more enlightened approach.

The Harper government's system does not accord with what Canadians believe themselves to be: compassionate, consensus-driven, generous, cooperative people who look for solutions based upon evidence and not upon unsubstantiated belief. Canadians will not continue to tolerate the antediluvian spectacle of their country imprisoning the mentally ill, the addicted, the poor, the homeless, the marginalized, and their children, just because their federal government thinks that this is how to be tough on crime.

"Tough on crime," as defined by the Harper government, is a chimera. "Tough on crime" is lazy. It is ill-informed and cruel. It will not succeed in its stated objectives. Canadians should reject the Harper crime agenda and demand a more thoughtful, evidence-based approach to criminal justice. We deserve no less.

ENDNOTES

CHAPTER 1

1   *Stand Up for Canada*, Conservative Party of Canada Federal Election Platform 2006. http://circ.jmellon.com/docs/html/stand_up_for_security_a_canadian_foreign_ intelligence_agency.html

2   Statistics Canada figures show that the crime rate, including severe crime, and including the homicide rate, has been dropping for about twenty years. See Chapter 2.

3   Remand facilities are the jails where accused persons are held until their trial, if they fail to obtain bail.

4   "Reverse onus" means that it is not up to the Crown prosecutor to prove why an accused should remain in custody until his or her trial. There is instead a presumption that the accused should be detained, unless a judge can be convinced that the accused should be released.

5   *Securing Canada's Success*, http://westernstandard.blogs.com/shotgun/files/platforme.pdf

6   www.cbc.ca/canadavotes2006/leadersparties/pdf/ndp_platform-en-final-web.pdf

7   www.blocquebecois.org/document.aspx

8   www.greenparty.ca/en/platform2006/justice

9   Report dated January 24, 2006, referred to by Tonda MacCharles, "Jails Fear PM's Justice Overhaul," *Toronto Star*, January 11, 2007.

10 Conrad Black, "Conrad Black: The Case Against Being Dumb on Crime," *National Post*, February 19, 2011.

11 Tom Flanagan, *Harper's Team: Behind the Scenes in the Conservative Rise to Power* (Montreal & Kingston: McGill-Queen's University Press, 2007), p. 247.

12 "We cannot be emotionless, but we are capable of rational debate," Comment, *Globe and Mail*, March 16, 2010, p. A13.

13 www.famm.org/Repository/Files/Boggs%20feature.pdf

14 Michael Tonry, "The Mostly Unintended Effects of Mandatory Penalties: Two Centuries of Consistent Findings," referred to in Bruce Cheadle, "Tories Ignore Taxpayer-funded Crime Research," *Canadian Press*, March 15, 2010.

15 Tonda MacCharles, "Tories Target Gun Crime. Prison Populations Would Swell under Measures in New Bills," *Toronto Star*, May 5, 2006.

16 I am indebted to Craig Jones, former executive director of the John Howard Society of Canada, for his comments on this report, "The Government Is Doing Something," *Inroads*, Summer/Fall 2010, pp. 58–69; and to Michael Jackson and Graham Stewart, *A Flawed Compass: A Human Rights Analysis of the Roadmap to Strengthening Public Safety* (September 2009). Michael Jackson has been a prisoners' rights advocate for thirty-five years and teaches in the Faculty of Law at the University of British Columbia. Graham Stewart worked for the John Howard Society for thirty-eight years, retiring from the post of Executive Director in 2007. http://www.cbc.ca/news/pdf/a-flawed-compass-final-web-distribution-sep25-09.pdf

17 "Day Denies Prison Privatization Plans But Is He Being Honest?" Opinion, *National Union*, April 29, 2007.

18 (Ottawa: Ministry of Public Works and Government Services, Canada, October 2007).

19 Craig Jones (ref. note 15, above).

20 Jackson and Stewart, *Flawed Compass*, p. xxxiv.

21 Conrad Black, "Harper's Inhumane Prison Plan," *National Post*, May 29, 2010.

22 *Integrated Overview: The Correctional Service of Canada Transformation Agenda* (Ottawa: The Correctional Service of Canada, November 2009).

23 Editorial, *Toronto Star*, July 19, 2008.

24 *The Current*, CBC Radio One, February 17, 2011.

25 *The True North Strong and Free: Stephen Harper's Plan for Canadians* www.conservative.ca/media/2008-Platform-e.pdf

26 *Richer, Fairer, Greener: An Action Plan for the 21st Century* www.scribd.com/doc/6308750/Liberal-Party-of-Canada-2008-English-Platform

27 *Strong Communities and Safe Neighbourhoods* www.mapleleafweb.com/feataures/2008-election-campaign-political-party-platforms

28 www.scribd.com/doc/6308738/Bloq-Quebecois-2008-English.Platform

29 www.votefortomorrow.ca

30 Bill C-25, the *Truth in Sentencing Act*, is analyzed in detail in Chapter 4.

31 Kirk Makin, "Canadian Crime and American Punishment," *Globe and Mail*, November 28, 2009, p. F1.

32 Gloria Galloway and Daniel Leblanc, "With Senate in His Grip, PM Drives Crime Agenda," *Globe and Mail*, January 30, 2010.

33 Letter to the Hon. Rob Nicholson, PC, MP, February 4, 2010.

34 One of them had reached the Senate only two weeks before the Christmas break, so there was insufficient time for the Senate to deal with it (the bill repealing the "faint hope" clause). One bill had been languishing in the Senate since June 2009, but was not really "urgent," since it only created a new offence for motor vehicle theft. Finally, the bill imposing mandatory minimum sentences for drug charges had in fact been modified by the Senate in December 2009. One amendment changed the amount of marijuana in a grow-op that would attract a six-month minimum sentence from one plant to six—not really an "evisceration."

35 "Government of Canada Enacts New Regulations to Help Fight Organized Crime," press release (Ottawa: Department of Justice Canada, August 4, 2010).

36 Lawrence Martin, "Puritanism Could Be a Winner," *Globe and Mail*, August 11, 2010.

37 Glen McGregor, *National Post*, February 20, 2011.

38 Kirk Makin, "Top Judges Rebuke Tories," *Globe and Mail*, November 10, 2006, p. A1; Kirk Makin, "Senior Lawyers Criticize Toews," *Globe and Mail*, November 16, 2006, p. A10; Editorial, "Meddling with Courts," *Toronto Star*, January 12, 2007, p. A18.

39 www.canada.com/edmontonjournal/news/story.html?id=01c0e854-3385-4561-8c86-43d160860cc9&k=0

40 Gloria Galloway, "Liberals Come Out Against Tory 'Dumb on Crime' Legislation," *Globe and Mail*, February 9, 2011.

41 Office of the Parliamentary Budget Officer, *The Funding Requirement and Impact of the Truth in Sentencing Act on the Correctional System in Canada* (Ottawa, June 22, 2010) p. 9.

42 www.conservative.ca/media/Conservative Platform2011_ENs.pdf

43 The others are job creation, helping families, eliminating the deficit, and defending the Arctic.

44 *Your Family. Your Future. Your Canada.* www.liberal.ca/platform

45 Gloria Galloway, "NDP Pledge Aims to Stamp Out Gang-Related Crime at Its Source," *Globe and Mail*, April 7, 2011.

46 Ibid.

47 The Conservatives have promised to scrap InSite.

48 Galloway, "NDP Pledge Aims..."

49 CBC *Newsworld*, April 12 and 13, 2011.

50 www.cbc.ca/news/politics/canadavotes2011/platforms/bloc

51 www.cbc.ca/news/politics/canadavotes2011/platforms/green

CHAPTER 2

1 Lawrence Martin, *Harperland: The Politics of Control* (Toronto: Viking Canada, 2010), p. 210.

2 "Corrections and Conditional Release Statistical Overview—2009," (Ottawa: Public Safety Canada). http://www.publicsafety.gc.ca/res/cor/rep/2009-ccrso-eng.aspx

3 Mia Dauvergne and John Turner, "Police-Reported Crime Statistics in Canada, 2009," *Juristat*, July 20, 2010. The homicide rate has remained stable over time, but is well below its peak in the mid-1970s. Attempted murder rates have been on a general decline over the past thirty years as well.

4 Lyne Casavant and Dominique Valiquet, "Bill C-4: An Act to Amend the YCJA and to Make Consequential and Related Amendments to Other Acts," *Legislative Summary*. (Ottawa: Parliamentary Information and Research Service, Ottawa, April 1, 2010.)

5 Tonda MacCharles, "Tories Target Gun Crime. Prison Population Would Swell under Measures in New Bills," *Toronto Star*, May 5, 2006.

6 Mia Dauvergne, "Use of Guns in Robberies Drops as Crime Locales Shift," *Juristat*, March 25, 2010.

7 Dauvergne and Turner, "Police-Reported Crime Statistics..."

8 "Corrections and Conditional Release Statistical Overview—2009," Public Safety Canada.

9 "Offences Against the Administration of Justice," *The Daily*, January 11, 2006.

10 Percentages that follow are rounded to the nearest whole number.

11 Jackson and Stewart, *Flawed Compass*, p. xxv.

12 *Corrections and Conditional Release Statistical Overview—2009*, Public Safety Canada. This source provides statistics on all of the forms of release referred to here.

13 Scott Newark, *Why Canadian Crime Statistics Don't Add Up. Not the Whole Truth*, (Ottawa: The Macdonald-Laurier Institute, January 29, 2011). It can be noted that Mr. Newark and the Macdonald-Laurier Institute have significant connections to the Conservative Party. According to *Globe and Mail* journalist John Ibbitson, most of the Macdonald-Laurier Institute's reports in its first year have supported policies of the Harper government, even though its managing director claims the institute is nonpartisan. Also, Scott Newark worked for Stockwell Day in 2006 when Mr. Day was minister of public safety. John

Ibbitson, "Think Tank Targets Statscan's Falling Crime Rate Claim," *Globe and Mail*, February 9, 2011.

14 *The Current*, CBC Radio One, February 15, 2011.

15 Dr. Doob is a Professor of Criminology at the Centre of Criminology, University of Toronto.

16 Edward Greenspan and Anthony Doob, "Crunch the Numbers: Crime Rates Are Going Down," *Globe and Mail*, February 22, 2011.

17 CBC Radio One *News*, January 31, 2011.

18 Jane Taber, "Stockwell Day Stands His Ground on Crime Stats," *Globe and Mail*, August 5, 2010.

19 Telephone interview with the author, January 25, 2010, and Ibbitson, "Think Tank Targets..."

20 Samuel Perreault and Shannon Brennan, "Criminal Victimization in Canada, 2009," *Juristat*, Summer 2010.

21 Tapio Lappi-Seppälä, *Trust, Welfare, and Political Culture: Explaining Differences in National Penal Policies*, February 18, 2008, p. 23.

22 Ibid., p. 30.

23 Telephone interview with the author, January 25, 2011.

24 The following four charts are from a PowerPoint presentation, "Crime and Punishment Trends" by Dr. Anthony N. Doob, January 25, 2011. See also Rosemary Gartner, Anthony N. Doob, and Franklin E. Zimring, "The Past as Prologue? Decarceration in California Then and Now," *Criminology and Public Policy*, Spring, 2011.

25 Gartner et al., "Past is Prologue..." p. 18.

26 See Chapter 3.

27 Warren Richey, "Supreme Court: Can Judges Tell California to Release 40,000 Prisoners?" *The Christian Science Monitor*, November 30, 2010.

28 Boyd, "Why More Prison Cells Are..."

29 The Finnish case is discussed in detail in Chapter 9.

30 The references are, respectively, "Punishment, Division of Labor, and Social Solidarity," *The Criminology of Criminal Law, Advances in Criminological Theory*, Vol. 8, edited by William S. Laufer and Freda Adler (Transaction Publishers, 1999), p. 283; "Prison Populations as Political Constructs: The Case of Finland, Holland and Sweden," *Journal of Scandinavian Studies in Criminology and Crime Prevention*, Vol. 4, 2003, p. 21; "The Political Economy of Imprisonment in Affluent Western Democracies 1960–1990," *American Sociological Review*, 2004, Vol. 69, p. 170; "Social Disruption, State Priorities, and Minority

Threat: A Cross-National Study of Imprisonment," *Punishment & Society. The International Journal of Penology*, Vol. 7, No. 1 (Sage Publications, 2005), p. 7.

31 Warren Silver, "Police Reported Crime Statistics in Canada, 2006," *Juristat* 27(5), pp. 1–15.

CHAPTER 3

1 Allan Manson, *The Law of Sentencing* (Toronto: Irwin Law, 2001) p. 370. Mr. Manson is an expert on sentencing and teaches law at Queen's University, Kingston.

2 Martin, *Harperland*, p. 118.

3 David Roberts, "Manitoba Bar Raps Justice Minister," *Winnipeg Free Press*, May 8, 1998, p. A17.

4 www.canada.com/ottawacitizen/news/story.html?id=20ab396c-23ad-403c-b8b7-179413f5f56f

5 Audrey Macklin and Lorne Waldman, "When Cabinet Ministers Attack Judges, They Attack Democracy," *Globe and Mail*, February 18, 2011.

6 *The Sunday Edition*, CBC Radio One, February 21, 2010.

7 Janice Tibbetts, "Lamer Stacks Alliance 'Yelping'," *National Post*, April 14, 2001, p. A01.

8 Nahlah Ayed, "Charter at 20 Still Brews a Storm in Canadian Politics as It Did at Birth," *Canadian Press*, April 11, 2002.

9 Frances Russell, "Toews is Conservatives' Weak Link," *Winnipeg Free Press*, February 8, 2006, p. A13.

10 *Canada (Prime Minister) v. Khadr*, [2010] 1 S.C.R. 44.

11 Kirk Makin, "Khadr Ruling Sees Top Court Clash with Tories," *Globe and Mail*, January 29, 2010.

12 Conrad Black, "Conrad Black: The Case Against Being Dumb on Crime," *National Post*, February 19, 2011.

13 Editorial, "Tories Twist Crime Stats to Build More Prisons," *Montreal Gazette*, February 28, 2011.

14 Julian V. Roberts, Nicole Crutcher, and Paul Verbrugge, "Public Attitudes to Sentencing in Canada: Exploring Recent Findings," *Canadian Journal of Criminology and Criminal Justice*, Vol. 49, January 2007, pp. 75–107.

15 *R. v. Proulx*, [2000] 1 S.C.R. 61.

16 Anthony N. Doob, *Crime and Punishment Trends*, PowerPoint presentation, January 25, 2011.

17 "Rough Justice," *The Economist*, July 24, 2010, p. 13.

18 Ibid., p. 29.

19 Ibid., p. 13

20 Kathleen O'Hara. "Conservatives' Crime-and-Punishment Plans Will Cost Us All," www.rabble.ca, February 4, 2011.

21 John Ivison, "With Crime Rates Falling, Building New Prisons Is an Expense This Country Doesn't Need," *National Post*, January 10, 2011, quoting Gingrich and Nolan.

22 Ibid.; and the editorial, "Harper Tories Split with Friends Abroad on Crime Policy," *Globe and Mail*, February 13, 2011.

23 Justice Policy Institute, "Finding Direction: Expanding Criminal Justice Options by Considering Policies of Other Nations." http://www.justicepolicy.org/research/2322

24 Editorial, "Harper Tories Split..."

25 *The Economist*, "Rough Justice," p. 13.

26 Ibid., p. 29.

27 *Prison Brief—Highest to Lowest Rates*, International Centre for Prison Studies, School of Law, King's College, London, March 18, 2010. www.kcl.ac.uk/depsta/law/research/icps/worldbrief/wpb_stats.php?area=all&category=wb_poptotal

28 National Criminal Justice Section, Canadian Bar Association, "Controlled Drugs and Substances Act Amendment," Submission to House of Commons Committee on Justice and Human Rights, May, 2009.

29 Kirk Makin, "Canadians' Views on Crime Are Hardening, Poll Finds," *Globe and Mail*, January 21, 2010.

30 Ibid.

31 National Criminal Justice Section, Canadian Bar Association, "Controlled Drugs and Substances..."

32 Steven N. Durlauf and Daniel S. Nagin, "Imprisonment and Crime: Can Both Be Reduced?" *Criminology and Public Policy* (2011) 11(1), pp. 9–54.

33 John Reilly, *Bad Medicine: A Judge's Struggle for Justice in a First Nations Community*, (Vancouver: Rocky Mountain Books, 2010), p. 42. Retired Judge Reilly ran in the 2011 election as a Liberal candidate, largely to oppose the tough-on-crime agenda.

34 Ibid., p. 172–173.

35 Tonda MacCharles, "Jailers Fear PM's Justice Overhaul," *Toronto Star*, January 11, 2007.

36 D. Champion, *Measuring Offender Risk* (Westport, Connecticut: Greenwood Press, 1994); Dan Weatherburn, "The Effect of Prison on Adult Re-Offending," *Crime and Justice Bulletin* (New South Wales, Bureau of Crime, Statistics, and Research), (2010) Number 143;

Rohan Lulham, Don Weatherburn, and Lorana Bartels, "The Recidivism of Offenders Given Suspended Sentences: A Comparison with Full-Time Imprisonment," *Crime and Justice Bulletin* (2009) Number 136.

37 S. Brody, *The Effectiveness of Sentencing* (London: Her Majesty's Stationery Office, 1976).

38 I. Brownlee, "Intensive Probation with Young Adult Offenders," *British Journal of Criminology*, Vol. 35, 1995, pp. 599–612.

39 P. Gendreau, C. Goggin, and F. T. Cullen, *The Effects of Prison Sentences on Recidivism* (Ottawa: Solicitor General, 1999).

40 Bruce Cheadle, "Tories Ignore Taxpayer-Funded Crime Research," *Canadian Press*, March 15, 2010.

41 Public Safety Canada, Research Summary, Vol. 4, No. 6, November 1999.

42 *Hansard*, May 3, 2010.

43 *The Badge and the Book. Building Effective Police/School Partnerships to Combat Youth Violence.* (Ottawa: Minister of the Solicitor General Canada, 1995.)

44 Harris MacLeod, "Justice Minister Nicholson Pushes Crime Bill He Used to Be Against," *Hill Times*, February 1, 2010.

45 "Rough Justice," (*Economist*) p. 29.

46 Cheadle, "Tories Ignore..."

47 *Criminological Highlights*, The Centre of Criminology, University of Toronto, Vol. 11, No. 2, Article 7, May, 2010, citing Judith Greene and Marc Mauer, "Downscaling Prisons: Lessons from Four States." The Sentencing Project. www.sentencingproject.org

48 Michael Tonry, referred to in Cheadle, "Tories Ignore..."

49 Bruce Cheadle, "Tory Prison Policy 'Wedge Politics': Study," *Globe and Mail*, September 24, 2009.

50 Makin, "Canadians' Views on Crime..."

51 Kirk Makin, "Canada: Mandatory Sentences Blamed for Boom in Cost of Prison," *Globe and Mail*, June 19, 2008.

52 Ibid.

53 Robert Matas, "Are Mandatory Minimum Sentences the Solution to Haphazard Justice?" *Globe and Mail*, December 16, 2010, quoting Robert Mulligan.

54 *R. v. Wust* (2000), 143 C.C.C. (3d) 129 (S.C.C.) at 139.

55 Makin, "Canada: Mandatory Sentences Blamed..."

56 *The Current*, CBC Radio One, December 15, 2010.

57 Kirk Makin, "Supreme Court Urged to Overhaul Sentencing Philosophy," *Globe and Mail*, December 8, 2010.

58 Makin, "Canadian Crime..."

59 Makin identifies this source as "a well-connected Justice Department insider who spoke on condition of anonymity," "Canadian Crime..."

CHAPTER 4

1   John Ibbitson, "Tories Hope Anti-Gang Fighter's Appointment to Senate Will Pay Dividends," *Globe and Mail*, December 21, 2010.

2   Adam Radwanski, "Julian Fantino: A Politician in Police Uniform," *Globe and Mail*, October 12, 2010.

3   "Federal Government Plans to Fight Crime," speech by Prime Minister Harper, April 3, 2006. www.pm.gc.ca/eng/media.asp?id=1088

4   *Proceedings* of the House of Commons Standing Committee on Justice and Human Rights, May 25, 2010.

5   Allan Manson, CBC Radio One, *The Sunday Edition*, February 21, 2010.

6   CBC Radio, *The Sunday Edition*, February 21, 2010.

7   Nicholas Hune-Brown, "Hell House," *Toronto Life*, December 2010, pp. 58–66.

8   *Proceedings* of the Senate Standing Committee on Legal and Constitutional Affairs, October 1, 2009.

9   Lyne Casavant and Domique Valiquet, "Bill C-25. The 'Truth in Sentencing Act'," *Legislative Summary*. (Ottawa: Legal and Legislative Affairs Division, Parliamentary Information and Research Service, April 24, 2009, revised January 25, 2010), referring to Radio-Canada and Presse canadienne, "Abolir le temps compté en double," March 25, 2009.

10 *The Sunday Edition*, CBC Radio One, February 21, 2010.

11 *Proceedings* of the House of Commons Standing Committee on Justice and Human Rights, June 1, 2009.

12 *Hansard*, April 20, 2009.

13 *Proceedings* of the Senate Standing Committee on Legal and Constitutional Affairs, September 17, 2009, testimony of witness Allan Manson.

14 Ibid., April 1, 2009.

15 Ibid.

16 Ibid., September 17, 2009.

17 *Proceedings* of the House of Commons Standing Committee, May 25, 2009, testimony of witness Andras Schreck, Director of the Criminal Lawyers Association of Ontario.

18 *Proceedings* of the Senate Standing Committee, September 16, 2009.

19 *R. v. Askov*, [1990] 2 S.C.R. 1199. The Supreme Court of Canada decided that a two-year delay breached the accused's right to trial within a reasonable time. The decision had huge repercussions, as thousands of similar cases had to be consequently stayed by Crown Attorneys.

20 Josh Weinstein, *Limiting Credit for Time in Pre-Sentence Custody*, Submission to House of Commons Standing Committee on Justice and Human Rights, Canadian Bar Association, May 22, 2009.

21 Commentary, "Aboriginals, Poor Hit Hardest by Tory Sentencing Law: Internal Report," *Globe and Mail*, September 26, 2010.

22 Ibid.

23 *Proceedings* of the Senate Standing Committee, September 17, 2009, testimony of Julian Roberts, Professor of Criminology, University of Oxford, and Dr. Anthony Doob, Professor of Criminology, University of Toronto.

24 Ian Robertson, "'Toronto 18' Terrorist Gets Only One More Day," *Toronto Sun*, January 20, 2010.

25 *The Funding Requirement and Impact of the "Truth in Sentencing Act" on the Correctional System in Canada"*(Ottawa: Office of the Parliamentary Budget Officer, June 22, 2010), p. 12.

26 Mia Rabson, "Showdown Over Crime Bill Looms. Cost of Bill C-25 Likely to Be Divisive," *Winnipeg Free Press*, May 11, 2010.

27 Standing Senate Committee on Legal and Constitutional Affairs, Issue 11—Evidence for February 25, 2008.

28 Makin, "Canadian Crime..."

29 Kirk Makin, "Court Upholds Tough-On-Crime Law, but Offers a Way around Sentencing Rules," *The Globe and Mail*, February 23, 2011.

30 Editorial, "The Last Laugh on Truth in Sentencing," *Globe and Mail*, February 24, 2011.

31 While the practice of naming legislation after a victim can be criticized, the new young offender law is referred to hereinafter, for convenience, as Sébastien's Law.

32 D. Merlin Nunn, *Spiralling Out of Control: Lessons Learned from a Boy in Trouble—Report of the Nunn Commission of Inquiry*," December 2006, p. 238. The commission was struck after a young offender with a long record was released from custody and within two days was responsible for a death in a motor vehicle accident.

33 Standing Committee on Justice and Human Rights, December 9, 2010.

34 Casavant and Valiquet, *Legislative Summary* re Bill C-4.

35 *Corrections and Conditional Release Statistical Overview—2009*.

36 *Hansard*, March 19, 2010.

37 "Submission to House of Commons Standing Committee on Justice and Human Rights, on Bill C-4: YCJA Amendments." National Criminal Justice Section, Criminal Bar Association, June 2010.

38 Janice Tibbetts, "Canada's Youth Crime Laws Hailed as Success," *Canwest News Service*, November 10, 2009.

39 Ibid.

40 Nicholas Bala, Peter J. Carrington, and Julian V. Roberts, "Evaluating the YCJA after Five Years: A Qualified Success," *Canadian Journal of Criminology and Criminal Justice*, April 2009, Vol. 51, #2, p. 159.

41 Ibid.

42 Ibid.

43 Caroline Alphonso, "Tory Bill Proposes Publicizing Names of Violent Young Offenders," *Globe and Mail*, March 17, 2010, p. A4.

44 Casavant and Valiquet, *Legislative Summary* re Bill C-4, quoting Nicholas Bala.

45 *R. v. B.W.P.; R. v. B.V.N.*, [2006]1 S.C.R. 941.

46 *R. v. D.B.*, [2008] 2 S.C.R. 3.

47 This is a quote from the Legislative Summary, and not from the Court decision.

48 *Proceedings* of the House of Commons Standing Committee on Justice and Human Rights, May 25, 2010.

49 Canadian Bar Association submission on Bill C-4.

50 *R. v. C.D.; R. v. C.D.K.*, [2005] 3 S.C.R. 688.

51 Ibid.

52 Kathleen Harris, "Youth Crime Bill Reaction Mixed," January 28, 2010. ca.new.canoe.ca/CNEWS/Politics/2010/10/28/12655596-qmi.html?cid=rssnewspolitics

53 *Proceedings* of the House of Commons Standing Committee, May 25, 2010.

54 Ibid.

55 Richard Tremblay and Frank Vitaro, "Iatrogenic Effect of Juvenile Justice," *Journal of Child Psychology and Psychiatry*, Vol. 50, No. 8, August 2009.

56 *Hansard*, May 3, 2010.

57 Ibid.

58 Robert Benzie and Diana Zlomislic, "Premier promises action on youth superjail," *The Toronto Star*, March 31, 2010.

59 Ibid.

60 *R. v. Proulx*, [2000] 1 S.C.R. 61.

61 Robin MacKay, "Ending Conditional Sentences for Property and Other Serious Crimes Act," *Legislative Summary*, Parliamentary Information and Research Division, Ottawa, April 28, 2010, quoting Joseph DiLuca, Vice-President, Criminal Lawyers Association.

62 Bruce Cheadle, "Tories Ignore Taxpayer-Funded Crime Research," *Canadian Press*, March 15, 2010.

63 MP Joe Comartin, *Hansard*, May 3, 2010.

64 *R. v. C.D.; R. v. C.D.K.*, [2005] 3 S.C.R. 688.

65 MacKay, *Ending Conditional Sentences*

66 Tonda MacCharles, "Jailers Fear..." quoting a Correctional Service of Canada report.

67 Parliamentary Budget Officer, *Funding Requirement*, p. 16.

68 Emile Therien, "Courts Need Conditional Sentencing," *Ottawa Citizen*, May 8, 2006, p. A9.

69 Emile Therien, "Canada's Increasingly Flawed Criminal Justice System," Letter to the Editor, *Hill Times*, June 22, 2009, p. 9.

70 This bill was originally introduced into the House of Commons as Bill C-36 and made its way to first reading in the Senate by November 2009. The bill died on the order paper when Mr. Harper prorogued Parliament, and was reintroduced by the Leader of the Government in the Senate in April 2010 as Bill S-6, receiving royal assent on March 23, 2011.

71 Robin MacKay, "An Act to amend the Criminal Code and another Act (Serious Time for the Most Serious Crime Act)," *Legislative Summary*. (Parliamentary Information and Research Division, Ottawa, April 30, 2010.)

72 It should be noted that Prime Minister Harper has declared himself in favour of capital punishment, despite what is now known about the incidence of wrongful convictions. Mentioned in an interview with Peter Mansbridge, CBC TV, January, 2010.

73 Josh Weinstein, "Serious Time for Serious Crime Act," Canadian Bar Association Submission to House of Commons Committee on Justice and Human Rights, November 2, 2009.

74 Jackson and Stewart, *Flawed Compass*, p. xxiv.

75 Julian V. Roberts, "'Faint Hope' in the Firing Line: Repeal of Section 745.6?," *Canadian Journal of Criminology and Criminal Justice*, Vol. 51, No. 4, October 2009, p. 537.

76 See discussion of victims' rights arguments at Chapter 7.

77 Tanya Dupuis and Lyne Casavant, "Bill C-39: An Act to Amend the Corrections and Conditional Release Act and to Make Consequential Amendments to Other Acts ("Ending Early Release for Criminals and Increasing Offender Accountability Act"), *Legislative Summary*, Parliamentary Information and Research Services, June 23, 2010. Bill C-39 was the precursor to Bill C-59.

78 Ibid.

79 Op. cit., p. 117.

80 *Annual Report of the Office of the Correctional Investigator 2009-2010* (Ottawa: Her Majesty the Queen in Right of Canada, 2010) p. 46.

81 Lyne Casavant and Dominique Valiquet, "Bill S-9: An Act to Amend the Criminal Code (Auto Theft and Trafficking in Property Obtained by Crime)," *Legislative Summary*. (Ottawa: Legal and Legislative Affairs Division, Parliamentary Information and Research Service, 2010).

82 Dominique Valiquet, "Bill C-19: An Act to Amend the Criminal Code (street racing) and to Make a Consequential Amendment to the Corrections and Conditional Release Act," *Legislative Summary*. (Ottawa: Legal and Legislative Affairs, Division, Parliamentary Information and Research Service, July 4, 2006, revised September 21, 2007), referring to Don Gardner, "Street Racing Legislation Will Do Nothing," *Windsor Star*, June 29, 2008, p. A8.

83 Ibid.

84 Ibid.

85 Gary Mason, "The Case for Legalizing Marijuana," *Globe and Mail*, October 7, 2010.

86 Cynthia Kirkby and Dominique Valiquet, "An Act to amend the Criminal Code (Sentencing for Fraud). ("Standing Up for Victims of White Collar Crime Act"). *Legislative Summary*. (Ottawa: Legal and Legislative Affairs Division, Parliamentary Information and Research Division, May 7, 2010.)

87 Lincoln Caylor and Joseph Groia, "Standing up for Canadian Victims of White-Collar Crime," *Globe and Mail*, December 23, 2010. Mr. Caylor practises commercial litigation, specializing in fraud in Toronto. Mr. Groia is a former director of enforcement for the Ontario Securities Commission.

88 Jeffrey Simpson, "Playing the Politics of Slogans and Fear," *Globe and Mail*, February 23, 2011.

89 "Citizen's Arrest Bill Announced by Harper," CBC News, February 17, 2011, quoting Myer Siemiatyki, Politics Professor at Ryerson University.

90 The $50 fee, which had stood since 1994, was increased to $150 in 2010. Jane Taber, "Hiking Pardon Fee Commercialized Justice System, NDP Warns," *Globe and Mail*, February 24, 2011.

91 Ibid.

92 "Tackling Recidivism: They All Come Home," *The Economist*, April 23, 2011, p. 34.

CHAPTER 5

1   Tom Flanagan, "Pariah Products Will Always Find Their Way," *Globe and Mail*, December 31, 2010.

2   http://www.youtube.com/watch?v=G5tWSMwhGkc&feature=topvideos

3   Tom Flanagan, "Guns and Grow-ops: Conservatives Should Be Consistent," *Globe and Mail*, September 20, 2010.

4   Neil Boyd, "We should not pretend that Bill S-10 has anything to do with evidence—or with making our country a safer place in which to live," *The Mark News*, March 1, 2011.

5   Dan Gardner, "Tough Justice: Is the Harper Agenda a Phony War on Crime?" *The Sunday Edition*, CBC Radio One, March 28, 2010.

6   *Proceedings* of the Standing Senate Committee on Legal and Constitutional Affairs, Issue 19—Evidence, November 19, 2009.

7   Ibid.

8   Kirk Makin, "Mandatory Sentences Blamed for Boom in Cost of Prisons," *Globe and Mail*, June 19, 2008.

9   www.justice.gc.ca/eng/news-nouv/nr-cp/2010/doc_32508.html

10 Proceedings of the Standing Senate Committee on Legal and Constitutional Affairs, Issue 19—Evidence, November 19, 2009.

11 Janice Tibbetts, "Plan for Minimum, Mandatory Drug Sentences Draws Fire," *Canwest News Service*, May 3, 2009.

12 Gloria Galloway, "Health Researchers Slam Tory Mandatory-Minimum-Sentence Proposal for Drug Crime," *Globe and Mail*, February 7, 2011.

13 Testimony at Standing Senate Committee, op. cit. Professor Fischer is a professor at Simon Fraser University and Research Chair for the Canadian Institutions of Health Research and the Public Health Agency of Canada.

14 "Canadians Split on Pot, Death Penalty: Poll," CBC News, March 18, 2010.

15 "Half of Canadians Support the Legalization of Marijuana," *Vision Critical*, Angus Reid Public Opinion, November 29, 2010.

16 Janice Tibbetts, "Minister Defends Mandatory Minimums," *National Post*, April 23, 2009.

17 Editorial, "When Jails Become a Jobs Program," *Globe and Mail*, February 14, 2011.

18 Benedikt Fischer. Testimony at the Standing Senate Committee, op cit., November 19, 2009.

19 Janice Tibbetts, op. cit., April 23, 2009.

20 Neil Boyd, in addressing the Standing Senate Committee, op. cit., estimated that the new drug legislation would result in the imprisonment for six months of "an additional 3,000 British Columbians."

21 Neil Boyd, op. cit.

22 Dr. Sharami Mami, *The Current*, CBC Radio One, December 23, 2010.

23 Tanya Dupuis and Robin MacKay, "Bill S-10: An Act to Amend the Controlled Drugs and Substances Act and to Make Related and Consequential Amendments to Other Acts," *Legislative Summary*. (Ottawa: Legal and Legislative Affairs Division, Parliamentary Information and Research Service, May 17, 2008.)

24 Katie De Rosa, "B.C. MP to Ask the Government to Decriminalize Marijuana," *National Post*, April 2, 2009.

25 Ibid., quoting Philippe Lucas, executive director of the Vancouver Island Compassion Society.

26 Neil Boyd, "Different Rules for Different Drugs," *The Mark*, September 21, 2010.

27 July 18–23, 2010.

28 Editorial, "Beyond the War on Drugs," *Globe and Mail*, August 28, 2010.

29 "Mexico's Drug War: Shallow Graves, Deepening Alarm," *The Economist*, April 30, 2011, p. 40.

30 Ibid.

31 "Thinking the Unthinkable," *The Economist*, August 14, 2010.

32 Ibid.

33 Ibid.

34 YouTube, op. cit.

35 Matthew McKinnon, "To Pot," *The Walrus*, April 2011, p. 15.

36 *Criminological Highlights*, The Centre of Criminology, University of Toronto, Vol. 11, No. 2, Article 5, May 2010. Reference: Buruma, Ybo (2007), "Dutch Tolerance: On Drugs, Prostitution, and Euthanasia."

37 Hélène Mulholland and agencies, "Ed Miliband Rebukes Bob Ainsworth over 'Legalise Drugs' Call," *The Guardian*, December 16, 2010.

38 Gloria Galloway, "Canada Warned Not to Follow U.S. Tough-on-Crime 'Mistakes'," *Globe and Mail*, March 3, 2011.

39 Megan McLemore, "Canada has been a regional leader in drug policy, but Bill S-10 would waste billions of dollars on ineffective approaches that only appear to be tough on crime," *The Mark News*, February 16, 2011. Megan McLemore is Senior Researcher, Health and Human Rights, Human Rights Watch.

40 Peter Hecht, "In Spite of Prop 19 Loss, California Cities Vote to Tax Pot,"*McClatchy Washington Bureau*, November 3, 2010.

41 Dick Polman, "Whiffs of Change," *McClatchy Tribune Services, Winnipeg Free Press*, April 10, 2010, p. H11.

42 *Globe and Mail*, October 2, 2010, p. A25. Rob Kampia, "Top Ten Marijuana Victories in 2010," Marijuana Policy Project, January 3, 2011.

43 Nick Wing, "Nathan Deal: Jailing Drug Addicts is 'Draining to Our State'," *Huffington Post*, January 10, 2011.

44 Kim Murphy, "Town Can't Find Jurors Willing to Convict in Pot Case," *Toronto Star*, December 26, 2010.

45 Kirk Johnson, "In Montana, an Economic Boon Repeal Effort," *New York Times*, March 5, 2011.

46 "Legalising Marijuana: The Law of the Weed," *The Economist*, July 17, 2010. p. 31.

47 Conrad Black, "My Prison Education," *National Post*, July 31, 2010.

48 CBC Radio One *News*, February 21, 2011.

49 According to a CBC Radio One news report May 6, 2011, in the first four months of 2011 there was an appreciable increase in overdose deaths in the vicinity of the Vancouver InSite program (which provides a safe place for addicts to inject heroin) due to a shipment of heroin that was twice as potent as usual. No users who injected at InSite died, since medical assistance is provided on site.

50 *The Current*, CBC Radio One, December 23, 2010.

51 Adrian Morrow, "Ontario Court Strikes Down Canada's Pot Laws," *Globe and Mail*, April 13, 2011.

52 CBC Radio One *News*, April 13, 2011.

53 Adrian Morrow, op. cit.

54 *The Current*, CBC Radio One, December 23, 2010.

55 *Hansard*, April 23, 2010.

56 *CBC News*, Radio One, April 18, 2011.

57 Angus Reid Strategies, "Majority of Canadians Would Legalize Marijuana, but Not Other Drugs," op. cit.

58 Angus Reid Strategies, "Half of Canadians Support the Legalization of Marijuana," Vision Critical, Angus Reid Public Opinion, November 29, 2010.

59 Proceedings of the Standing Senate Committee on Legal and Constitutional Affairs, November 19, 2009, op. cit.

60 The hepatitis C rate among newly admitted prisoners is 9 per cent for males and 31 per cent for females. In the prison population, the rates are 27 per cent and 36 per cent respectively. Similarly, the HIV/AIDS rate among newly admitted prisoners is 0.8 per cent for males and 1.9 per cent for females. In the prison population, the rates are 1.5 per cent and 4.5 per cent respectively. André Picard, "The Lack of Needles and the Damage Done,"

Globe and Mail, February 18, 2010, p. L4.

61 Ibid., citing conclusions of the Public Health Agency of Canada.

62 Annual Report of the Office of the Correctional Investigator 2009-2010, op. cit., pp. 23 and 80.

63 Urban Health Research Initiative, Vancouver, reported by Randy Shore, "Doctors, Scientists Want Proposed Federal Drug Law Scrapped," *Vancouver Sun*, February 7, 2011.

CHAPTER 6

1 Carol Goar, "Tough on Crime but Soft on Logic," *Toronto Star*, March 19, 2010.

2 Heather Scoffield, "Tory Law-and-Order Agenda Costs up to $10-Billion, Budget Office Says," *Globe and Mail*, April 27, 2010.

3 Gloria Galloway, "Opposition Balks at Steep Price of Tory Crime Bills," *Globe and Mail*, May 17, 2010.

4 *Power and Politics*, CBC News Network, June 23, 2010; *The Agenda*, TV Ontario, November 23, 2010.

5 Janice Tibbetts, "Crime Laws Will Cost Billions: Minister," *National Post*, April 29, 2010.

6 Parliamentary Budget Officer, *Funding Requirement*.

7 Ibid., p. 12.

8 *The Agenda*, TV Ontario, November 23, 2010.

9 Parliamentary Budget Officer, *Funding Requirement*, p. 19.

10 Ibid.

11 Jeffrey Simpson, "The True Costs of 'Truth in Sentencing'," *Globe and Mail*, June 29, 2010.

12 Parliamentary Budget Officer, *Funding Requirement*, p. 71.

13 *Proceedings* of the Senate Standing Committee on Legal and Constitutional Affairs, September 30, 2009.

14 The Correctional Service of Canada says the number will increase by 3,445 within the next three years—an increase of about 33 per cent. David McKie, "Inmate Programs Fall Short of Capital Spending," CBC News, January 14, 2011.

15 Parliamentary Budget Officer, *Funding Requirement*, p. 22, 25.

16 Janice Tibbetts, "Minister Downplays Prison Double-Bunking," *National Post*, May 4, 2010.

17 Bill Curry, "Tough-on-Crime Policies Worsening Prison Conditions, Guards Say," *Globe and Mail*, February 15, 2011.

18 *Annual Report of the Office of the Correctional Investigator 2009–2010*, op. cit, pp. 34–35.

19 Ibid., p. 6.

20 Held at Geneva in 1955, and approved by the Economic and Social Council by its Resolutions 663C (XXIV) of 31 July 1957 and 2076 (LXII) of 13 May 1977, s. 9(1).

21 Bill Curry, "Fight Over Cost of Tory Crime Bills Sets Up Commons Confrontation," *Globe and Mail*, February 11, 2011.

22 Summary of Capital Spending, *Reports on Plans and Priorities*, Correctional Service Canada, Ottawa (2005–2006 to 2010–2011). The figures relate to four programs within the CSC: custody, correctional interventions, community supervision, and internal services. www.tbs-sct.gc.ca/rpp/2010-2011/inst/pen/st-tso5-eng.asp

23 "2011–12 Estimates. The Government Expenditure Plan and the Main Estimates," p. 299. www.tbs-sct.gc.ca/est-pre/20112012/me-bpd/docs/me-bpd-eng.pdf

24 Gloria Galloway, "Ombudsman Paints Grim Prison Picture," *Globe and Mail*, November 6, 2010, p. A6.

25 Parliamentary Budget Officer, *Funding Requirement*, p. 16.

26 Ibid., p. 94.

27 Ibid., p. 102. This number does not include provincial or territorial budgets.

28 2011–12 *Estimates*, p. 299.

29 Richard Cleroux, "The Real Cost of New Crime Laws," *Law Times*, March 7, 2011.

30 David McKie, "Tory Crime Plan Fails Victims, Inmates: Critics," CBC News, February 15, 2011.

31 Cleroux, "Real Cost..."

32 2011–12 *Estimates*, p. 230.

33 Ibid.

34 Justin Piché, "Tracking the Politics of 'Crime' and Punishment in Canada." http://tpcp-canada.blogspot.com/ In conducting his research on provincial prisons, doctoral candidate Justin Piché of Carleton University has obtained data directly from the governments of the provinces and territories. Also, see Gloria Galloway and Karen Howlett, "Provinces Want Ottawa to Help Pay Additional Costs for Prisons," *Globe and Mail*, February 16, 2011.

35 Parliamentary Budget Officer, *Funding Requirement*, p. 84.

36 Galloway and Howlett, "Provinces Want Ottawa..."

37 Dr. Anthony Doob, *As It Happens*, CBC Radio One, February 16, 2011.

38 *Proceedings* of the Standing Senate Committee, November 19, 2009. Others estimate the number at seven hundred per year in British Columbia: Dupuis and MacKay, Bill S-10, *Legislative Summary*.

39 The Parliamentary Budget Officer's estimate of $84,225 per year includes the high costs of imprisonment of prisoners in the territorial system as well as the provincial system.

40 Casavant and Valiquet, *Legislative Summary* re Bill C-4.

41 Tim Naumetz, "Mass detention of 300 Tamil migrants cost $18-million, says Canada Border Services Agency," *The Hill Times*, February 14, 2011.

42 Sara Beattie, *Police Resources in Canada, 2009.* (Ottawa: Statistics Canada, Ministry of Industry, 2009.) Catalogue Number 85-225-X, p. 7.

43 Ibid., p. 9.

44 Stephen Thorne, "Ottawa's Law-and-Order Agenda Costly, Police Say," *Toronto Star*, April 20, 2010.

45 "2011–12 *Estimates*, p. 230. This is at a time when money laundering is reaching new levels of sophistication as online gaming becomes the medium of choice.

46 Bill Curry, "Public-Service Unions are Bracing for Cuts," *Globe and Mail*, December 23, 2009, quoting figures from the Public Service Commission of Canada annual report.

47 Curry, "Tough-on-Crime Worsening..."

48 Justice Paul Bentley, *The Current*, CBC Radio One, February 17, 2011.

49 "Stay Out of Jail Clean,"*The Economist*, February 26, 2011.

50 http://www.promisingpractices.net/program.asp?programid=128

51 www.publicsafety.gc.ca/res/cor/apc/apc-20-eng.aspx

52 www.vcn.bc.ca/august10/politics/facts_stats.html

53 www.thestar.com/special Sections/crime/article/460773

54 Editorial, *Globe and Mail*, February 14, 2011.

55 Editorial, *Globe and Mail*, February 16, 2011.

56 Editorial, *Toronto Star*, February 22, 2011.

CHAPTER 7

1 Examples of self-harming would be choking, overdosing, or slashing with a razor or other sharp object. *Annual Report of the Office of the Correctional Investigator 2009–2010*, Ottawa, 2010, p. 18.

2 Ibid., p. 40.

3 Ibid., p. 7.

4 Janice Tibbetts, "Canadian Prisons Lacking Rehabilitation," *National Post*, November 5, 2010.

5 *Report of the Office of the Correctional Investigator 2009–2010*, p. 6.

6   Ibid., p. 46.

7   Gloria Galloway, "Ombudsman Paints Grim Prison Picture. Report Describes Aging and Overcrowded Correctional Facilities that Undermine Rehabilitation," *Globe and Mail*, November 6, 2010.

8   Parliamentary Budget Officer, *Funding Requirement*, p. 37.

9   Michael Jackson, *Justice Behind the Walls: Human Rights in Canadian Prisons* (Vancouver: Douglas & McIntyre, 2002) p. 167.

10 Mark MacGuigan, Chairman, House of Commons Sub-Committee on the Penitentiary System in Canada, *Report to Parliament*. (Ottawa: Minister of Supply and Services, 1977). Mr. MacGuigan travelled the country, visiting penitentiaries in response to the series of riots and other violent events in prisons during the 1970s. His report was severely critical of the system.

11 Parliamentary Budget Officer, *Funding Requirement*, p. 32.

12 Tibbetts, "Canadian Prisons Lacking..."

13 Conrad Black, *Power Play*, CTV, January 10, 2011.

14 Stewart and Jackson, *Flawed Compass*.

15 Ibid., pp. 34–35.

16 Robin MacKay, "Ending Conditional Sentences for Property and Other Serious Crimes Act," *Legislative Summary*. (Ottawa: Legal and Legislative Affairs, Division, Parliamentary Information and Research Division, Ottawa, August 6, 2009.)

17 Jackson and Stewart, *Flawed Compass*, p. xv.

18 Ibid., p. xxv.

19 Conrad Black, "Harper's Inhumane Prison Plan," *National Post*, May 30, 2010.

20 The Correctional Service of Canada, "Report on Plans and Priorities," 2010–2011. (Ottawa: Correctional Service of Canada, 2010).

21 Ibid., p. 17.

22 Correctional Investigator, *Report, 2009-2010*, p. 10.

23 Kirk Makin, "Mentally Ill Offenders Swamping Prisons," *Globe and Mail*, November 17, 2010.

24 Ibid. The Ontario Review Board is responsible for offenders who have been found not criminally responsible for committing offences. It had more than 1,500 patients under its purview in 2009, 400 per cent more than in 1992. Almost three hundred offenders are added annually, far more than the number being released.

25 Michael MacDonald, "Mentally Ill Youth Needing Treatment Get It Through Criminal Justice System," *Globe and Mail*, December 15, 2010.

26 Kirk Makin, "To Heal and Protect," *Globe and Mail*, January 22, 2011, p. F6.

27 Ibid.

28 Terri Theodore, "After Their release, Most Mentally Ill Offenders Left Unchecked," *Globe and Mail*, December 13, 2010.

29 Correctional Investigator, *Report, 2009–2010*, p. 10.

30 Report of the Standing Committee on Public Safety and National Security, *Mental Health and Drugs and Alcohol Addiction in the Federal Correctional System*, Kevin Sorensen, chair, December 2010.

31 Ibid., p. 69.

32 Ibid., p. 92.

33 Michael MacDonald, op. cit.

34 CBC Radio One, May 4, 2011.

35 Makin, "Mentally Ill Offenders..."

36 Ibid.

37 Correctional Investigator, *Report, 2009–2010*, p. 12.

38 Makin, "To Heal and Protect."

39 Correctional Investigator, *Report, 2009–2010*, p. 13.

40 Makin, "To Heal and Protect."

41 Committee on Public Safety, *Mental Health and Drugs*, p. 20.

42 Makin, "Mentally Ill Offenders..."

43 Committee on Public Safety, *Mental Health and Drugs*, p. 93.

44 Ibid., p. 41.

45 Correctional Investigator, *Report, 2009–2010*, p. 22.

46 Committee on Public Safety, *Mental Health and Drugs*, p. 93–94.

47 [1999] 1 S.C.R. 688 at paragraph 58ff.

48 Kirk Makin, "Courts Falling Short on Effort to Keep Natives Out of Jail," *Globe and Mail*, December 27, 2009.

49 Correctional Investigator, *Report, 2009–2010*, p. 43.

50 Jeffrey Simpson, "The True Costs of 'Truth in Sentencing'," *Globe and Mail*, June 29, 2010.

51 Reilly, *Bad Medicine*, p. 168.

52 Makin, "Courts Falling Short..."

53 Ibid.

54 *Good Intentions, Disappointing Results: A Progress Report on Federal Aboriginal Corrections* (Ottawa: Office of the Correctional Investigator) November 2009, p. 43.

55 Makin, "Courts Falling Short..."

56 Correctional Investigator, *Report, 2009–2010*, p. 44–45.

57 Ibid., p. 49ff.

58 Kirk Makin, "Incarcerated Women Twice as Likely as Men to Be Diagnosed With a Mental Illness," *Globe and Mail*, January 26, 2011.

59 Gloria Galloway, "Coalition of Churches Condemns Ottawa's Justice Plan," *Globe and Mail*, January 26, 2011.

60 Canadian Resource Centre for Victims of Crime, Annual Report, 2010.

61 Telephone interview with the author, April 4, 2011.

62 Gloria Galloway, "Coalition of Churches..."

63 Presentation by the Church Council on Justice and Corrections to the Senate Committee on Legal and Constitutional Affairs regarding Bill C-2, the *Tackling Violent Crime Act*, February 22, 2008.

64 Ibid., p. 3.

65 Submission to House of Commons Standing Committee on Justice and Human Rights, May 13, 2010.

66 Allan Young is a professor and legal expert who did this research for the Department of Justice of Canada in 2001.

67 Submission to the Standing Committee, quoting Steve Sullivan.

68 "Steve Sullivan: Victim Rights Still Get Short Shrift," *National Post*, August 31, 2010.

69 2011–12 *Estimates*, op. cit. p. 230.d

CHAPTER 8

1 MacGuigan *Report*, p. 156.

2 Reilly, *Bad Medicine*, p. 174.

3 Wanda Jamieson and Liz Hart, *Compendium of Promising Crime Prevention Practices in Canada* (Ottawa: Caledon Institute of Public Policy, 2003).

4 MP Irene Mathyssen, *Hansard*, May 3, 2010.

5 *Hansard*, April 23, 2010.

6 See Chapter 6.

7 Ibid.

8 Editorial, *Toronto Star*, July 19, 2008.

9 Editorial, "Let's Build Opportunity, Not Prisons," *Globe and Mail*, February 18, 2011.

10 Editorial, *Globe and Mail*, March 19, 2011.

11 Research shows that "the proportion of recent immigrants lowers the violent crime rate;

it acts as a protective factor," according to Statistics Canada. However, second- and third-generation immigrant children are somewhat more likely than first-generation to get into trouble with the law. Rachel Giese, "Arrival of the Fittest: Canada's Crime Rate Is Dropping as Immigration Increases. Is There a Connection?" *The Walrus*, June 2011, p. 28.

12 Jim Rankin, "More People Released from Jail Face Homelessness: Report," *Toronto Star*, August 10, 2010.

13 Steve Sullivan, "Victim Rights Still Get Short Shrift," *National Post*, August 31, 2010.

14 www.tbs-sct.gc.ca/est-pre/20112012/me-bpd/docs/me-bpd-eng.pdf

15 www.justice.gc.ca/eng/pi/yj-jj/

16 *Power Play*, CTV, January 10, 2011.

17 Rick Hansen, Calgary Chief of Police, *The Current*, CBC Radio One, February 17, 2011; Bill Blair, Toronto Chief of Police, quoted in Editorial, "Jail 'A Lazy Response to Poverty'," *Toronto Star*, July 19, 2008.

18 www.tbs-sct.gc.ca

19 Elizabeth Comack, Lawrence Deane, Larry Morrissette, and Jim Silver, *If You Want to Change Violence in the 'Hood, You Have to Change the 'Hood: Violence and Street Gangs in Winnipeg's Inner City*, Report presented to the Minister of Justice and Attorney General, Government of Manitoba. (Winnipeg: Canadian Centre for Policy Alternatives—Manitoba, 2009).

20 Ibid., p. 1.

21 Ibid., p. 4.

22 Irvin Waller, *Less Law More Order: The Truth about Reducing Crime* (Ancaster: Manor House Publishing Inc., 2008), p. 72.

23 Dawn Moore and Erin Donohue, "Harper and Crime: The Great Distraction," in Teresa Healy (ed.) *The Harper Record* (Ottawa: Canadian Centre for Policy Alternatives, 2008).

24 Ibid., p. 10.

25 John Geddes, "Are We Really Soft on Crime?" *Macleans*, November 9, 2009.

26 Comack et al., *If You Want to Change Violence.*

27 "Winnipeg Anti-Gang Programs at Risk," CBC News, January 26, 2011.

28 Akua Schatz, "The Value of Safety: Unwrapping Crime and Urban Space," essay, n.d. www.dramatispersonae.org/EnterpriseOfTheCity/HomePage/TheCrimeInSafety.htm

29 Waller, *Less Law*, p. 114–115.

30 Ibid., quoting *New York Times*.

31 According to Waller, the number per 100,000 was thirty in 2008, still an improvement on the thirty-six in Washington, DC.

32 *Proceso*, November 2010.

33 Waller, *Less Law*, p. 80–81.

34 *The Sunday Edition*, CBC Radio One, April 17, 2011.

35 James Morton, "'Tough on Crime' Stance Needs Scrutiny," *Toronto Star*, January 3, 2010.

36 There is a Centre for Restorative Justice within the School of Criminology at Simon Fraser University in British Columbia. It is devoted to working with schools and communities, and it posts stories of individual successes in restorative justice on its website. www.sfu.ca/cru/stories.html

37 www.publicsafety.gc.ca

38 Manson, *Law of Sentencing*, pp. 371ff.

39 *R. v. Gladue*, op. cit., p. 726.

40 Julian V. Roberts et al., "Public Attitudes..." pp. 75–107.

41 Jarem Sawatsky, *The Ethic of Traditional Communities and the Spirit of Healing Justice* (London: Jessica Kingsley Publishers, 2009).

42 News Release, September 18, 2009. ww2.news.gov.bc.ca

43 *CBC News*, CBC Radio One, February 20, 2011.

44 Jeremy Hainsworth, "Vancouver's Innovative Community Court Evaluated," *Lawyers Weekly*, October 1, 2010.

45 Thomas Gove, "Community Court Shows Encouraging Results on Second Anniversary," *Vancouver Sun*, September 2010.

46 "Community court opens in Vancouver Downtown Eastside," CBC Radio News, September 10, 2008.

47 *The Current*, CBC Radio One, February 17, 2011.

48 Ibid.

49 "Drug Treatment Courts' Future up in Air," *CBC News*, March 10, 2009.

50 Jeff Latimer, Kelly Morton-Bourgon, and Jo-Anne Chrétien, *A Meta-Analytic Examination of Drug Treatment Courts: Do They Reduce Recidivism?* (Ottawa: a report prepared for Department of Justice, Research and Statistics Division, August 2006.)

51 Department of Justice, *Backgrounder*, June 2, 2005.

52 "Stay Out of Jail Clean," *The Economist*, February 26, 2011, p. 38.

53 MP Bill Siksay, *Hansard*, May 3, 2010.

54 Ibid., referring to Ritchie Eppink and Scott Peterson in *Law Now*.

55 "Misunderstood," *The Economist*, March 8, 1997, p. 64.

56 *Criminological Highlights*, Vol. 11, No. 5, January 2011, referring to Hilde Wermink, Arjan Blokland, Paul Nieuwbeerta, Daniel Nagin, and Nikolaj Tollenaar, "Comparing the Effects

of Community Service and Short-Term Imprisonment on Recidivism: A Matched Samples Approach," *Journal of Experimental Criminology*, 6 (2010) pp. 325–349.

57 Justice Policy Institute, "Finding Direction..."

58 Paula Mallea, *Getting Tough on Kids: Young Offenders and the "Law and Order Agenda,"* (Winnipeg: Canadian Centre for Policy Alternatives—Manitoba, November, 1999), p. 21–22.

59 Reilly, *Bad Medicine*, p. 41, 42, 46, 120, 129–130.

60 David C. Anderson, "Let His Children Go," *New York Times*, January 26, 1992; Mallea, *Getting Tough*, p. 21.

61 Florida's population in 1989 was 12,637,718; Massachusetts's was 6,015,478 (United States Census Bureau, Population Division).

CHAPTER 9

1 www.cjibc.org

2 Mallea, *Getting Tough*, p. 23.

3 Ibid., p. 26.

4 The MacGuigan Report, cited in Jackson, *Justice Behind the Walls*, p. 18.

5 Jackson, *Justice Behind the Walls*, p. 83, from an interview with Jim Mackie, Kent Institution, 1998.

6 Ibid., from an interview with Doug Cassin, September 1995, p. 85.

7 Ibid., from an interview with Warden Ken Peterson, p. 91.

8 Committee on Public Safety, Mental Health and Drugs, p. 48.

9 Steven J. Stack and Olga Tsoudis, "Suicide risk among correctional officers: A logistic regression analysis," *Archives of Suicide Research*, Vol. 3, No. 3, pp. 183–186.

10 Ibid., from an interview with Dave Humphries, 1993, p. 98.

11 Committee on Public Safety, *Mental Health and Drugs*, p. 48.

12 The Honourable Louise Arbour, Commissioner, *Commission of Inquiry into Certain Events at the Prison for Women in Kingston* (Ottawa: Solicitor General of Canada, 1996).

13 Jackson, *Justice Behind the Walls*, p. 88.

14 Jackson and Stewart, *Flawed Compass*, pp. vi, xiv, and xv.

15 *Roadmap*, p. 59.

16 Jackson and Stewart, *Flawed Compass*, pp. xxvff.

17 Ibid., p. 137, referring to research by Stephen Duguid.

18 *The Current*, CBC Radio One, February 2, 2011. The inmate said that the Grand

Valley Institution in Kitchener had in fact added some additional units, but that the overcrowding still interfered with access to all programs, including access to family visits.

19 Jackson and Stewart, op. cit., p. 77.

20 Conrad Black, "Harper's Inhumane Prison Plan," *National Post*, May 30, 2010.

21 Correctional Investigator, *Report, 2009–2010*, p. 46.

22 Gloria Galloway, op. cit., November 6, 2010, quoting the January 2006 Correctional Service of Canada publication *Let's Talk*.

23 Colin Perkel, "Critics Claim Closing Prison Farms Would Create $1-million Milk Bill," *Globe and Mail*, May 5, 2010.

24 Ibid.

25 "Adult Basic Education: Can It Help Reduce Recidivism?" *Forum on Corrections Research*. (Ottawa: Correctional Service of Canada, n.d.) http://www.csc-scc.gc.ca/text/pblct/forum/e031/e031c-eng.shtml.

26 Roger Boe, "A Two-Year Release Follow-Up of Federal Offenders Who Participated in the Adult Basic Education (ABE) Program." (Ottawa: Research Branch, Correctional Service of Canada, February 1998).

27 Black, "Harper's Inhumane Prison Plan."

28 Conrad Black, "Playing to the Reactionaries," *National Post*, August 7, 2010.

29 John Howard Society of Kingston and District, "Community Intake and Outreach." http://www.johnhowardkingston.ca/Intake.html.

30 John R. Hipp, Joan Petersilia and Susan Turner, "Parolee Recidivism in California: the Effect of Neighbourhood Context and Social Service Agency Characteristics," *Criminology* (2010) 48(4), pp. 947–979.

31 Ibid.

32 Lise McKean and Charles Ransford, "Current Strategies for Reducing Recidivism," (Chicago: Center for Impact Research, August 2004). www.impactresearch.org/documents/recidivismfullreport.pdf

33 "Tackling Recidivism: They All Come Home," *The Economist*, April 23, 2011, p. 34.

34 http://www.gosonyc.org/

35 www.eoyja.ca/programs

36 Dan Gardner, "Why Finland is Soft on Crime," *Ottawa Citizen*, March 18, 2002.

37 Young offenders in Canada, by contrast, serve their entire sentences. There is no provision for parole or any kind of early release.

38 www.prisonpolicy.org/scans/sp/usno1.pdf

39 Waller, *Less Law*, p. 119, referring to governments in general.

CONCLUSION

1   Craig Jones, "The Government is Doing Something," *Inroads*, Summer/Fall 2010, pp. 58–69.

2   Journalist Don Gardner, quoted in Jackson and Stewart, p. 131.

3   Jane B. Sprott, "Understanding Public Views of Youth Crime and the Youth Justice System," *Canadian Journal of Criminology*, July 1996, pp. 271–290; Kate Warner, Julia David, Maggie Walter, Rebecca Bradfield, and Rachel Vermey, "Public Judgement on Sentencing: Final Results from the Tasmanian Jury Sentencing Study. Australian Institute of Criminology, *Trends & Issues in Crime and Justice*, (2011) No. 407.

4   Flanagan, *Harper's Team*, p. 274.

5   Barbara Yaffe, "Opinion: Running Party Like War Machine Is Key for Harper," *Vancouver Sun*, December 15, 2010, quoting Tom Flanagan in *Inroads*.

6   *The Current*, CBC Radio One, July 26, 2010.

7   Geddes, "Are We Really Soft...?"

8   *A Framework for Sentencing, Corrections and Conditional Release: Direction for Reform* (Ottawa, 1990), p. 9.

INDEX